STRATEGIC LEADERSHIP

Part of the American Council on Education, Series on Higher Education

Susan Slesinger, Executive Editor

Other selected titles in the series:

STRATEGIC LEADERSHIP

Integrating Strategy and Leadership in Colleges and Universities

Richard L. Morrill

Published in partnership with the

AMERICAN COUNCIL ON EDUCATION
® The Unifying Voice for Higher Education

ROWMAN & LITTLEFIELD PUBLISHERS, INC.
Lanham • New York • Toronto • Plymouth, UK

Published in partnership with the American Council on Education

Published by Rowman & Littlefield Publishers, Inc.
A wholly owned subsidiary of The Rowman & Littlefield Publishing Group, Inc.
4501 Forbes Boulevard, Suite 200, Lanham, Maryland 20706
http://www.rowmanlittlefield.com

Estover Road, Plymouth PL6 7PY, United Kingdom

British Library Cataloguing in Publication Information Available

Library of Congress Cataloging-in-Publication Data

Morrill, Richard L.
   Strategic leadership : integrating strategy and leadership in colleges and universities / Richard L. Morrill.
     p. cm. — (ACE/Praeger series on higher education)
   Includes bibliographical references and index.
   ISBN–13: 978–0–275–99391–7
   ISBN–10: 0–275–99391–4
   1. Universities and colleges—Administration. 2. Universities and colleges—Planning. 3. Educational leadership. I. Title.
   LB2341.M6376 2007
   378.1'01—dc22   2007013449

ISBN: 978-1-60709-654-2 (pbk. : alk. paper)
ISBN: 978-1-60709-655-9 (electronic)

Printed in the United States of America

To Nicholas, Charles, William, Eleanor, and Charlotte

Mes petits-enfants extraordinaires

CONTENTS

PREFACE

The purpose of this book is to describe why and how to use the process of strategy as a form of leadership in colleges and universities. For some time now, strategy has been seen as one of the major disciplines of management. I make the claim that it also can be practiced as a systematic process and discipline of leadership, hence the term "strategic leadership."

STRATEGIC LEADERSHIP

Although the term "strategic leadership" has appeared frequently in the literature of management, the military, and higher education, it has not yet developed a settled meaning (Chaffee 1991; Chaffee and Tierney 1988; Freedman and Tregoe 2003; Ganz 2005; Goethals, Swenson, and Burns 2004; Morrill 2002; Neumann 1989; Peterson 1997). As understood here, strategic leadership designates the use of the strategy process as a systematic method of decision making that integrates reciprocal leadership into its concepts and practices. Strategy is not just a tool of management used by leaders who hold positions of authority but is as well a method of interactive leadership that clarifies purposes and priorities, mobilizes motivation and resources, and sets directions for the future.

Although strategy is relevant in a variety of organizational contexts, the focus here is on strategic leadership in colleges and universities. Given their distinctive collegial decision-making culture and systems, the process holds particular promise for institutions of higher learning. To be sure, leadership is a highly complex combination of many factors, characteristics, and circumstances that decidedly cannot be reduced to one dimension or defined by a single method. Nonetheless, one of its important organizational aspects is a collaborative process of strategic decision making that engages an academic community in defining and achieving a vision for its future.

THE RENEWAL OF STRATEGIC PLANNING

From any number of perspectives, it is clear that "strategic planning" has become the standard term to define the work of strategy in higher education. In point of fact, as we shall see, planning represents just one of several forms of strategy. Nonetheless, this is the terminology that is primarily used on campus.

As we shall review and document at greater length in several contexts, there is no matching or parallel consensus about how strategic planning should be practiced, nor the worth of doing so. Although the broad outlines of the process are often similar, the similarities end there. It is more a category than a specific method, and planning often functions as a figure of speech. Ironically, the term became popular in the corporate world in the 1960s to designate a process of detailed programmatic design and control that few colleges and universities have ever actually used.

If the form of planning can vary, so do the opinions about its worth. Critics lament its vagueness and the absence of empirical evidence for its effectiveness, even as governing boards and others on campus find it to be a useful or even invaluable process. Many faculty members, and not a few administrators, see it as a managerial threat to academic governance or as a colossal waste of time. Perhaps the most common lament is that strategic planning fails to make any difference in the way institutions actually do things.

One of my primary motivations is a desire to respond to this mixed experience with the use of strategic planning in higher education. I prefer the more basic terms "strategy" or "strategy process," although I also use and differentiate the meaning of "strategic planning" in various contexts. If we can take George Keller's influential work *Academic Strategy* (1983) as a point of reference, we can see the 1980s as the period when strategic planning emerged in higher learning as a method of projecting future goals in response to a changing context. With the help of Keller and others, colleges and universities began to see strategy as a distinctive form of decision making differentiated from long-range planning and ad hoc choice. As strategic planning became widespread in the late 1980s and 1990s, it evolved into a comprehensive collaborative process that increasingly shifted its attention to the implementation of plans through strategic management. We might think of this shift as a second major phase in the evolution of the process in higher education.

In the early years of the new millennium, it has become clear to this author that strategic planning and management, or better, the strategy process, needs to be reconceptualized and reformulated. When it fails, it is often because it has not been clearly defined and related to the values, mental models, and complex leadership and governance systems of colleges and universities. To do so has become a pressing priority, as the issues that cloud higher education's future require ever-more adept forms of decision making. One of the tasks that this book sets for itself is precisely this redefinition of the role of strategy in the participatory decision making configurations of the academy.

CONCEPTUAL MODEL AND METHODOLOGY

Strategic planning needs to be renewed by being set into a much deeper conceptual framework than ordinarily occurs. By moving the conceptual register from management to leadership, we can achieve much of the intellectual repositioning that is required. Yet to make the transition is demanding and requires the use of insights from several sources and disciplines. No single language or method, whether empirical, cultural, managerial, or otherwise, is adequate to this task. We have to cross boundaries and integrate methods to see strategy as both an *integrated* and *integral* process, one that is whole, complete, and entire in the range of its intellectual foundations and practical applications. I ask readers to understand that I am using the term "strategy" to include issues of fundamental importance such as organizational identity, values, and vision, not only to refer to a set of managerial methods or the competitive positioning of brands in a marketplace.

To refashion itself as strategic leadership, strategy has to consider deep questions, many of which have been raised by contemporary students of leadership (Goethals and Sorenson 2006). There is no way around the complex issues of the meaning of leadership and strategy with reference to human agency, the notion that humans are in charge of their own conduct and determine the meaning and direction of their lives through the enactment of their values and beliefs. Considered in this light, leadership includes various forms of organizational sense-making and sense-giving that depend on a process of mutual influence between leaders and those led. Drawing on insights from Weick (1995), I emphasize two dimensions of sense making. The passive motif of "sense" refers to our discovery of the meaning of a situation, and the active dimension of "making" shifts our focus to the agency required in constructing meaning, including the elements of enactment. "Sense-making is about authoring as well as interpretation, creation as well as discovery" (Weick 1995, 8). As becomes clear in many places in this book, the conceptual model has several interwoven components. One of these is the assumption that the deeper dimensions of strategy and leadership are centrally related to the enactment of values as standards of choice concerning what matters decisively to us. Values are powerful in shaping the culture and the decision-making patterns of organizations, especially colleges and universities. I am also persuaded by both study and experience that organizational narratives of identity and aspiration are critical dimensions of strategic leadership and are essential for understanding human agency and leadership as interactive processes. Finally, I find that paradigms as basic assumptions of thought and belief are the keys to gaining awareness of the frames of reference that are often hidden in organizational decision making. The three intertwined motifs of values, narratives, and paradigms provide the conceptual framework for both the theory and the practice of strategic leadership.

By shining this new conceptual light on the development of strategy, we are able to see more clearly the tacit forms of leadership that are present in the work of strategy in collegiate settings, such as in the shaping and articulation of a sense of purpose and vision. Schools and universities are loosely organized or "coupled" and do not have a uniform hierarchical structure of authority to define their purposes. As a result, they need to have sensitive and effective ways to understand and to tell their stories of identity, which is an important dimension of leadership (H. Gardner 1995; Weick 1991, 2001). Sense making includes but goes beyond the articulation of rational principles, the application of managerial systems, or the development of empirical explanations and focuses on an understanding of values and narratives as organizational enactments. So, the book's argument moves forward by analyzing information, connecting concepts, drawing out presuppositions and paradigms, searching out values and narratives, and tracing the deeper implications of practices in academic decision making. I try to make explicit the way stories and commitments shape the ordinary flow of experience as well as the formal decision-making systems of academic cultures. The argument I use to perform these tasks is philosophical in form, though not technical in content. It intends to avoid speculation but aims to provide a description of meanings that are embedded in the work of strategy as both a tacit and conscious activity.

To understand fully the possibilities and the limits of strategic leadership, it is essential to consider it at the intersection of theory and practice. The way we think about the deeper meaning of strategy obviously affects the way we enact strategy. Without a strong conceptual foundation, strategy remains a set of managerial techniques that are unable to connect systematically with the larger demands of leadership in academic communities. Conversely, without the defined steps of an applied discipline and a process of implementation, leadership cannot consistently shape the actual decisions of an organization. So, the reconceptualization of strategy leads to its reformulation and the effort to redefine and to integrate a number of its procedures, mechanisms, and processes. Although the work turns on conceptual arguments, it never leaves for long the realities and procedures of academic decision making. In many ways, the book is intended to be a conceptual and practical guide to a new approach to strategy. We might think of it as representing one aspect of another stage in the evolution of strategy that integrates strategic planning and management with leadership.

The evidence to support this integrative argument comes in several forms. Much of the work is analytical and draws conclusions, makes connections, and offers interpretations of a variety of other works, some of which are empirical, and others case based or interpretive. The adequacy and relevance of the analysis is open to scrutiny, criticism, and correction. Other tests of the argument are largely philosophical and concern its consistency and coherence. A related form of evaluation involves checking the capacity of the ideas to represent and describe personal and professional experience adequately and accurately. In particular, does the analysis illuminate others' experiences and understanding of strategy in terms of the motifs of organizational values, sense making, and leadership? I try to show that a good strategy process builds a case for change from many sources, including the organizational narrative. In doing so it may persuade and engage a good cross-section of a campus community about the organization's identity and prospects (cf. H. Gardner 2004).

The book also includes advice and a large number of recommendations for effective and useful ways to develop a strategy process. In many instances, these claims are supported by the study of cases or have become part of the research and literature on strategy. Many of the suggestions about best practices have been shaped and reinforced by my professional experience as a faculty and staff member, college president, corporate and nonprofit board member and chairman, seminar leader, and consultant on strategy.

I am fully aware that the book's arguments and recommendations add up to a significant reorientation of the work of strategy in academic settings. Although the argument is emphasized consistently to make the case for strategic leadership, I know that the effort is exploratory and that many of its claims need to be confirmed by a variety of forms of experience, research, and analysis. My aim is to integrate a variety of insights about strategy and leadership that have been developed in various contexts, and to encourage others to explore this and other models.

CONTENTS OF THE STUDY

The work is divided into four parts and thirteen chapters. Part I, **Issues in Leadership and Governance**, is an effort to provide the conceptual foundations for strategic leadership in higher education. In chapter 1, I offer a brief analysis of the portrayal of leadership in recent scholarship. In doing so, I seek to discover some of the defining elements of leadership as a relationship of mutual engagement and influence, an understanding that will guide my orientation to the tasks of strategy. Then, in the second chapter, I analyze leadership in higher education by focusing on presidential leadership, which introduces us as well to the challenges and conflicts of collegial governance and decision making. Subsequently, in the third chapter, I offer my own interpretation of values as standards of choice and explore the structural conflict between the values of academic autonomy and organizational authority in the culture of academic decision making.

Part II, **Preparing for Strategic Leadership**, consists of two chapters that set the stage for the practice of strategy. Chapter 4 analyzes recent understandings of strategy in business and higher education, situates strategy in the value system and paradigms of the academy, and provides an outline of an integrated approach to the strategy process. I propose the paradigm of responsibility (or "response-ability") as a way to think about and situate the work of strategy effectively within institutions of higher learning. Chapter 5 provides a detailed description of the ways that strategic planning can be successfully related to the governance of colleges and universities while respecting the commitment to collegial decision making. It focuses on the importance of a strategic planning council or its equivalent to coordinate the strategy process and suggests practical ways to orient the council's work, including the use of a set of strategic indicators.

Part III, **Practicing Strategic Leadership**, focuses each chapter on the components of an effective strategy process and suggests methods to orient them to leadership. Chapter 6 is the book's center of gravity, since it roots strategic leadership conceptually and practically in narratives of identity. It discusses and illustrates the power of narrative in organizational experience and analyzes the central place of stories of identity in leadership. In the following chapter the essential content of strategy is considered in terms of institutional identity, mission, and vision. In this context, the connection between strategy and leadership becomes explicit and inescapable, given the commanding importance of mission and vision for both practices. The next four chapters describe how each of the major components of strategic planning is reformulated as they are developed in the context of the process and discipline of strategic leadership. Chapter 9 suggests the importance of interpreting institutional identity in strategic terms as a repertoire of capabilities, explores the usefulness of the idea of core competencies, and examines the possibilities of environmental scans, SWOT analyses, and scenarios for exploring and responding to change in the wider world. The tenth chapter examines how strategic leadership provides a helpful orientation to the different levels of strategy as it moves from strategic initiatives and imperatives to measurable goals and actions. The following chapter provides a series of illustrations of the implications of strategic leadership for decision making in different spheres of organizational life, from student learning to finances. Chapter 12 describes the important transition from leadership to management and suggests ways to embed the process of strategic leadership in the operations of an academic institution.

Part IV, **The Limits and Possibilities of Strategic Leadership**, consists of two chapters, the first of which focuses on the central problems of the leadership of change and conflict, issues that have been both explicit and implicit throughout the study. The chapter shows the capacities of strategic leadership to deal effectively with change and structural conflict, as well as its limits concerning adversarial conflict and crisis management. The conclusion offers a recapitulation of each of the major elements of the discipline and the process of strategic leadership and explores other central issues, including the strategic integration of various dimensions and forms of leadership.

SOURCES OF THE STUDY

In developing the many-sided arguments of the work, I have explored literature and research in several overlapping areas. These include studies on leadership in general, and on leadership and governance in higher education in particular. It goes without saying that there is now a vast popular and scholarly body of literature on leadership, with some interesting points of convergence in the best of the work. In particular, I have developed several important facets of the book's argument in response to the groundbreaking ideas of James MacGregor Burns in *Leadership* (1978) and *Transforming Leadership* (2003). By situating the phenomenon of leadership squarely within the deepest dimensions of human moral agency and identity, he has opened a new approach to the contemporary study of leadership. My own reflection on human moral experience has been shaped through studies, research, and other writings on values (Morrill 1980). H. Richard Niebuhr has been the primary inspiration for much of this reflection. The analyses of Burton Clark have been of capital importance in my understanding of the culture of organizations of higher learning. His work on institutional sagas has stimulated and reinforced my own reflections on narratives of identity, which have been influenced by the work of Howard Gardner.

The other primary sources that I have used are institutional strategy reports and related documents. Many of these can now be found on institutional Web sites, and I have studied and printed parts or all of more than fifty such sources and have read many others that have come to me in other ways. Not surprisingly, I rely especially on those strategic plans in which I have been involved directly as a participant, leader, or consultant.

AUDIENCE

This work is addressed to a wide audience, in effect, to the faculty, administrators, and board members who study, lead, or participate in the strategic decision-making processes of colleges and universities. One of the premises of this book, as explained in several contexts, is that leadership as a process occurs throughout organizations of higher education and is frequently a collaborative activity. As a consequence, strategic leadership is relevant to virtually any faculty member or administrator who makes recommendations or significant decisions about the future—nearly everyone who chairs or serves on a committee, leads a department, or exercises more formal authority as a dean, director, vice president, or president.

Also included in the process of strategic leadership, as the text emphasizes on several occasions, are governing boards. The board's role in leadership extends well beyond its formal responsibility as the institution's ultimate legal authority. As governing boards come to understand more fully the organizational dynamics and commitments of the institutions they serve, they become more effective participants in strategic governance and strategic leadership.

Scholars and students interested in leadership and strategy in higher education in particular and in professional and nonprofit organizations in general will also find much of the argument relevant to their concerns.

ACKNOWLEDGMENTS

Although this book has its roots in many forms of study and practice over the years, it would not have been written without the generosity of the Board of Trustees of the University of Richmond. When I completed a decade of service and retired from the presidency, I was honored with appointment as chancellor, and a professorship carrying my name that enabled me to do the initial research and writing required for the book. Austin Brockenbrough III and Gilbert Rosenthal, rector and vice-rector respectively, as well as Elaine Yeatts, Lewis Booker, and Robert Burrus, were the trustee leaders who proposed these opportunities. I am deeply grateful for their support and friendship.

One of the university's trustees, Robert Jepson, has been more instrumental in this work than he knows. Early in my presidency at Richmond, he finalized a gift of $20 million to create the Jepson School of Leadership Studies. The establishment of the school was among the most satisfying aspects of my work, and it has attracted an exceptionally talented group of faculty members and students. I owe Bob Jepson my enduring gratitude for being a deeply generous benefactor, a visionary leader, and a friend.

One of the reasons that this project has gone forward is the result of my teaching seminars on the topic in the Jepson School. I am happy to express my sincere thanks to my students for their lively involvement and responsiveness to many of the concepts surrounding strategic leadership. One of my former students, Anne Williamson, worked intensively with me for several weeks to begin to document references and to shape the rough draft into a useful document. I am thankful for her insights, efficiency, and encouragement. Another former student, Joshua Parrett, served as a research assistant, summarized various studies, and ingeniously chased down a large number of strategic plans on the Internet. I appreciate his assistance.

I am grateful to Nancy Nock for her skillful typing in creating a first draft of the text, and especially to Barbara Morgan, my assistant, for stepping in to help at critical points. Other thoughtful staff members at the university, including Terri Weaver and Marion Dieterich, assisted when needed.

Colleagues too numerous to mention have read parts of the text and have encouraged me in my work. David Leary, university professor; Andrew Newcomb, dean of arts and sciences; and Susan Johnson, associate dean, all at the University of Richmond, have provided feedback and support on many occasions. At Centre College, President John Roush, Vice President Richard Trollinger, and Professor Clarence Wyatt have shown a special interest in my work. I am indebted to all of these individuals and many others for their friendship and colleagueship.

Susan Slesinger, executive editor for the ACE/Praeger series, has offered insightful advice and great support during the review and editing process, and I am very thankful for her assistance.

PART I

Issues in Leadership and Governance

CHAPTER

The Phenomenon of Leadership

erhaps uniquely in the world, contemporary America has become increasingly captivated by the possibilities and mysteries of leadership. From tiny human-service agencies to vast multinational corporations, from the halls of government to the local schoolhouse, there is vital interest in both the theory and the practice of leadership. Books on leadership flood the shelves of libraries and bookstores, and every organization searches for ways to develop the leadership skills of its members. Whether as citizens, professionals, or volunteers, people want to understand the meaning of effective leadership and how to practice it (Bligh and Mendl 2005).

THE UNCERTAIN PLACE OF LEADERSHIP IN HIGHER EDUCATION

When it comes to institutions of higher learning, there are several ironies concerning the phenomenon of leadership—as an area of study, as a goal of education, and as an organizational process. In one form or another, the theme has long been a subject of inquiry in both the social sciences and the humanities. Studies in these fields provide various accounts of leaders and leadership as a part of their intellectual stock in trade. Without doubt, the motif has recently become much more explicit in many disciplines and cross-disciplines, and the study of leadership is increasingly the subject of organized curricular and campus programs (Goethals, Swenson, and Burns 2004). Further, colleges and universities often turn to the language of leadership to describe how their educational programs will prepare students to exercise intellectual and social responsibilities in the future. Yet, at the same time, many academicians resist the endorsement of the leadership theme, for it continues to be associated with vague and unattainable educational objectives, and it is suspiciously tied to the moral ambiguities of privilege and power—to which history's leaders often bear bloody testimony.

Perhaps the culminating irony is that colleges and universities, the institutions that study leadership analytically and empirically, rarely make their own decision-making and leadership processes and practices the object of formal programs of development or inquiry. There are notable and growing exceptions concerning leadership development programs in larger institutions, but even in these cases the emphasis is often on the responsibilities of designated positions of authority (Ruben 2004b). They often focus more on management than leadership, at least understood as a process that involves setting directions, motivating others, and coping with change.

When we turn to academic decision making proper, the idiom in currency in higher education is governance rather than leadership. The authoritative texts and documents that define campus decision making say much about "joint effort" or "shared governance," but little about leadership. Bringing various forms of campus authority and the decision-making process into proper balance, and parsing texts and delineating practices to do so, is often the focus of faculty and administrative activity. The larger and often-pressing question of leadership—of the ways, for instance, to develop a shared vision for the future—is pursued obliquely through activities such as strategic planning that have an awkward place in the formal governance system itself. Leadership as a process of change and motivation remains a repressed theme.

This is a peculiar and troubling form of neglect, especially given the ever-intensifying demands on colleges and universities in a challenging environment. Frank Rhodes, president emeritus of Cornell, voices a recurrent theme: "The development of responsible, effective, and balanced governance, leadership, and management is one of the most urgent priorities for the American university as it enters the new Millennium" (2001, 201).

If we are to bring new resources to bear on this complex set of issues, it will be in some measure because of the convergent understandings of leadership that have emerged in a variety of fields in the last several decades. Although the work on leadership is of very mixed quality and importance, from self-aggrandizing memoirs to groundbreaking scholarship, there is much to be learned from the best of the literature. It gives us reason to believe that it is worthwhile to look closely again at leadership in colleges and universities through the lens of these perspectives. As we review and synthesize some of these studies of leadership, we shall keep before ourselves a central question. What can we learn about leadership that will increase our understanding and improve the practice of it in colleges and universities?

MOTIFS IN LEADERSHIP

We use the words "leadership" and "leaders" in everyday language to describe an enormous variety of relationships and contexts in which certain individuals and groups influence the thought and action of others. Leadership scholars have developed a dizzying array of schools, categories, and taxonomies of leadership and leadership theories to differentiate various approaches and concepts (Wren 2006). In order to get our bearings for the task, it is worth the effort to sort out briefly several threads of common and academic usage before providing a more formal analysis.

In many contexts we refer to leadership as a *pattern of influence* that resides in an individual's or a group's innovative ideas and creative achievements outside the bounds of formal institutions. Leadership in this sense can be indirect and distant, as when we point to the leader of a school of thought, the innovator of a set of professional practices or to the dominant figure in an artistic or social movement. We readily understand, for instance, the meaning of the claims that Albert Einstein was a leader in the development of modern physics, or Paul Cézanne in the evolution of twentieth-century painting, or Martin Luther King, Jr., in civil rights, though none of them did so by virtue of holding a formal position of authority. In *Leading Minds*, Howard Gardner (1995) suggests that this form of leadership is real but indirect.

As we evoke the motif of leadership in organizations and institutions, and in many social movements, quite different themes come to light. This form of leadership is more direct and involving, for it occurs in smaller or larger groups in which the participants have various roles, responsibilities, and mutual expectations defined by the collective itself. Perhaps the most familiar use of the terminology of leadership is when it is used to refer to formal positions of authority, as exemplified by those who hold political office or carry major responsibilities in a complex organization. These uses of the words "leader" and "leadership" turn around power and authority and are the stuff of everyday life and language.

Any sketch of common usages would not be complete if it did not acknowledge the traditional belief that leadership is variously defined by the exceptional attributes of leaders, which we can categorize as skills and personal characteristics. In this perspective, leaders are special individuals marked by fixed attributes and abilities, such as high resolve, energy, intelligence, expertise, persuasiveness, and a forceful or magnetic personality, which is often called *charisma*. Great leaders are often depicted as those who turn the pages of history. As the memoirs, biographies, and studies of business and political leaders attest, many in the contemporary world continue to believe that leaders possess special qualities and skills, such as assertiveness, decisiveness, and confidence. In the public mind, they are often understood to provide a compelling vision that gives purpose and direction to the groups that they lead. It would be unwise not to reckon with the broad appeal and continuing influence of this perspective. Although recent scholarship offers a much more nuanced, penetrating, and contextual understanding of the attributes of leadership, strong echoes of these traditional ideas can be heard in many of the contemporary discussions of leadership.

One of the leading scholars in the field, Bernard Bass, uses the word "charisma" as a way to describe one of the characteristics of those he calls "transformational" leaders (Bass and Aviolio 1993; Bass and Riggio 2006). He uses the word to refer to leaders whose followers in a given organizational context feel a magnetic attraction to them, so charisma is not a fixed personality trait.

Other scholars have published numerous studies to show that leadership effectiveness is contingent on situation or circumstance, an insight that has become a common assumption in the scholarly literature and in many spheres of practice. Fiedler (1993), for instance, has shown in many studies that the task-oriented style of leadership seems more effective when circumstances are less orderly or verging on a crisis, while a more relationship oriented style fits better when conditions are more normal. As Clark Kerr and Marian L. Gade (1986) have suggested, effective presidential leadership in colleges and universities is highly situational since it depends on the right match between circumstance, individual, and institution. A hero in one institution could be a failure in another.

As we shall explore throughout this study, leadership recently has been differentiated both theoretically and practically from the possession of formal authority and personal attributes. Many scholars have focused on the tasks or practices of leaders, what some would call a behavioral orientation. More important than what leaders are or the positions that they hold is what they do. They do such things as define purpose, envision the future, set high ethical standards, and renew the organization under many different circumstances (J. Gardner 1990; Kouzes and Posner 1990).

Perhaps the most widely shared understanding among contemporary theorists is that leadership is primarily a *relationship* between leaders and followers. The relationship is interactive and involves a variety of social processes, practices, and engagements through which followers respond to the influence of leaders, and leaders attend to the needs and values of their followers. My concerns for leadership will center precisely on the development of a collaborative and interactive method of strategic leadership as a systematic organizational process. Though I by no means exclude a focus on the significance of authority, nor a concern for the skills, styles, qualities, and practices of leaders, the components of strategic leadership as an interactive form of direction setting and decision making will be our central preoccupation.

GOOD TO GREAT: A CASE STUDY IN LEADERSHIP

In order to gain an understanding of the changing interpretations of the phenomenon, it will be useful to look briefly at the findings of one influential analysis of leadership in business, the widely read book by James Collins (2001), *Good to Great.* Using long-term superior performance in earnings and stock appreciation as indicators of success, the book attempts to find the characteristics that differentiate good companies from great ones. The work's findings about leadership are striking because they are counterintuitive, at least in terms of popular expectations. The author offers a typology of leadership with five levels of talent and effectiveness that culminate in the motif of the executive leader who builds greatness into an organization. Yet, ironically, the leaders of the great companies were not characterized as having particularly strong or forceful personalities, nor were they seen as visionaries. Often shy and self-effacing, they were typically uncomfortable in the limelight and did not call attention to themselves or their personal achievements. Collins describes this as the paradox of personal humility and professional will. These executives brought a powerful level of commitment, unparalleled determination, and excellent managerial skills to their responsibilities, but the focus was always primarily on organizational purposes and goals. These chief executives tended to lead by (1) raising questions, not providing answers; (2) using debate and dialogue, not coercion; (3) conducting autopsies on mistakes without placing blame; and (4) building red-flag problem indicators into their systems of information.

To be sure, a simple, compelling vision was a crucial component of leadership in these cases, but it was the result of a collective process, open debate, and intense discussions, often over a long period of time. The focus of the dialogue was not rhetoric about being the best company in the industry. Rather, the preoccupation was using analytical methods and collaborative processes to find those specific spheres of activity or product lines in which the company actually excelled, or could excel, to become the very best in the world. The idea that a bold leader imposes a dazzling vision on an acquiescent organization would ring false to the top executives of these companies. "Yes, leadership is about vision. But leadership is equally about creating a climate where truth is heard and the brutal facts confronted" (Collins 2001, 74). Drawing these findings together in a sharp, ironic reversal of traditional thinking about leadership, Collins offers these conclusions: "The moment a leader allows himself to become the primary reality people worry about ... you have a recipe for mediocrity, or worse.... Less charismatic leaders often produce better long-term results than their more charismatic counterparts" (2001, 72). So, charisma is a liability that effective leadership can overcome!

As we shall see in the brief phenomenology of relational leadership that follows, Collins's findings are largely consistent with the interpretations of leadership that have emerged in the past several decades in many fields. The personalities and styles of effective leaders come in all sizes and shapes. Often they are skilled in delegating authority, but not infrequently they are immersed in the details of the enterprise. What matters most are their practices and commitments and the disciplined processes of leadership that they embed in their organizations.

TOWARD A PHENOMENOLOGY OF RELATIONAL LEADERSHIP

This sample of Collins's research and reflection opens up a vast sea of contemporary findings about leaders and leadership. Some twenty-five years ago one of the most influential students of leadership, James MacGregor Burns, made a succinct claim to which scholars have tried to respond ever since: "Leadership is one of the most observed and least understood phenomena on earth" (1978, 2).

Over the past several decades, efforts to remedy this deficit have been made in a variety of academic forms and organizational contexts.

As one reads some of the more influential studies of leadership, it soon becomes obvious that there are any number of common insights and shared findings, though no single dominant systematic theory (Goethals and Sorenson 2006). Without claiming anything like an exhaustive explanation of an ever-enlarging body of knowledge and inquiry, it nevertheless becomes possible to discover common themes and parallel conclusions, especially concerning the reciprocal relationship between leaders and followers. Although this is often called the "social exchange" theory of leadership, the terminology is misleading, for the relationship is typically much more significant and engaging than the rather mechanical term "exchange" suggests (Hoyt, Goethals, and Riggio 2006; Messick 2005). A primary focus on the skills, qualities, practices, styles, contexts, and authority of leaders usually still involves interpreting leadership as what leaders do *to* or *for* others rather than as engaging definitively *with* others. Some of the most interesting and promising motifs for understanding and exercising leadership in academic communities flow from a relational understanding of leadership.

In order to reveal the core meanings of relational leadership that emerge from recent studies, we shall use some of the techniques of phenomenological analysis and description. From this perspective, our task is to ask: What are the defining characteristics of leadership as a human relational phenomenon? What conditions of possibility have to be satisfied for it to occur? How is it constituted? As a consequence, what basic meanings does it convey, both tacitly and explicitly?

Leadership as Agency

We discover first that many modern scholars tend to depict leadership as an activity, as a form of human agency. As agents, humans are self-determining beings who are in charge of their own conduct. They give form and purpose to their lives through their choices and actions, as carried out within various systems of meaning. In this context, leadership is primarily a pattern of engagement and a relational process within a larger framework of human sense making, rather than a position of authority in an institutional hierarchy. Leadership is situated in that sphere of life in which humans forge meanings with others and work towards common social and institutional goals to fulfill their needs and realize their values. For Burns (2003), interactive leadership is the crux of historical causality itself, so leadership as agency is on display in the record of human striving.

Leadership as Fundamental

"Leadership" is both a fundamental and a relational term. It describes the dynamics of an inescapable form of social interaction by naming the relationship that occurs between certain individuals (and groups) and those whom they influence and by whom they are influenced. The relationship has several features, one of which is that leadership is a basic ingredient of human social organization, not an elective addition to it. As Thomas Wren puts it, "If leadership is viewed as a process by which groups, organizations, and societies attempt to achieve common goals, it encompasses one of the fundamental currents of the human experience" (1995, x). One does not first create an institution and then search for ways to introduce leadership into it. Rather, leadership occurs simultaneously with social organization.

Leadership as Relational

One consequence of this perspective is that the term "leadership" always involves the idea of followership. If no one is following, no one is leading. Leaders and followers (in the generic sense, not as a form of dependency) require one another for either side of the leadership equation to make sense (Hollander 1993). According to Joseph Rost, "Followers and leaders develop a relationship wherein they influence one another as well as the organization and society, and that is leadership. They do not do the same things in the relationship...but they are both essential to leadership" (1995, 192). The relationship has characteristic features and patterns of interaction that give it texture and meaning.

Leadership as Sense Making

One of the central forms of reciprocity is effective communication between leaders and followers about the challenges and issues that they face together. Leaders seek to influence their followers to adopt the leader's interpretations of their shared experience, and they use a variety of linguistic and nonlinguistic forms of communication to do so. They use symbols and metaphors and tell stories of identity and aspiration to construct a shared sense of meaning (Bennis and Nanus 1997; H. Gardner 1995; Goethals 2005). In communicating with followers, leaders typically express a compelling sense of vision for the future. "A leader does not tell it 'as it is'; he [or she] tells it as it *might* be.... The leader is a sense-giver" (Thayer, quoted in Weick 1995, 10). Sense giving and sense making offer people a sense of possibility that an otherwise hostile, indifferent, or incomprehensible world can be brought under their control.

Moral Leadership

As has become clear in the modern scholarship on leadership, followers or constituents, especially in a democratic context, are not empty vessels who are filled by content provided by the leader. At a minimum, followers have to give their consent to the leader's goals and priorities. When they are fully engaged, they are committed to the leader's program, and frequently to his or her person. Yet it is clear that followers do not lend their support blindly but do so in terms of needs and interests of their own that are satisfied by the leader.

Followers bring expectations and criteria to the relationship based on mutual respect between them and the leader. As James O'Toole suggests, "Treating people with respect is what moral leadership is about" (1995, 12). People expect their voices to be heard, their problems to be addressed, their needs to be satisfied, and their hopes to be fulfilled. They seek security and protection from threatening circumstances (Messick 2005). If the goals they entered into the relationship in order to secure are not reached, in time their support will dissolve. It is at their own peril that leaders forget that support is always conditional. Authority is not an absolute but is always *conveyed* in the name of larger social and organizational ends, and measured by the criteria that those purposes entail (Heifetz 1994). Leaders and followers together serve a "third thing," a common cause that defines their relationship. Whatever the social context, followers always have means to influence and to assess the effectiveness and legitimacy of their leaders (cf. Hollander 1993). From the gathering of the elders to the ballot box, from passive resistance to violence in the streets, followers know how to influence and replace their leaders.

Because of the depths to which leadership reaches, followers have explicit moral expectations of their leaders. The support of followers is conditioned on the leader's legitimacy, trustworthiness, and credibility. Should there be many false notes, the leader's credibility soon begins to fade. If lies or duplicity are revealed, the leader's trustworthiness vanishes overnight. Nor is trustworthiness just accuracy in communication, for it involves integrity in the leader's conduct and commitment as well. To be credible, the leader must embody the values for which the institution stands, or the leadership relationship will be weakened or broken (cf. Hogg 2005). When leaders use careful ethical reasoning, establish and enforce high standards, live the values that they claim, and sacrifice their own interests to do so, they become respected or even hallowed figures in the eyes of their followers. Contemporary leadership scholars such as James O'Toole (1995), Ronald Heifetz (1994), Joanne Ciulla (1998, 2002, 2005), Douglas Hicks and Terry Price (2006) Terry Price (2005), Howard Gardner (1995), John Gardner (1990), and James MacGregor Burns (1978, 2003) place ethics and moral integrity at the heart of leadership.

Leadership, Conflict, and Change

Invariably, changing circumstances or the leader's chosen directions will stir up resistance and engender conflicting interests among some constituents, which reveals another defining characteristic of leadership. Since the resources of time, space, attention, and money are always strictly limited, and everyone's values, interests, and appetites can never be fully reconciled, inequality and conflict are at the heart of social experience. Leaders work tirelessly to resolve conflict in a variety of forms and at every level of the organization.

The leader also has to address threatening forms of change that create fear and resistance and that may stir up bitter conflict of its own. So leadership is always a gritty affair that engages leaders in a perpetual process of responding to conflict and change. They expend considerable energy in motivating, persuading, influencing, and manipulating others to join them in responding to tension and change; or they may use more assertive methods to enact their purposes. Historical experience shows that leaders will use a large range of harsh sanctions, the logical end point of which is coercion and violence, to achieve their goals. Where leadership ends and domination begins becomes a compelling and complex issue of historical and ethical interpretation.

Leadership and Empowerment

In the contemporary scholarship on leadership, there is often an emphasis on the ways that the leadership relationship leads to the explicit empowerment of followers. In political contexts, of course, empowerment is a central feature of democratic systems. Increasingly, however, the meaning of the word has broadened. It now refers as well to the ways that leaders seek to place more decision-making authority and responsibility in the hands of individuals and teams throughout the organization. The focus is often on ways to improve processes that are best understood by those closest to them. Empowerment in this sense often opens other doors of human development and personal fulfillment, for it leads to the creation of ways to improve the motivation, decision-making skills, and capabilities of the total workforce or community. When work takes on a deeper sense of purpose, people become far more engaged in their responsibilities (George 2003). As success is achieved, they develop more self-confidence, optimism, and self-respect (Messick 2005). Leadership at this level appears to touch a person's sense of identity and self-esteem, so it triggers a range of strong intrinsic motivations for achievement and for effectiveness in working with others (House and Shamir 1993).

The more decisions are dispersed, the more individuals and groups become directly accountable for their performance. The roles of leader and follower become fluid, as individuals and groups both respond to the influence of others and exercise their own leadership. Leadership scholar Gill Hickman makes a point that has special relevance for academic communities: "Individuals move from participant to leader or leader to participant based on capabilities, expertise, motivation, ideas, and circumstances, not solely on position or authority" (1998, xiii). Leadership becomes a disposition and a process that is incorporated into the workings of the organization.

In an influential study of adaptive leadership, Ronald Heifetz focuses on some of the complexities of placing responsibility in the hands of constituents that they may prefer to avoid, a phenomenon that is common in academic communities. He emphasizes the leader's role in focusing, analyzing, diagnosing, and interpreting challenges to the group's values and effectiveness that have to be faced. The leader's task is many sided but must take into account Heifetz's counsel to "Give the work back to people, but at a rate they can stand. Place and develop responsibility by putting pressure on the people with the problem" (1994, 128).

Leadership and Positions of Authority

These comments on empowerment make explicit an important theme about authority that has substantial implications for the exercise of leadership in institutions of higher learning. Academic professionals carry much of the authority and responsibility for leadership in various units and activities—schools, departments, committees, programs—spread throughout the organization. Given our description of leadership, we can see clearly why those who hold positions of formal authority such as president, dean, or chairperson are not thereby necessarily the only leaders, or even the most effective leaders, in academic organizations. Based on this understanding, it is perfectly consistent to say that a person can be the titular head of an organization, but not the leader of it. Under some circumstances, such an individual might be better described as an authority figure, a manager, a figurehead, or a paper shuffler. At one extreme, they may function as autocrats who glory in imposing their will on others, or at the other pole as mere figureheads who cannot make decisions. Conversely, individuals with little formal power or authority may play vital roles in leadership. The exercise of leadership can be found at every level of an institution's formal hierarchy, especially in academic communities where authority is diffuse and widely dispersed.

We should not, of course, rush to break the link between leadership, power, and authority. Effective leaders are often known by their ability to use their administrative, legal, coercive, and symbolic power responsibly and effectively (cf. Hughes, Ginnett, and Curphy 1995). The capacity to do so is no mean accomplishment but is dense with organizational and moral significance. Both designated and other kinds of leaders also gain power informally by means of relationships, talents, expertise, and political skills. As we shall see more than once, the critical question for leadership in colleges and universities becomes the way power, authority, and influence are exercised to define and to achieve common purposes. Governance is one thing and reciprocal leadership is another; but those who have been granted authority have the opportunity and the responsibility to transform it into interactive leadership. As we shall see, embedding strategic leadership processes throughout the organization is one of the ways to accomplish this transformation systematically.

Transactional and Transforming Leadership

As we continue to explore the nuclear elements of reciprocal leadership, we will do well to pause over an important distinction between transactional and transforming leadership. First articulated in Burns's groundbreaking 1978 study *Leadership*, and reformulated in his 2003 book *Transforming Leadership*, these concepts have become a pivotal organizing theme for much of the research and writing on leadership. For Burns, and now many others, one basic form of leadership involves a mutuality of immediate interests and exchange of benefits between leaders and followers that can be called "a transaction" and is therefore termed "transactional leadership." Leaders meet the conscious needs and interests of their followers and are rewarded with their support, or punished by its withdrawal. Leaders in turn use rewards and sanctions to build their power base and to create discipline in the ranks. Classic examples of these types of exchanges come readily to mind: the politician elected to office rewards his supporters with jobs and punishes his opponents by reducing their influence, a manager gains or loses the confidence of an operating unit by providing or withholding capital resources, and a college dean is judged to be effective if she increases faculty salaries and budget lines. This form of leadership meets the basic test of reciprocity, for the mutuality of the relationship is clear. Yet transactional leadership tends to accept the status quo, and to avoid or deflect important forms of conflict over purposes and values. It lacks the ability to respond creatively to the forces of change, to inspire followers to superior performance, or to challenge the community or the organization to meet demanding moral commitments.

In *Leadership*, Burns characterizes transforming leadership in primarily moral terms. It involves the leader's ability to summon followers to a higher level of ethical understanding and commitment, the capacity, for example, to move the group or the society to the more elevated concerns of justice and equality, rather than just the satisfaction of material wants and needs. The transforming leader who engages followers at these encompassing levels of values and purposes also creates pervasive, enduring, and fundamental changes in organizations and societies, a conclusion introduced by Burns in *Transforming Leadership*.

As Burns's ideas have been pursued by other scholars, such as Bernard Bass, they have been translated into different idioms and contexts. For Bass, transformational leadership becomes a pattern of relationship between leaders and followers in business, the military, and other organizations. Transformational leaders challenge their subordinates' thinking, show personal interest in their development, inspire them to higher levels of achievement, and represent a magnetic source of attraction. Bass makes it clear that transformational and transactional leadership are not exclusive alternatives, for most leaders show both characteristics in their work (Bass 1990; Bass and Aviolio 1993).

In terms of leadership in higher education, it is clear that the words "transactional" and "transformational" can be misleading if they are used to classify leaders or their influence in exclusive categories. They are better seen as motifs and methods of leadership that are largely intertwined in practice, not as rigid categories to be glibly applied to all the work of an individual or group. In Burns's (2003) terms, many transforming changes may take decades and can be the result of incremental achievements over time. For colleges and universities, the key question becomes the shape and intent of the processes of leadership and their potential to motivate an academic community to respond effectively to change.

Leadership as Service

For a number of contemporary commentators, these ideas lead to the conclusion that leadership is best understood as a form of service to others and to shared values. The influential reflections of Robert Greenleaf have given the notion of servant leadership an important place in discussions of the role and responsibilities of leaders. As he puts it, "A new moral principle is emerging which holds that the only authority deserving one's allegiance is that which is freely and knowingly granted by the led to the leader in response to, and in proportion to, the clearly evident servant stature of the leader" (1977, 10). The practices of leading through deep listening, persuasion, and empathy, and by articulating a vision of new moral possibilities, are some of the components of servant leadership.

Implications of the Contemporary Concepts of Leadership

Our description of some of the defining elements of relational leadership points in many directions both to understand and practice leadership. To offer a working definition for our purposes, we propose that leadership is an interactive relationship of sense making and sense giving in which certain individuals and groups influence and motivate others to adopt and to enact common values and purposes, and to pursue shared goals in responding to change and conflict.

If leadership takes us to the fundamental conditions of human self-enactment in groups, it also reveals essential human possibilities and needs. Leadership ultimately has to do with the human condition (Goethals and Sorenson 2006). A person does not live without values and commitments that make the human enterprise itself worthwhile in facing the limits and threats with which he or she must contend. Ultimately it is the protection and flourishing of their values that humans seek in the leadership of their organizations and institutions. The ultimate tests of leadership end up as moral and spiritual criteria because of the way humans are constituted.

Implications for Higher Education

The framework that we have constructed gives us the insights, concepts, and vocabulary to assess and to critique various theories of leadership in higher education, and to draw useful perspectives from them. Most importantly, our phenomenology of relational leadership will serve as a central point of reference in our efforts to describe a process of strategic leadership. We can already see in broad terms the criteria that it will have to satisfy. The process will have to be

- Sense making and sense giving
- Collaborative and empowering
- Direction setting and values driven

- Change oriented and conflict resolving
- Motivating and influential

When we reach the campus, we shall find again the familiar leadership themes of reciprocity and responsiveness to the needs and values of participants, now arrayed in the colorful and complicated regalia of collegial governance. The process of academic decision making rests on academic values and professional norms that have powerful ethical force. Yet leadership in colleges and universities is typically problematic and unsure of itself both in theory and in practice. Structural conflict is a given of the decision-making system, often frustrating the tasks of leadership. Thus, these preliminary ideas about leadership will be put to the test as we investigate the possibilities of strategic leadership.

LEARNING LEADERSHIP

One of the persistent questions about reciprocal leadership concerns the relationship between the characteristics of individual leaders and the process of leadership. We have spoken repeatedly of leadership, but little of leaders. Yet at one pole of the relationship are those we call leaders. What can we say about leaders as part of the leadership equation? Though not simply defined by fixed traits or the possession of formal authority, leaders nonetheless logically must have some set of attributes and qualities that give meaning to the term. The characteristics and skills of leaders may vary widely with context and circumstance, but it is still impossible to avoid some generalizations about them. We need to focus on these factors in order to give precision to a formal method of strategic leadership. An answer must finally be given to the questions, Who will use the process? What skills will they require? How will they learn them?

In this context, a number of questions regularly present themselves concerning the genetic, psychological, experiential, and educational formation of leaders. Are they born or made? Can leadership be taught, or, put more precisely, how is it learned? In serious studies, the answer to these questions is always equivocal, always both yes and no (Bass 1990; K. E. Clark and M. B. Clark 1990, 1994; J. Gardner 1990; Kouzes and Posner 1990; Padilla 2005). The ambiguity comes from the fact that, as we have seen, leadership involves a wide variety of forms of intelligence, knowledge, skills, practices, commitments, and personal characteristics. The talent for leadership is widely but not equally distributed in the species. While much can be taught and learned about both the nature and the practice of leadership, some of its crucial components—consider courage and resilience—are largely beyond the influence of formal education.

Needless to say, those issues relating to the different dimensions of leadership, and how and whether it can be taught and learned, touch on a series of complex and difficult questions. Relying on the work of Bass, Hollander, and others, John Gardner (1990) has synthesized a list of attributes of leadership that includes general competencies, skills, and qualities that are shaped in practice by context and circumstance. As we examine many of these broad characteristics of leadership, we also begin to get a good sense of how different aspects of leadership can be learned and taught, and the place and potential for learning a structured process of strategic leadership.

A Spectrum of Leadership Characteristics

In effect, the possibility for both attributes and practices of leadership to be learned can be considered as points along an uneven and disjointed spectrum, punctuated by the unpredictability of the influence of circumstances on individuals and groups. Although subject to a great deal of fluctuation and variation, it is helpful to think of three broad zones along the leadership spectrum: (1) fixed characteristics, (2) forms of practice and behavior, and (3) methods of thinking, problem solving, and deciding. As one moves along the spectrum, the characteristics of leadership become more predictably subject to different forms of experience, intentional development, and formal education.

Fixed Characteristics

Consider some of the categories that seem to describe a person's ways of being, or the fixed elements of identity that are more or less defined by genetic predisposition, the stable characteristics of personality, the influences of powerful formative experiences, and the deepest commitments to values and beliefs. Attributes of this sort noted by Gardner include high intelligence, courage and resolution, the need to achieve, the willingness to accept responsibility, confidence and assertiveness, adaptability, and physical stamina. Although there are undoubtedly many exceptional cases and circumstances, these characteristics are difficult to change intentionally or fundamentally through teaching and learning in the adult years.

Forms of Practice and Behavior

At the midpoint along the spectrum, the characteristics of leadership tend to consist of forms of practice, action, and behavior. Thus, we find on Gardner's list skills in dealing with people, the ability to motivate others, the understanding of followers' needs, and the capacity to win and maintain trust. These patterns of action and forms of relationship are in large measure learned through a variety

Table 1.1
The Spectrum of Leadership Characteristics

Fixed characteristics	Forms of practice and behavior	Methods: knowledge, skills, and expertise

of social, educational, and personal experiences throughout life, including both classroom and experiential education. Yet unlike most aspects of a person's fixed characteristics, they are subject to continuous reinterpretation and modification, as mediated by new experiences, the powers of practical intelligence, and formal programs of education and personal development. Although highly variable according to each individual, few would claim that thoughtful efforts to develop the appropriate interpersonal and behavioral competencies are without effect. Knowledge about leadership can be appropriated for the practice of it, especially if it is tied to an effective set of systematic methods, as one finds in an effective strategy process.

Knowledge, Skills, and Expertise

At the other end of the spectrum are attributes of leadership that are clearly subject to conventional forms of teaching and learning. Always within limits set by motivation and talent, it is obviously possible to teach people how to improve judgment through knowledge, to achieve expertise in complex fields, and to use complicated systems of decision making and management—all of which are required in a strategy process. In these contexts, the exercise of leadership itself is closely tied to acquiring and applying knowledge through basic and applied disciplines. Leaders in any walk of life will only be able to lead their colleagues if they have a mastery of the intellectual and practical tools of their trade, whether they work on Main Street or Wall Street, in a courtroom or a classroom.

Leadership Education and Development

The possibilities of leadership education and development have been seized by virtually every large organization, so that it has become something of a profession unto itself. Leadership programs of all sorts are now offered in most corporations and government agencies, and in many colleges and universities. We should emphasize, however, that many of the programs do not instruct us consistently or precisely about the possibilities of teaching leadership as a way to motivate change and to set directions for the future. They sometimes appear to have a confused and confusing agenda, much of which consists of different forms of management training or executive development that focus on the skills needed for a specific position. They can include everything from computer literacy to running a successful meeting to deepening personal self-awareness. Many corporations use a variety of developmental methods, including mentoring, coaching, formal education, and developmental assignments, to enhance an executive's leadership readiness.

In effect, the activities and programs that go under the name of leadership development are often quite distinct enterprises. Most of them are valid and valuable in their own ways. As long as expectations are realistic, there is good reason to believe that such efforts can make an incremental contribution to a person's effectiveness as a positional leader, especially in terms of enlarged self-understanding, broadened professional experience, and a larger repertoire of skills.

Yet any assessment of the capacity of these programs' success in developing the attributes or methods of engaging, relational leadership requires a careful sorting out of their actual goals and practices. They must serve a larger end if they are to reach the heart of leadership—which is to mobilize and motivate the members of an organization to enact shared values and purposes.

Much of the burden of our argument goes toward showing that an important dimension of reciprocal leadership can be taught and learned as a process and discipline of decision making. We have tried to go beyond the common effort to list the characteristics of exceptional leaders as the primary way to understand leadership. In his compelling account of authentic leadership as the chief executive of a major corporation, Bill George relates, "In my desire to become a leader, I studied the biographies of world leaders, as well as great business leaders of my era, attempting to develop the leadership characteristics they displayed. It didn't work" (2003, 29).

To be sure, there is no leadership without leaders; yet many of the skills and abilities of leaders become effective dimensions of leadership only as they are woven into a more encompassing process of decision making oriented to the fulfillment of the purposes of the organization. In the context of a relational theory of leadership, we can see the skills and talents of leaders in a new and dialectical perspective. Until the capacities of leadership are woven into the realization of shared purposes and commitments, they are resources waiting to be defined and given content. Unless the leader's abilities carry and inspire a larger meaning than individual virtuosity, they do not meet the tests of leadership as a reciprocal process oriented to values. At the same time, engaging and intentional leadership cannot be sustained without the hard and effective work of skilled leaders whose competencies and qualities are necessary, but not sufficient to inspire commitment to shared purposes.

THE CONTEXT FOR THE DISCIPLINE OF STRATEGIC LEADERSHIP

These reflections allow us to anticipate the possibilities of a formal and systematic process of strategic leadership. As a structured, collaborative method and discipline of decision making, it can be taught and learned. Like all processes and disciplines, it will be practiced more effectively by some than others. As we shall see, it requires integrative and systemic thinking, quantitative reasoning, collaborative decision making, effective communication, sensitivity to narratives and values, and a capacity to work in structured group processes. As suggested by our analysis of the attributes of leadership, these are not abilities that everyone has in the same measure, but each step in the total process is part of an applied discipline that can be learned.

Perhaps the most promising possibility for a systematic process of leadership is its use by those who have been charged with strategic decision-making responsibilities. As we turn our inquiry in this direction, we shift our attention to the

actual choice processes of academic organizations. In a collegiate setting, strategic decision making involves the governing board, the president and other top
officers, much of the administrative staff, and at one time or another many of the
faculty. Whether in committees, departments, schools, or the university itself,
issues that touch on questions of purpose and direction always raise the question
of leadership.

In all these contexts and many others, both the faculty and the administration
know the need for effective leadership but are also keenly aware of their peculiar
lack of authority. It is in the nature of things that most colleges and universities do
not have mechanisms of authority that can readily create or implement a vision
of the future. In hierarchical organizations, on the other hand, the development
of a vision may require involvement from many quarters, but once adopted it is
implemented through a clear system of authority.

One symptom of the tension in academic organizations is that leaders often
yearn for clearer authority and support in a chain of expectations that ends, for
presidents, with the governing board. Many other leaders reason tacitly that if
only they could improve their skills in leadership, they could create far better
results for their organization. Although the goal is worthy and important, even if
they could transform themselves and their talents, leadership as the creation and
enactment of a shared vision for the future is disproportionate to the skills
and practices of leaders considered in isolation. The dialectic between leaders and
leadership beckons us to move in a new direction and to draw systematically
on contemporary insights about leadership. By attending to relational leadership
and its role in both empowering and engaging individuals and groups in a collaborative strategy process, it offers a new way of thinking about both the tasks
and the authority of leadership. In this approach, leadership can be closely tied
to the methods and systems of decision making in a legitimate institutionalized
process. Effectively implementing the steps in the process does not require decision makers to reinvent themselves or their responsibilities, but it enables them
to mobilize and to amplify their existing authority and talents by drawing them
into a method of leadership.

Some years ago, James MacGregor Burns signaled with some urgency the need
to better understand and evaluate leadership as a phenomenon that shapes our
lives profoundly—in politics, the professions, science, the academy, and the arts.
He went on to lament that "There is ... no school of leadership, intellectual or
practical" (1978, 2). Since that claim was made, schools, centers, and programs
on leadership have proliferated within and beyond universities, and resources for
understanding it have continued to grow through the efforts of many scholars and
reflective practitioners. Leadership has become a self-conscious interdisciplinary field of study with a range of theoretical and practical achievements. Yet we
would go further. Theory gives rise not just to knowledge *about* leadership, but to
methods of decision making *for* leadership. An understanding of leadership as the
enactment of shared purposes can frame the construction of an applied and integrative discipline for the exercise of strategic leadership. To effect that translation
between theory and practice is the aim and the subject of this work.

CHAPTER

The Ambiguities and Possibilities of Leadership in Higher Education

I f strategic leadership is to be an effective method, it has to pass several critical tests. One is its ability to function effectively in the culture and systems of academic decision making. In this chapter I will explore the norms, practices, and expectations of academic governance and leadership. I will also analyze some of the most influential interpretations of leadership of the past couple of decades, principally concerning the college presidency. One of my primary goals will be to relate these ideas to the contemporary models of leadership analyzed in the last chapter. In doing so, I will ask several basic questions. How does a particular form of leadership choose to address the complexities of academic decision making, in particular, the protocols and norms of shared governance? What methods and practices does a particular approach to leadership propose or entail? What does it expect to achieve? What are its assumptions? As I pursue the analysis, I shall also uncover the roots of strategic leadership in the decision-making systems of the academy, as well as the challenges it must surmount to be robust and effective.

FORMS OF LEADERSHIP IN HIGHER EDUCATION

Leadership as Knowledge and Skills

Higher education's leadership library is growing rapidly and will soon need more shelf space. After a long period when the dominant focus was on presidential leadership, authors and publishers are now creating a long list of books with "leadership" in their titles, often centered on the concerns of practitioners. Many of them focus on the qualities, expertise, and skills required for effectiveness in specific positions of authority, such as chief academic officer or department chair. In this regard, they are close to the traditional motifs of management education, and development, as a sampling of the enormous number of recent books makes clear (see, e.g., Diamond 2002; Ferren and Stanton 2004; Gmelch and Miskin 2004; Green and McDade 1994; Gunsalis 2006; Hoppe and Speck 2003; Krahenbuhl 2004; Ramsden 1998; Ruben 2004b, especially chapter 8). Although these works may consider broader findings and theories concerning leadership, their primary attention goes to the tasks and operational responsibilities of a given academic position. They may cover such topics as faculty appointment, evaluation, development and tenure, curricular change, affirmative action and equity, legal questions, planning, budgets, compensation, group dynamics, and conflict resolution. Especially useful for academic professionals who may have little or no administrative experience, these books address one aspect of the leadership equation: "What skills and knowledge do I need to exercise my responsibilities effectively?" (The American Council of Education has led the way over many years in developing materials, programs, and bibliographies on leadership development in this vein.[1])

Interactive Leadership

The contemporary motif of leadership as a process of mutual influence between leaders and followers that mobilizes commitment to common purposes also has emerged clearly as a theme in the literature (see, e.g., Davis 2003, Kouzes and Posner 2003, Shaw 2006). Peter Eckel and Adrianna Kezar (2003) describe a transformational change model that parallels several aspects of interactive direction-setting leadership. In using the motif of legitimacy as the threshold condition for transformative presidential leadership, Rita Bornstein (2003) demonstrates how the concept answers to the multiple expectations of key campus participants and other constituencies. The publications of the Institutional Leadership Project, directed by Robert Birnbaum (1988, 1992) in the late 1980s, also show a clear understanding of many aspects of interactive leadership. In none of these cases, though, have the implications of reciprocal leadership been fashioned into a systematic method of organizational decision making and leadership (Bensimon, Neumann, and Birnbaum 1991). Paul Ramsden (1998) comes close to doing so, yet he also considers leadership as a set of qualities, skills, and characteristics. As we shall see, the guidebooks to strategic planning in higher education move largely within the orbit of management, though the motif of interactive leadership is sometimes a tacit and emergent theme (Sevier 2000). Representative articles and collections of studies from journals and other sources on governance, management, and leadership also reflect several of the motifs of interactive leadership (M. C. Brown 2000; Kezar 2000; Peterson, Chaffee, and White 1991; Peterson, Dill, Mets, et al. 1997). They offer a variety of insights on themes that have a direct or indirect bearing on strategic leadership, such as symbols and sense making, gender and multiculturalism, and strategic change. As descriptive analyses, however, the primary aim of these publications is to provide research and findings that have implications for leadership, rather than to propose a systematic method for practicing it.

LEADERSHIP AS AUTHORITY: THE CASE OF THE COLLEGE PRESIDENCY

The central issue of authority in collegiate leadership takes us logically to a consideration of the college presidency, which has been the focus of the most concentrated, systematic, and influential scholarship on leadership over the past several decades. Books and studies related to the presidency continue to appear, so the topic remains a focus of investigation (Association of Governing Boards of Universities and Colleges 1996, 2006; Bornstein 2003; D. G. Brown 2006; Fisher and Koch 2004; Keohane 2006; Padilla 2005; Shaw 2006).

We are drawn to this literature for several reasons. In the first place, it offers a test case to scrutinize the theories and the language of leadership in higher education, and in the second, it provides recommendations for the practice of leadership. Most importantly, presidential leadership is the mirror image of the campus system and culture of authority and decision making. It reflects the quite particular ways in which academic organizations carry out their purposes through the work of decentralized and autonomous groups of knowledge professionals. If strategic leadership is to flourish in the values and practices of the academy, it must first understand how academic governance works.

The Weakness of the Presidency

The most influential analyses of the college presidency conclude that it is structurally weak in authority, beyond whatever strengths and talents a given individual may bring to it. In the words of the Association of Governing Boards of Universities and Colleges' influential 1996 Commission on the State of the Presidency, "University presidents operate from one of the most anemic power bases in any of the major institutions in American society" (9). In language that is even more pointed, Cohen and March claim in their classic study of the presidency: "The presidency is an illusion. Important aspects of the role seem to disappear on close examination.... The president has modest control over the events of college life" (1986, 2). These arguments and the research that supports them may be challenged, but they have set the terms for debate on the presidency for several decades.

Loosely Coupled Systems

It is worth examining a series of structural characteristics of academic and organizational governance, from shared authority to what Cohen and March

(1986) call "organized anarchy," that explain these sobering appraisals of presidential authority and leadership. To begin, presidents preside over two separate systems of authority within the same institution, one for academic affairs and one for administration. The administrative system is organized hierarchically and operates with many of the same patterns of managerial authority, control, and coordination that one finds in other organizations. In today's world, the span of administrative authority itself includes an ever-expanding set of complex operations, from technology to athletics, from venture capital spin-offs to arts centers. These activities may themselves be only loosely and incidentally tied to one another, heavily complicating the contemporary tasks of university management.

The academic system of governance is loosely coupled both within itself and with the world of administration. The two systems have episodic, complicated, and often controversial connections around issues like financial and physical resources that are of critical importance in both spheres. The academic domain functions through highly decentralized departments and programs that are largely governed independently by academic professionals. The units embody intellectual and professional norms as well as territorial boundaries. Most academic units do not need each other to do their work, and most faculty members do most of their teaching and much of their research independently of one another. The interaction of academic professionals in carrying out their tasks is unpredictable, uncertain, and infrequent, the epitome of loose coupling (Birnbaum 1988, 1992; Weick 1991).

Presidential authority over the academic system is usually a form of oversight and is filtered through several layers of faculty committees and other protocols of collegial decision making. Usually these collegial mechanisms themselves are weakly related to one another, and they typically resist efforts to be more closely connected.

In much of the president's work, responsibility is split from authority (cf. Birnbaum 1989). Presidents are often perplexed or frustrated because they are held responsible for decisions or events over which they have little authority and no control. For instance, they do not hire and cannot fire the faculty, most of whom hold permanent appointments. The most important decisions about everything from finances to student discipline are made through some type of participatory process, which often gives the president little margin for independent action. Faculty members who scuttle a worthy new academic proposal, sometimes working in the shadows, do not have to answer personally for their decisions, while presidents seeking change without the authority to enact it are held responsible for failing to achieve it. Presidents may be blamed by the trustees for the failures of an academic program, by legislators for the offensive comments of a faculty member, or by neighbors for the crude behavior of intoxicated students.

Leadership scholars can help presidents to understand, though not alter, these circumstances. They suggest that most stakeholders and participants hold their own image about what they can expect leaders to do and use it to evaluate the president's performance, whether the attribution is relevant or irrelevant, accurate or inaccurate (Birnbaum 1988, 1989; Hollander 1993).

Shared Governance

Many of the challenges to strong presidential leadership are summed up in the practices of shared governance. The classic statement that often is taken to be its charter is the 1967 "Statement on Government of Colleges and Universities." Ironically, the phrase "joint effort" is the touchstone of the document, not "shared authority" or "shared governance." The statement defines expectations for joint effort on central matters of institutional purpose, direction, and program. The notions of advice, consent, consultation, initiation, and decision are the variable forms of shared authority depending on the type of question under consideration. The initiation and approval of decisions differ in various spheres of decision making, from academic areas, where the faculty will have primacy, but not total control, to different administrative issues (facilities, budgets, planning) where faculty members advise and, sometimes, also consent. Institutions should determine "differences in the weight of each voice, from one point to the next . . . by reference to the responsibility of each component for the particular matter at hand" (American Association of University Professors, 1991; Association of Governing Boards, American Council on Education, 1967, p. 158).

Whatever else, the statement establishes the expectation that the faculty's voice will be heard on all issues of consequence, even as it affirms the president's ultimate managerial responsibility. The document portrays the president primarily as a "positional," leader not as an intellectual and educational partner with the faculty (Keller 2004).

The theory and the practice of shared governance are often at variance, since faculty and administrative expectations about its meaning are in constant flux and are often clouded by distrust (Association of Governing Boards of Universities and Colleges 1996; Tierney 2004; Tierney and Lechuga 2004). When decisions are considered to be important regardless of their content, the expectation for broad consultation is often stressed by faculty, and increasingly by staff members. Failure to consult with all interested parties is perceived as arbitrary, even when decisions are made by well-established protocols that include representatives from various groups. As the Association of Governing Boards of Universities and Colleges' report *Renewing the Academic Presidency* puts it, "'Consultation' is often a code word for consent. . . . Any one of the three groups [faculty, president, board] can effectively veto proposals for action" (1996, 8). This leads to the conclusion that "At a time when higher education should be alert and nimble, it is slow and cautious. . . . The need for reform [in shared governance] is urgent" (1996, 7). Many analysts and practitioners offer similar views of the challenges of shared governance for leadership (see, e.g., Benjamin and Carroll 1998; Duderstadt 2004; Keller 2004; Tierney 2004).

Authority in "Organized Anarchies"

If we are to grasp the depth of the issues concerning leadership and shared governance, we need to go below the surface to understand other dimensions of academic processes of choice. In their classic study of the presidency, Cohen and March (1986) use the mordant phrase "organized anarchy" to describe several of the defining features of university decision making. This does not mean that universities are filled with marauding bands of teachers and students, but that they have several formal "anarchic" properties, one of which is having problematic goals (Cohen and March 1986). What this means in a collegiate context is explained in two lines worthy of immortality: "Almost any educated person can deliver a lecture entitled 'The Goals of the University.' Almost no one will listen to the lecture voluntarily" (Cohen and March 1986, 195). Why? Because in order to gain acceptance and avoid controversy, the goals have to be stated so broadly that they become ambiguous or vacuous.

Another defining characteristic of colleges and universities is that their basic educational processes are unclear (Cohen and March 1986). There are no standard methods of collegiate education, but rather a vast number of divergent and autonomous approaches to teaching, learning, and research. As these are carried on by custom, trial and error, preference, and intuition, professors do not really understand the effects of their methods of teaching and learning and resist efforts to assess the results (cf. Bok 2006).

Colleges and universities also are characterized by fluid participation in their systems of governance. Many professors show minimal interest in organizational matters and prefer to be left alone to do their work. They wander in and out of the decision-making process depending on circumstance and inclination. Cohen and March conclude that these characteristics do not "make a university a bad organization or a disorganized one; but they do make it a problem to describe, understand, and lead" (1986, 3).

Decoupled Choice Processes

Cohen and March also offer an influential analysis of a decoupled pattern of organizational choice making that they refer to as the "garbage can" process. Organizational decision making is not simply what it appears to be, that is, a set of rational procedures for making decisions and for resolving conflicts through rational argumentation and negotiation. It may be these things, but it is something quite different as well (Cohen and March 1986).

The graphic image of garbage (a better metaphor might be baggage) is used to indicate that the opinions, problems, and solutions that are always flowing through an organization typically do not have a necessary connection to a specific choice under consideration. Due to their ambiguities of purpose, the absence of an authority to define rules of relevance, and fluid participation in governance, universities exemplify decoupled patterns of choice.

On many, if not most, campuses, for example, virtually any specific decision, from relocating a parking lot to issuing a new admissions pamphlet, can become a heated debate about shared governance. The search for a vice president for development may lead to lively exchanges about the true meaning of liberal education. In other words, people tie their passions and preoccupations to any likely proposal or decision, whether it is relevant or not.

Multiple Constituencies: The President as Juggler-in-Chief

Trustees are often bewildered as they come to discover that a president's leadership is highly circumscribed by a large variety of interests on and off the campus. Not only does the president answer to many internal participants and external constituencies, but many of the groups have an influential voice or a formal role in the decision-making process. Most of them—faculty, staff, alumni, athletic boosters, students, parents, legislators, the media, local residents, and public officials—expect the president to advance their interests, and he or she is evaluated by his or her capacity to do so. Increasingly those who have an ax to grind with the president make their complaints public though e-mail networks, anonymous opinion blogs, and Web sites. If the president takes a tough stand, there is no guarantee that the board or the faculty will support the decision. "As a result, presidents run the risk of being whipsawed by an ever-expanding list of concerns and interests. Instead of a leader, the president has gradually become juggler-in-chief" (Association of Governing Boards of Universities and Colleges 1996, 9–10).

These structural features of split authority and shared governance, decoupled systems, anarchic organization, disconnected choice processes, and multiple constituencies together define the dense set of organizational realities within which presidential leadership is exercised in higher education. These factors explain why the president's leadership through authority can be interpreted as strictly limited and even illusory, even though the position is at the top of the institutional hierarchy.

These interpretations do not mean that the work that presidents perform is insignificant. They are the most influential individuals on a campus and play important administrative, legal, and symbolic roles. If the president tries to do the right things in the right ways, the benefits of presidential leadership will operate at the margin for the good of the institution. But the influence of the individual is not likely to be decisive or to last long after the president's term (Birnbaum 1988, 1989, 1992; Cohen and March 1986). The position is essential but can be played by many individuals with comparable results. As March once put it, presidents are both necessary and "interchangeable," like lightbulbs (quoted in

Kerr and Gade, 1986, p. 11) Humility about the role and its possibilities is the
beginning of wisdom.

LEADING WITH LIMITED AUTHORITY
Tactics of Administration

What finally, then, becomes of leadership when it is so limited and fragmented?
The answers come in several different forms, one of which is the systematic and
detailed counsel to employ "tactics of administrative action" (Cohen and March
1986, 205). These tactics display "how a leader with a purpose can operate within
an organization that is without one" (Cohen and March 1986, 205).

The proposed tactics are conclusions drawn from the characteristics of the
university as an organized anarchy. In this case, knowledge gives birth strictly to
tactics of administration, not to processes of leadership. To gain advantage in decision making, administrators should (1) spend time on issues, because most people
will tire of them; (2) persist because circumstances may change; (3) exchange
status for substance and give others the credit; (4) involve the opposition and
give them status; (5) overload the system, ensuring that some things will pass;
(6) create processes and issues (to serve as garbage cans) that will take free-floating
interest and energy (the garbage) away from important projects; (7) manage unob-
trusively; (8) reinterpret history, since interest in the record of campus events is
usually minimal (Cohen and March 1986).

It is compelling that the recommendations of a highly influential study of
presidential leadership consist of potentially cynical tactics to manipulate the
practices of decision making. They represent the repudiation of most conventional ideas of leadership, no matter how they are defined. The transactional,
transforming, engaging, interactive, or strategic forms of leadership described
in studies of political leaders or business executives are nowhere to be found.
There is a clear lesson to be learned from this methodology and its conclusions.
If we presuppose that holding authority is the defining form of leadership, it
becomes difficult to discern and describe the interactive and strategic forms of
leadership that are at work throughout collegiate organizations. We may be left
only with administrative tactics unless we change our assumptions about the
nature of leadership.

Lessons for Leadership

Having found limitations in the authority of the president that broadly concur
with the conclusions of Cohen and March, Birnbaum (1998, 1989, 1992) offers
a decidedly different set of interpretations about the possibilities of presidential
leadership. He presents his ideas as cognitive insights derived from empirical
studies of presidential attitudes, performance, and relationships with key constituencies. They are lessons that can serve as guides to more effective presidential leadership, though they are offered as prudential principles rather than laws

or systematic methods. They are rooted in a concept of cultural leadership that involves "influencing perceptions of reality" by creating a shared understanding of the values, traditions, and purposes of the organization (Birnbaum 1992, 55). In this cultural context, appraisals of presidential performance by trustees, staff, and faculty are taken to be reliable measures of presidential success. More quantifiable indicators of organizational performance may be less valid since they could be the results of the efforts of others or of circumstances over which the president has no real control (Birnbaum 1992).

Birnbaum's principles of leadership suggest ways to use the real but limited authority of college presidents contextually within their distinctive cultural and organizational worlds. So, presidents should make a good first impression, learn how to listen, balance governance systems, avoid simplistic thinking, deemphasize bureaucracy, affirm core values, focus on strengths, evaluate personal performance, and know the right time to leave (Birnbaum 1992). This approach makes clear that the use of authority by itself is not leadership but can be a key resource in the larger cultural task of shaping a shared sense of values and purposes. It is clear that Birnbaum's cultural and cognitive lessons may help presidents to achieve organizational equilibrium, but they do not add up to a method of leadership for strategic change (Birnbaum 1988).

Differentiating and Affirming Presidential Authority

We found that the Association of Governing Boards of Universities and Colleges' report *Renewing the Presidency* (1996) offered a perceptive diagnosis of the complications of presidential leadership. When it turns to proposals for action to address the problems, it recommends the reform of shared governance by a careful differentiation of the process. "It should not be impossible to clarify and define areas where faculty decision-making is primary, and subject to reversal only by justifiable exception [curriculum . . . , appointment, tenure]. In important areas like the budget and planning, faculty should be involved and consulted, but will not have determinative authority. In other areas, faculty will not be involved, but will be kept informed of developments" (Association of Governing Boards of Universities and Colleges 1996, 26). Following its own example, in 1998 the Association of Governing Boards issued a new *Institutional Governance Statement*, which makes clear assertions of the board's ultimate authority in governance.

As to the president's authority, no new structural elements or decision-making powers are proposed, either by the 1996 commission or the 2006 Association of Governing Boards of Universities and Colleges Task Force on the State of the Presidency. The reports of both bodies, each chaired by former governor Gerald Baliles of Virginia, strongly advise governing boards to support and evaluate presidents systematically and regularly. Presidents are counseled to exercise the full authority of the office that they hold and to find "the courage to persist with initiatives . . . for change" (27).

Consistent with our emphasis on strategic leadership, it is interesting to note the following central recommendation concerning the role of the president: "It is...to provide strong and comprehensive leadership for the institution by developing a shared vision of its role and mission, forging a consensus on goals derived from the mission, developing and allocating resources in accordance with a plan for reaching those goals" (Association of Governing Boards of Universities and Colleges 1996, 19). Several of the emphases in the 2006 report have the same strategic focus. The president's role includes "pursuing a shared academic vision" with the faculty and developing a strategic plan as key components in what the report calls "integral leadership" (Association of Governing Boards of Universities and Colleges 2006, 9). It is worth emphasizing that these responsibilities cannot be accomplished simply by reaffirming the president's authority, no matter how much the role is clarified and strengthened. Effective methods of collaborative strategic leadership have to be joined to the president's formal role to fulfill each set of the Association of Governing Boards of Universities and Colleges' recommendations.

The Strong Presidency

The Association of Governing Boards of Universities and Colleges commission's belief in the desirability and possibility of stronger presidential leadership is not a solitary view but has confident echoes in the literature. James Fisher and James Koch argue in their 1996 work, *Presidential Leadership: Making a Difference*, that much of the research that plays down presidential influence and authority is misleading and inaccurate. In a striking reversal of most of the views we have examined, they claim: "The effective leader will learn how to use authority and recognize its value.... To lead, to influence, and to use authority is to be powerful" (Fisher and Koch 1996, 22). In coming to these conclusions, they draw on research and personal experiences that contradict the interpretations of the weakness of the presidential office (Fisher 1984; Fisher, Tack, and Wheeler 1988). They argue that presidential vision and inspiration should be central components of leadership, which does not have to detract from collaborative processes. A vision is decidedly of the president's own making and is given to the campus more than derived from it. A number of personal traits are important for the president as well, including charisma. The ability to keep a proper social distance and manage campus appearances, even while projecting an image of warmth and friendliness, is a valuable skill and an important part of a systematic effort to manage the presidential image (Fisher and Koch 1996). Ironically, Birnbaum (1992) explicitly singles out each of these points as a myth of presidential leadership.

In *The Entrepreneurial College President*, Fisher and Koch (2004) continue to develop their case concerning the significant impact of presidential leadership, this time using the notions of entrepreneurial and transforming leadership as their key categories. Based on statistical analyses of questionnaires from "effective" and "representative" presidents, as defined by peer nominations, they argue that leaders who are willing to pursue change, take risks, and challenge the status quo, and who do not let organizational structures discourage their efforts, are typically more successful and effective collegiate leaders. They pointedly repudiate Birnbaum's systematic critique of strong presidential leadership.

The methods and assumptions used to study the entrepreneurial approach raise many questions, starting with the authors' ambiguous connection of entrepreneurial with transforming leadership, which are very different things. The content of their questionnaire is also problematic, since it tests a relatively narrow set of self-attributed attitudes as opposed to more objective assessments of presidential decisions and achievements, or the evaluations of others within the institution. One also has to wonder how presidents acquire the qualities necessary for entrepreneurial leadership if they do not already have them, particularly since they appear to be personal characteristics that are hard or impossible to acquire. Entrepreneurial leadership does not seem to be a method or process of decision making that can be learned. It also appears to be the norm of leadership under all circumstances, rather than having to do with the match between the leader and the situation of the organization.

Our primary interest in the study, however, concerns not its accuracy but what it represents in the study of leadership. Unlike the "weak" presidential theories, the focus here is on the way the legitimate authority of the presidential office can be combined with the personal characteristics, expertise, and skills of the president to create a strong form of leadership. More than other analysts, Fisher and Koch offer a perspective that integrates different dimensions of leadership, including self-managed behavior, into a single theory.

THE MULTIPLE FRAMES AND STYLES OF LEADERSHIP

Students of organizations have developed theories about the ways that the structures, politics, people, and cultures of organizations are woven together into complex patterns. In *Reframing Organizations*, Lee Bolman and Terrence Deal (2003) describe what they call four frames, each of which describes a dimension of an organization, as well as a cognitive lens, a "way of seeing," that privileges that dimension in our thinking and experience. This perspective has been adapted and applied to the analysis of presidential leadership by investigators such as Birnbaum (1988, 1992), Estella Bensimon (1991), and William G. Tierney (1991). The four modified frames are (1) the bureaucratic (or administrative), (2) the political, (3) the collegial, (4) and the symbolic. They are illuminating categories with clear implications for practice.

As the research suggests, and as experience confirms, individuals apprehend organizational life and decision-making processes in quite different ways. Some leaders look through cognitive windows and see *political* interactions as primary and pervasive, while others are partially blind to the issues of power, persuasion, and influence. For other leaders, nothing is more self-evident than formal organizational authority and structures, and the dependence of effective leadership on good *administrative systems* and controls, especially in today's complex organizations. Administrative leaders often think and act in these terms, while many of their faculty colleagues are far more sensitive to the procedures and protocols of *collegial* decision making, which is reinforced by its own system of professional values and norms. Academic leaders who understand and respect those norms are able to motivate change through collaborative processes. Other leaders in academic communities are especially concerned with the values and expectations of the organization's culture, its *symbolic* frame. By drawing on its stories, metaphors, norms, rituals, and traditional practices, they make sense of the world and influence others to move in a common direction.

Leadership Styles: Using Multiple Frames of Interpretation

It is worth emphasizing that interpretive frames are not just a way of understanding organizational experience, for they also shape decisions and actions. If we regard the world as essentially political, for example, we shall act on it in those terms. Since organizations cannot, in fact, be reduced to a single dimension, leaders will be more effective to the extent that they can master the skills and cognitive abilities both to understand and to make decisions with regard to multiple frames and dimensions. In interviews with presidents of thirty-two institutions, Bensimon (1989) has shown that most presidents—about two-thirds—conceive of their responsibilities by combining two or three of the leadership orientations. This greater conceptual complexity seems to be associated with experienced presidents who may have served as chief executive in more than one institution, as well as those who serve in the larger and more complex four-year universities.

Interestingly, as we focus on frameworks of interpretation, we shift our attention away from seeing leadership primarily as formal authority toward the cognitive capacities and orientations of individuals. In turn, these characteristics relate in various ways to the needs and values of other participants in the organization, so they become aspects of a reciprocal process of leadership. Because of these multiple characteristics, we can think of the frames as contributing to particular styles of leadership.

From the perspective of leadership education and development, it also becomes clear that gaining awareness of one's own orientation to the tasks of leadership is a valuable form of self-discovery. It provides insights about self and circumstance that help a leader to understand the characteristics of his or her strengths and weaknesses, problems, and frustrations. Most importantly, the process of self-awareness can initiate steps to correct imbalances in order to create a more integrated method of leadership.

INTEGRATIVE LEADERSHIP

Our discussion of the frames of leadership has suggested that leaders with only one or two sets of cognitive abilities will find it hard to respond effectively to the multiple realities that they face. Those, for example, who live by political insights and skills will be confounded by the unyielding commitment of faculty members to academic values and to collaborative processes. To lead through administrative authority and expertise alone is to force managerial methods beyond their proper domain, and to reduce every human and academic problem to a rational one or to a cost-benefit analysis. Whatever else, the studies of the presidency show the severe limitation of authority alone as a model of campus leadership. Yet to emphasize the inspiration of symbolic leadership to the exclusion of other abilities can lead to a worship of the past and to a sentimental celebration of the artifacts of community. If administrative systems are dysfunctional, the celebration will not last very long. The collegial model may function well by itself in a static world, but its tendency toward insularity and stasis requires other models of decision making to deal with the realities of change and competition.

Clearly, both adequately describing and leading organizations of higher learning requires the integration of the various frames. Integration means more than deploying a serial combination of skills and insights, using political abilities for one set of issues, and shifting to other frames as circumstances dictate. Such an approach might create a stable organization, but it cannot produce a coherent form of leadership. Nor can truly integrated leadership be achieved by another common pattern, that in which one approach becomes dominant while others play supporting roles. Such a model would produce less than a true integration, since some elements of a situation would be distorted to fit the dominant orientation (Bensimon 1991).

Yet if complexity in both thought and action is likely to be more effective as a form of leadership, we should press harder to consider an integration of the different models of leadership. To be integrative, the model of leadership will have to draw elements from the various frames into a new and coherent whole. To find a new integrative logic for their relationship to each other, the cognitive frames will need to be situated within a different and larger perspective on leadership. We will have to find methods of leadership that enable an institution to be true to its deepest values at the same time that it deals effectively with change and conflict.

A Cybernetic Model

Birnbaum proposes an integrative theory that he calls cybernetic leadership. A cybernetic system is self-regulatory and automatically adjusts the activity that it controls to stay within an acceptable range. Birnbaum (1988) uses the example of a thermostat, which is a cybernetic device since it keeps a room's temperature at a given setting by automatically turning the heating system on or off. Translating this idea to a university, we see that each sphere of administration uses a series of monitors to regulate its performance. So, if a department overspends its budget, its purchase orders may be refused until steps are taken to bring things back into balance. Similarly, if an admissions office misses its enrollment target of first-year students, it adjusts automatically by accepting more transfers. As we have seen, in a loosely coupled administrative system, decisions and actions in various units are often quite independent of one another. Self-regulation can usually accomplish its purposes because it does not affect the total system. One key role for leadership is to make sure that the monitoring systems are effective. Leaders need to make sure as well that a good communications system is in place so that signals about problems get to the right people, especially if issues in one area have a ripple effect on other units (Birnbaum 1988).

At times, leaders may need to intervene more dramatically in the system. Processes may have to be shocked or reengineered to come back into balance. Nonetheless, it is always advisable to exercise caution in disturbing a cybernetic system too drastically. "Good cybernetic leaders are modest.... They adopt three laws of medicine. 'If it's working, keep doing it. If it's not working, stop doing it. If you don't know what to do, don't do anything'" (Konner, quoted in Birnbaum 1988, 21).

The Limits of the Cybernetic Model

Does the cybernetic model offer an integrative approach to leadership, as it proposes to do? After a fashion it does, but not with the type of interpenetration or systematic relationship of the frames that one might expect. "The objective of the bureaucratic administrator is rationality. The collegial administrator searches for consensus, the political administrator for peace, and the symbolic administrator for sense. But the major aim of the cybernetic administrator is balance" (Birnbaum 1988, 226).

This is leadership as oversight. Cybernetic leadership does not involve an internal restructuring or reorganization of the four cognitive frames, for they continue to function as discreet systems. Integration produces an equilibrium in which the frames have a proportionate influence. They operate as a series of separate approaches triggered by a control mechanism that balances their activity without a content of its own. So, the integration of cybernetic leadership is a passive one, if we can speak of integration at all.

As Birnbaum claims in several places, cybernetic leadership is modest. Except under special conditions such as a crisis, or in smaller colleges, or when there is ripeness for long-deferred change to take place, leaders should not delude themselves by expecting transforming change (Birnbaum 1988). Since cybernetic leadership responds to signals of operational problems, it does not have the capacity to create and implement "disruptive" new possibilities, or to motivate others to set new directions in response to change. It provides cognitive insights and wise counsel about methods of administration and management, not processes of leadership.

A Story: From Cybernetics to Strategy

These final points can be made through a simple story. Take the example of the thermostat as a self-regulating device. No matter where one sets the temperature, the thermostat will work. The more interesting issue is what the temperature means to the family who lives in the house, not just as a measure but as a value, as part of a way of life, as an indicator of purpose. Assume that the family is trying to save money on energy costs, so they lower the temperature to sixty degrees in winter and raise it to seventy-five in the summer. The parents and teenage children argue constantly among themselves about the settings, framing the issues in different ways.

As debates about the best temperature unfold, it becomes evident that the problem is not the temperature at all, nor the old furnace, and certainly not the thermostat. The family finds itself involved in a decision that keeps expanding to encompass wider issues of values, priorities, and purposes. It turns out that the temperature is only symptomatic of much larger concerns. The region's cold winters, high-energy costs, and low salaries surface as the real problem. Given their vision of the life they want to live, they decide to move to a warmer climate with a lower cost of living.

This example suggests how strategic thinking probes issues to find the source of the problem. If we translate the family's situation into the admissions example used earlier, we can see the parallels. What may appear to be a minor operational problem with a lower number of entering students could be a strategic indicator of the need for a basic change in the college's academic program. The response to competition in the marketplace may require not just new programs, but a refashioning of the frame of collegial decision making as well. Cybernetic balance cannot provide the integrative leadership required to anticipate and to address these broader forms of change.

In these examples, we learn that the fragmentation of operational decision making gives way to the systemic patterns of strategic thinking and leadership. This means that we have to reveal and bring to awareness the values and purposes that are embedded in the forms of organizational life and in the ways we do business as usual. At the strategic level, leadership means systematically making sense of our organization's identity and its place in the wider world in order to define its best possibilities for the future. Along the way, monitoring systems of all sorts are needed to tell us whether we are reaching our goals, but in themselves they are mechanisms of management, not leadership. These conclusions make it clear that it is essential to develop a process of strategic decision making that can effectively integrate the complex patterns and frames of organizational decision making. While making sense of purposes and values, it will also have to bind together complicated forms of knowing and acting. As a form of leadership, it also will be expected to create a vision of the future and translate it into reality.

DIVERGING AND CONVERGING CONCLUSIONS

Several of the influential sources that we have consulted see the college presidency as weak in authority, albeit for different reasons. In the views of organizational theorists, the reasons for the weakness are given with the structural elements and choice processes of academic organizations. Although the president's role is administratively essential, it is an illusion to expect the dominant forms of leadership that may appear in other types of institutions. The responsibilities of symbolic interpretation and legal authority, of administrative coordination and collegial facilitation, are necessary forms of leadership that come with the position. Add to these shrewd political insights and tactics, and presidents will be able to get things done. So, personal characteristics, knowledge, and abilities as well as authority count in the leadership role. Nonetheless, except in periods of crisis or in a few special kinds of organizations, modest and passing presidential influence is all that is possible. Rhetoric, nostalgia, and desire notwithstanding, the basics of the situation cannot be changed.

Not everyone shares the same interpretation of the president's authority and leadership. The 1996 and 2006 reports of the Association of Governing Boards of Universities and Colleges suggest that the weakness of the presidency and the confusion of shared governance are real but remediable. Presidential authority can be affirmed and asserted, governance clarified, strategy processes implemented, a vision adopted, and the influence of politics reduced. A summons to moral and professional responsibility can motivate change. The presidency may often be weak and ineffective, but it can be made stronger to achieve integral leadership (Association of Governing Boards of Universities and Colleges 2006).

According to Fisher and Koch, the assertion of presidential authority does not need remediation of the powers of the office. They describe the effectiveness of presidents who have entrepreneurial characteristics and who know how to use the power inherent in their role. They believe that when charisma, expertise, confidence, and risk taking are combined with legitimate authority, the result is transforming and entrepreneurial leadership.

Leadership. Governance. Authority. Decision Making.

As we look below the surface of the various studies, analyses, and proposals that we have reviewed, we find several central themes: leadership, governance, authority, and organizational decision making. In many ways, the challenge of understanding leadership in higher education reduces to ways of reconceptualizing these interwoven themes, both to grasp each more fully in itself and to consider the relationships among them. Taken together, these factors produce a number of ironies for the study of leadership. Whereas we might expect that concepts of distributed and reciprocal leadership would be dominant, we find instead a central focus on leadership as the exercise of the responsibilities of the presidential position, whether it is conceived as weak or strong. In terms of leadership practices, the research primarily proposes administrative tactics to manipulate and cognitive principles to interpret an otherwise daunting system of shared authority. Recent literature offers practical guidance about how to manage the responsibilities of academic positions, yet analyses of more encompassing and systematic processes of influential and engaging leadership are not in evidence. A genuine integration of different styles or frames of leadership also waits be achieved, as does the articulation of a method of strategic leadership that touches the deeper currents of organizational narratives and values. In sum, the agenda for understanding leadership needs to be enlarged, and the methods for practicing it more robust.

To achieve these goals we have to find new intellectual bearings. Some of those new ways of thinking have come to light in our review of the concept of relational leadership in contemporary scholarship, and we will put these findings to good use. As we do so, we shall examine what we take to be the deeper roots of the perennial challenges of shared governance in higher education. Much of the problem of leadership in academic institutions resides in the need to reconceptualize and to reconfigure collegial authority and decision making. In tracing these new conceptual elements, we shall also be setting in place the framework for an integral approach to strategy as a process and discipline of leadership.

NOTE

1. For a good bibliography on the tasks of academic management and leadership in various positions, see the American Council on Education's workshop notebook on "Chairing the Academic Department" (Washington, DC: American Council on Education, 2004), which is periodically reissued.

CHAPTER

The System and Culture of
Academic Decision Making

We have learned that leadership is a complex phenomenon and is doubly so if we seek to understand it more fully in order to exercise it more effectively. As we have explored the literature to address these issues, we have not found fully satisfying answers. In part because it is an interdisciplinary field, leadership studies often has a difficult time creating an integrated set of conclusions, especially concerning the transition from knowledge about leadership to the practice of it.

WAYS OF THINKING ABOUT LEADERSHIP

We have also discovered that interpretive methods and models produce powerful insights but also distort what they study. They serve as filters for what counts as significant but only give us access to the aspects of experience that they privilege. Models like entrepreneurial leadership, cultural leadership, organized anarchy, garbage-can processes, and cybernetic leadership all seem to function in this way. Empirical studies that help to produce or support the model provide valuable knowledge about leadership, but they can only control two or three variables at a time. As a result, their conclusions often seem to reach beyond their specific findings, giving rise to theories that take on a life of their own. As this occurs, the integrated aspects of human experience and leadership that do not fit the model of analysis become distorted or lost from view.

Playfulness and Foolishness

It turns out that there is an illuminating irony in a concluding section of *Leadership and Ambiguity* that hints at the possibility of leadership as a contextual process of sense making rather than as the exercise of authority. Cohen and March (1986) describe a "technology of foolishness" and a reflective "playfulness" that expands on some of their earlier suggestions about the limits to rational decision making. In questioning the rational model, they emphasize the unpredictability of translating goals into actions.

Reflective playfulness involves the idea that goals should be seen more as exploratory hypotheses to be tested than as rigid objectives to be achieved. They suggest as well that our goals might arise more from our actions than the reverse. They affirm that planning may be more of a discovery of the meaning of the past in the present than the definition of future outcomes. This involves treating "experience as a theory," meaning that past events are subject to reinterpretation as a way to gain new self-understandings (Cohen and March 1986, 229). In keeping with these notions, they see leadership more as a journey of search and discovery than as the calculated voyage of ships marshalling their resources for battle.

These perspectives are entirely consistent with leadership as an interactive process that is focused on the complex interplay of human rationality, values, and narratives. In their pursuit of "foolishness," Cohen and March have touched on some of the deeper layers of human experience and agency.

Toward Contextual Leadership

Were we to start with contextual questions about the actual patterns and processes of leadership at work in organizations rather than with authority, our conclusions would be decidedly different. How is influence actually exercised by presidents and by others throughout the organization when universities or programs within them achieve the goals that they set for themselves? How are effective strategies for change actually developed and implemented? Whether in the leadership of presidents or, as likely, in leadership and decision-making processes distributed throughout colleges and universities, something has happened in much of the world to create institutions of higher learning that are purposeful and productive centers of learning. To be sure, purpose cannot be preconceived to be like a monarch in exile waiting to be summoned home by college presidents to perform a sovereign's duties. Purposes are often buried in the work being done and need to be attentively excavated from that source. In spite of enormous challenges, complexities, and deficiencies, many academic organizations, and especially specific programs and the people within them, continue to respond effectively to change. How is this possible without various forms of contextual, distributed strategic leadership?

HUMAN AGENCY AND VALUES

We have described leadership as an integrative process of sense making, choice, and action that influences groups and individuals to pursue shared goals in the context of change and conflict. Some aspects of the process are so contingent on personal characteristics and expertise, on context and culture, and on authority and power, whether formal or otherwise, that they resist easy appropriation for use in other settings. Yet many features of the leadership relationship lend themselves to translation into methods of strategic decision making. Aspects of leadership can be taught and learned if we can find the right conceptual framework with which to interpret and apply them.

To locate those features of leadership, we need to shift our intellectual gears toward the conceptual model of human agency, and to values as patterns and norms of self-enactment. The word "values" itself is slippery and is used to refer to many things, including opinions on controversial moral questions or, at another pole of usage, personal preferences. I intend a different yet common meaning. As persons, as agents of our own lives, we make choices in the name of centered values, in spite of the continuous change and conflict in the values that we hold. Even though we are not always conscious of our values as the standards of our choices, we can easily find them by asking a basic question that comes in many forms. To locate our values, we must ask ourselves: what matters decisively to us as we give shape to our lives and form to our experience? We can block this question from our thoughts, but not our lives.

Values provide the standards of choice that guide individuals, organizations, and communities toward satisfaction, fulfillment, and meaning (Morrill 1980). As a consequence, they have critical importance for both understanding and practicing relational leadership. Although values may seem to be abstractions because we often use abstract terms to name them, they are inescapably immersed in the choices we make and the lives we lead, more gerunds than nouns. Whether august values such as liberty and equality, or more earthy pursuits like ambition and status, they orient and shape our thinking, feeling, and acting. Our values are both expressed in and influenced by what we believe, feel, and do. We find them in the ways that we push ourselves this way and that, in bestirring ourselves to have more of whatever attracts us, whether love, justice, knowledge, pleasure, wealth, or reputation. We know them as claims on us, as sources of authority over us, as well as forms of desire and aspiration. Each type of value, whether moral, intellectual, aesthetic, personal, or professional, has its own weight and texture, but as a value it both attracts and judges us. No matter how we touch the life of a person or of an organization, we find values as demands and goals. In real life they do not fall easily into neat hierarchies, as much as we wish they would, for we both wisely and unwisely shift our values in different situations.

Respect as a Value

A quick example may help to illustrate these points. Consider a value such as respect for others, a pattern of comportment that many would see as central to leadership. As a value, respect is the activity of respecting, so it is a form of agency. It is a specific pattern of valuing another person as an end in him- or herself. Respect as a value involves a pattern of choice and action that determines how a self constructs relationships with others. In this account, respect does not fully exist as a value for us as selves, nor as leaders, unless we shape our intentions and actions by it, no matter how much we know about it, espouse it verbally, or feel positively about it. As a value, respect provides a pattern of intentionality and motivation that shapes our actions.

For a leader, or for anyone, valuing the other as an end rather than an object is not a simple possibility. The self as agent is constantly and forever solicited by thoughts and feelings—anxieties, insecurities, obsessions, stereotypes—that push and pull away from the enactment of respect. In effect, the self is continuously offered emotional, psychic, and ideological chances to satisfy other needs or compulsions that may be disrespectful and harmful to the other. If it is to prevail as a way of valuing another person, respect has to exercise sovereignty over the self's choices among the conflicting possibilities that flood a person's intentions and actions.

Values and Identity

As we consider the full reach of personal agency and fulfillment, it becomes clear that the choice of a specific constellation of values defines an individual's identity as a self. The constitution of the self coincides with the choice of a set of values (Mehl 1957; Ricoeur 1992). As the distinguished philosopher Charles Taylor puts it, when the question "Who am I?" is posed, "This can't necessarily be answered by giving name and genealogy. What does answer this question for us is an understanding of what is of crucial importance to us. To know who I am is a species of knowing where I stand" (1989, 27).

Although this evocation of values as the activity of valuing has been cast in terms of individual identity, cultural and organizational identities clearly function in similar ways. They represent shared and institutionalized value commitments that finally must be enacted through the agency of individuals. It makes perfect sense to ask of participants in organizations, "What matters decisively to this institution?" Questions of this sort trigger the process of self-discovery and the articulation of organizational identity, which is the birthplace for the work of strategy.

Values and Leadership

As we give a central place to understanding the dynamics of human agency and valuing, we also open new perspectives on leadership. We see more clearly that the meaning of leadership at a fundamental level turns on human values, specifically as the effort to understand and to respond to the values and needs of constituent groups and individuals in a variety of different forms.

Leadership occurs precisely in the relations between leaders and followers in matters that are of decisive importance to both parties. To be sure, the shape and scope of the leadership process and the way it deals with values depend decidedly on context. Nonetheless, with a value-centric orientation, we understand more fully why many contemporary students of leadership refer to the moral dimension as the heart of the matter. This does not mean that leaders are especially gifted in deciding controversial moral dilemmas or that their personal lives are exemplary. Rather, it suggests that leadership involves fulfilling the values that the organization exists to serve, and ensuring the authenticity of the commitment to those purposes.

The values theme also provides one of the conceptual foundations for building an integrative process of leadership. It offers a center of gravity for finding institutional identity in what may otherwise appear to be so many disparate beliefs, facts, and artifacts of institutional history and culture, programs, and resources. Just as a person expresses his values in the fabric of his life, so do institutions incorporate their commitments in all their tangible and intangible forms of organizational sense making and decision making.

STRUCTURAL CONFLICT IN ACADEMIC DECISION MAKING

In the preceding chapter we analyzed some of the complexities and conflicts in collegial authority, leadership, and governance. We return to those issues here but reexamine them through the conceptual lens provided by our analysis of agency and values. With this optic we can gain a new perspective on many of the conundrums of academic decision making. We shall seek to show that there is a series of structural conflicts embedded in the basic values of the academic decision-making system itself. To examine the way participants experience various forms of conflict, we shall begin with a case study that has its roots in my own experience.

A New Dean

After a national search for a new dean at a selective liberal arts college, the faculty search committee recommends a local candidate to the president. Since the individual is the highly respected and amiable chairperson of a small department, the president quickly clears the appointment with the board, to be effective in three moths. After the announcement, the dean-elect receives enthusiastic calls and messages from many colleagues celebrating her appointment. She also notices that the chairman and two senior colleagues from the history department have scheduled a meeting with her. Since she knows and likes all of them, she looks forward to the occasion.

After some pleasant bantering about her "moving to the dark side," she discovers that the trio is on a mission. They voice their concerns about the erosion of departmental autonomy and faculty governance during the tenure of the retiring dean, expressing confidence that she will redress the balance. Her colleagues go on to express their deep personal and professional distress over a decision recently taken by the outgoing dean not to fill a vacant tenure-track position in the history department. With courteous asides and apologies for bringing this to her prematurely, they make it clear that they want the dean-elect to intervene before the decision is enacted. Although they indicate that they did not initially take the deliberations about budgetary problems too seriously, they have come to believe that the process was arbitrary and flawed by the use of irrelevant credit-hour costs. They are convinced that if the decision is implemented, the quality of the history program will be irreparably damaged.

The dean-elect is taken aback by the request but tries to respond with equanimity. She knows several positions had to be cut by her predecessor because of a serious budgetary problem. She is also aware that the retiring dean used a consultative process to come to the final decisions, and that he has confessed to having little success in getting the budget advisory committee to focus on the data about the hard choices concerning priorities. The dean-elect thinks, therefore, that it is appropriate to show empathy for the department's situation; she suggests her openness to explore better processes of measurement and governance and asks for their involvement. She also indicates cordially but clearly that it is awkward and inappropriate for her to raise the issue directly with the president or the current dean during this interim period.

Suddenly the tone changes. Her colleagues begin to look at her in a new way and exchange sideways glances. Civility prevails, but suspicion, doubt, and uncertainty steal into the room. As the historians depart, they indicate their disappointment that she cannot find a way to remedy such a clear case of flawed priorities and processes. The dean-elect sits alone, bewildered at what has just happened.

Interpretations of the Dean's Conflict

Based on what we have learned about academic decision making from our earlier analyses, what can we tell the new dean that might be helpful to her? How can the various accounts of authority and leadership shed light on the situation and offer resources for the dean-elect? Which of them would most assist her to think through the implications of her responsibilities, especially in terms of the opportunity to exercise leadership?

A fundamental question begins to emerge. How can leadership reach to the source of the conflict in order to come to terms with it effectively? To achieve this, much depends both on the way we interpret leadership and the conflict that it seeks to reconcile. The language of leadership is not often heard in campus debates and discussions about governance and decision making, so a new idiom will have to be introduced to move the conversation forward.

As we recall, our earlier profile of leadership placed the issue of conflict at the heart of the leader's agenda. Leadership always appears at the contact points of change, competition, contradictions, and disputed priorities. The precise shape that leadership takes in a society or an organization is determined, as much as anything, by the nature of the conflict to which it seeks to bring resolution.

Drawing from our earlier discussion of organized anarchies, the frames of leadership, and shared governance, we can suggest several different ways in which leadership can be understood and practiced in terms of how the basic form of conflict is interpreted. Many would suggest, for instance, that responding effectively to the conflicting interests of a college or a university's multiple constituencies is the essence of leadership. In a number of cases—consider large public institutions—it appears that balancing the demands of the intricate network of campus and public interests and expectations is the sine qua non of effective leadership. Political skills move to the top of the leader's repertoire. The dean-elect has already learned that she will need to sharpen her skills of negotiation and conflict resolution, even though she has always been gifted in balancing the needs of different groups and individuals.

In other contexts—the small, selective college comes to mind—there are elevated expectations for participatory governance. Everything from the institutional operating budget to the schedules of athletic teams is a matter for shared faculty and administrative deliberation. If and when the protocols of shared governance begin to falter and conflict intensifies, a proper task of leadership is to redefine the methods and structures of collaborative decision making. In the name of collegial norms, the institution may reexamine the responsibilities of its faculty, the authority of its administration, and the content of its board's bylaws. As suggested earlier, the aim is to bring greater definition and legitimacy to the exercise of various forms of authority. Behind the effort is a belief in collegiate constitutionalism, the assumption that improving the forms and mechanisms of governance is the way to deal with conflicts. As a case in point, our dean-elect has been quick to suggest to her colleagues that a review of the methods for setting budgetary priorities is in order.

We also have seen how conflict is handled in organized anarchies. In the hands of seasoned administrators, conflict is disarmed through tactical maneuvers such as delay and deflection. Tactical leaders get things done by playing the system against itself, by knowing, for instance, that faculty interest and participation in governance is episodic and fluid. They provide opportunities (garbage cans) for people to deliberate on big issues like strategic plans that may not lead to action but will give them a feeling of importance. Our dean-elect is clearly aware of the need for tactical skill as she tries to deflect the substance of the issue that her colleagues have brought to her. As a longtime member of the community, she also knows that she must find ways to connect her work with the norms and symbols of the organization's identity and traditions, so symbolic sensitivities will be a critical part of her leadership.

To be sure, it is appropriate and helpful to understand various dimensions of conflict and their resolution by drawing on different sources of knowledge and frames of analysis. Any academic officer, new to the post or otherwise, must constantly attend to all these facets of a complex system of decision making. The problem is that each of these diagnoses and proposed resolutions fails to penetrate to the core of the issue. No matter how skilled the leader of constituencies, how deft the drafter of collegial bylaws, how skilled the storyteller, or how shrewd the tactician, conflict persists. These forms of leadership have not yet found the conflict with which they must fundamentally contend.

STRUCTURAL CONFLICT IN VALUES

To grasp the full texture of the problem of structural conflict, we need to understand it in terms of the decision-making culture or meta-culture of colleges and universities. "Culture" can mean many things, but here it refers to the shared paradigms, values, and norms through which organizations of higher learning build their systems of decision making. They apply widely, even around much of the globe (Ramsden 1998; Tabatoni 1996; Watson 2000). By penetrating the level of culture as a system of beliefs and practices, we find the place at which people understand themselves to be exercising their moral commitments and professional responsibilities in academic communities. We reach them at the point of their investment in a set of values and processes that comprise the foundations of a decision-making culture. We should seek first to understand academic professionals as participants in shaping a culture rather than explain them by their behavior or their bylaws.

To be sure, every organization also has its own distinctive culture. Practices like shared governance are markedly different in tone, emphasis, and content from one college to the next. One of the most influential writers in the field, Edgar Schein, defines the culture of a group as "a pattern of shared basic assumptions that the group learned as it solved its problems of external adaptation and internal integration, that has worked well enough to be considered valid and, therefore, to be taught to new members as the correct way to perceive, think, and feel in relation to those problems" (1992, 12). Many contemporary scholars of higher education have written in similar ways on the importance of campus culture and climate, including issues of race and gender (see, e.g., Birnbaum 1992; Chaffee and Tierney 1988; B. R. Clark 1987, 1991,1998; Dill 1997; Gumport 2000; Hortado 2000; Kuh and Whitt 2000; Peterson and Spencer 1991; Tierney 1991; Toma, Dubrow, and Hartley 2005). One of the tasks of effective leadership is to understand and mobilize the norms and practices of the culture in solving problems and setting directions for the future. Schein suggests that it is possible "that the only thing of real importance that leaders do is create and manage cultures" (1985, 2).

The common culture of academic decision making shapes the self-understanding of academic professionals at deep levels of their values and beliefs. Until that level is reached, efforts to develop an integrative understanding and process of leadership will be frustrated. The way to move beyond these frustrations is to locate the problems of academic decision making in a structural conflict of values.

Autonomy and Authority[1]

As organizations, colleges and universities try to mix oil and water by combining the academic value of autonomy with the institutional value of authority. The university itself draws its first breath from freedom of inquiry and builds its life around academic autonomy both for itself and its faculty members, both individually and collectively. The creativity of intellectual work and its inestimable value to society depend on academic freedom for each individual. Yet freedom and autonomy apply to collectives as well. Only those who know the special language, methods, and content of an academic discipline, which are first inculcated in the rites of passage of graduate study, can judge the work of others in the same field. The autonomy and the prerogatives of each academic department have deep cultural and professional roots. Yet, as academic professionals become members of formal organizations, they experience the structural tension in value systems. Just as professionals embrace autonomy, institutions emphasize authority, order, and accountability, values that are exercised through systems of controls. Organizations must control—define, systematize, regulate, and legitimize—what otherwise would be the chaos of freedom without boundaries (Morrill 2002). Many controls, from class schedules to budgets, are taken for granted as annoyances, until they begin to press hard against the requirements of autonomy. Should they ever touch the content of teaching or research, the academic heart of things, then the conflict becomes a deep crisis in fundamental values. So it is that academic authority plays out uncomfortably within the organization.

Intrinsic and Instrumental Values: Measuring the Immeasurable

The same rudimentary conflict appears in a parallel form in the conflicting ways that knowledge professionals and their institutions define and measure worth. Faculty members are driven by a commitment to the intrinsic value of teaching and research. At their core, the worth of the discovery and transmission of knowledge is self-authenticating and intrinsically motivating. It is not determined by measurement. Academic institutions respect these basic values but still must construe and measure value instrumentally to balance competing claims on their resources and responsibilities. The procedures of managerial decision making and the criteria of the market continually try to determine the value of the pursuit of knowledge. Judgment become quantified in costs and credit hours, and systems of measurement become normative, even though most academic people have little confidence in the ability of any system to measure what matters most to them (Morrill 2002). Courses and programs are dropped or added, and new initiatives pursued or forsaken, in ways and by measures that assault the academic values and sensibilities of scholars and teachers committed to their fields. These polarities are woven into the culture of academic decision making itself, which is understood as a system of values, beliefs, and practices.

Professional and Personal Identity:
Self and Role

At its best, academic life is a true calling (B. R. Clark 1987). The sense of self and the identity of the academic professional are interwoven. The academic professional says easily, "I am what I do." Even though faculty members are like other humans in that they value money and power, the profession's self-definition involves a sense of service to the cause of learning that transcends narrow self-interest. It carries the responsibility to address fundamental and enabling dimensions of human development and experience. Because of this, decisions that relate to the academic standing, effectiveness, and reputation of faculty members touch on personal identity and professional purpose. This shows itself in a variety of ways, especially in decisions related to academic programs and to appointment, promotion, and tenure. If a negative decision is made in areas that define professional status, especially regarding tenure, it is felt as a punishing blow to the person's sense of identity and self-worth. We meet in a different form the problem of disproportion in the measures of worth in academic decision making. Integrating the functional dimensions of organizations with the identities of academic professionals proves again to be a daunting task.

A deeper understanding of the sources of conflict in this cultural system does not provide anyone, including our new dean, with a ready formula to respond to disputes over priorities. But it gives rise to insights about the true dimensions of the world of decision making in which all academic men and women take up their duties. With this new point of departure, we can reconceptualize the issues and seek ways to reconcile the conflict through the integrative methods of strategic leadership.

SHARED GOVERNANCE AND
ITS DISCONTENTS

If we look again at the issues of shared governance through the lens of the structural conflict in values, several new dimensions come to light. Many members of academic communities would suggest that the value tensions in academic decision making are real, but that they can be effectively balanced precisely through the traditions of shared governance. Some institutions seem to have found effective and constructive ways to live with conflicting values. Over the years they have created, often more by practice than design, a series of councils and committees to address institutional issues. Following this model, a workable balance in university governance seems possible (cf. Birnbaum 2004).

Observation of shared governance in a variety of contexts reveals several other widespread beliefs concerning the exercise of academic decision making that are important for our development of a model of strategic leadership. Among other things, shared governance is understood by academic professionals to incorporate moral imperatives as well as formal processes. Those who try to exercise leadership in strictly political terms by currying favor or assembling changing coalitions of convenience quickly lose an academic community's respect. Similarly, administrative officers who are unwilling to press legitimate claims of collegial authority are perceived to be weak or ineffectual (Morrill 1990).

If, on the other hand, decisions are made unilaterally, they violate norms that have ethical force. They threaten canons of legitimacy that have their roots in the professional self-consciousness and self-respect of the faculty (cf. Bornstein 2003). Those canons also have the symbolic force of tradition, and the legal and administrative weight of formal codification in bylaws and operating procedures. Any member of the academic community who violates these norms does so at great peril, for they invariably translate into sanctions of distrust, protest, and recrimination against those who are seen to have abused them. The unprecedented 2005 vote of no confidence in President Lawrence Summers by the Harvard Faculty of Arts and Sciences—and in his subsequent resignation in 2006—focused on the values of mutual respect and collegiality. Harvard professors complained bitterly of Summers's perceived lack of respect for their intellectual expertise and his inability to appreciate the "basic civility" that is a moral and cultural norm of the Harvard faculty and staff (Healy and Rimer 2005).

While academic leaders at all levels need to understand the criteria of ethical legitimacy embodied in shared governance, they also come to learn the limits of the process. As the 1996 Association of Governing Boards of Universities and Colleges commission suggests, the system works tolerably well on many campuses when leadership is effective and conditions are stable. Yet when pressures for change begin to mount, fault lines quickly appear in the system. Then the fuzziness of the delineations of shared responsibility becomes glaringly visible and the conflicts in values palpable, especially if significant changes in academic programs themselves are at stake (cf. Benjamin and Carroll 1998; Duderstadt 2004; Keller 2004; Longin 2002).

Perhaps the most significant challenge of shared governance is its inability to address systematically and coherently the deepest and most comprehensive strategic challenges that confront an institution. Deep strategic questions of identity and purpose are always systemic and integrated, while the faculty committee structure is typically fragmented, complex, and cumbersome. Ironically and perilously, an academic decision-making system intended to give weight to the faculty's voice actually dissipates its influence through fragmentation and complexity. Those who hold formal positions of academic authority are equally frustrated, because they do not have effective vehicles to address the fundamental educational and organizational issues that will define the institution's future. We have come upon the fact that the motif of strategic leadership is intimately related to the issue of strategic governance.

LEADERSHIP AND THE RECONCILIATION OF THE CONFLICT IN VALUES

We have reflected on values to deepen our understanding of the decision-making culture of colleges and universities and have done so for several reasons.

One is to complement and supplement other accounts of decision making in order to provide a fuller description of a complex organizational culture. By going more deeply into the choices of persons as agents, as participants who enact values through their choices, we enrich our understanding of collegiate decision making.

This orientation opens up a number of promising possibilities. It helps all the stakeholders in higher education to give voice explicitly to what they know tacitly, which is intellectually satisfying in itself. But, for many who are caught in the frustrations of the system—consider again our new dean—the insights also serve as a kind of cognitive therapy. Conflict is depersonalized when it is seen as structural, and the natural tendency to place blame on oneself or others can be transcended. More importantly, insights at this level release energy and open up possibilities for action. The mind is set free to think of new approaches to the problem, and novel ways to both understand and reconcile structural conflict. When the sphere of action is as complex and demanding as the exercise of leadership in a university, the task of designing new approaches needs all the insights and resources that it can muster. Even though the process will never be complete, it helps to invest intellectual capital in reconceptualizing the issues.

Our explorations bring to light some of the conditions that must be met in order for a process of strategic leadership to deal effectively with structural conflict. Even as I have argued that shared governance needs to be reconceptualized, it would be illusory to think that the tension between professional autonomy and organizational authority can ever be eliminated. As a true polarity, both sides of the relationship are required to address the realities with which academic decision making must contend. An effective strategy process can mediate the conflict, not eliminate it.

On a substantive level, it is also an aim of strategic leadership to find and to articulate shared values that transcend the structural conflict in the culture of academic decision making. As we shall explore in detail in subsequent chapters, knowing and articulating the narratives, images, and metaphors in an institution's life story are crucial aspects of leadership. In his widely influential article on the loose coupling of decision making in schools, Weick (1991, 1995, 2001) notes that a worthy aim of research is to understand how people make sense of their experience in such unpredictable and ambiguous organizational contexts. He notes that in constructing their social reality, one would expect members of educational organizations to use the resources of language to create organizational myths and stories.

Narratives are indeed crucial in sense making because they carry wider meaning and convey the common values that have shaped an organization's identity. Through the discovery of the ways these defining values are incorporated into the work of the organization, a common set of commitments can be raised to awareness, given voice, and celebrated. As this occurs, diverse members of the campus community find substantive values that provide worthy common ground for their commitment, narrowing the gap between autonomy and authority. The common values exemplify the specific forms in which the organization has pursued its commitment to quality, to learning, to service, to innovation, to diversity, and to its other central values. These values can be given powerful expression and distinctive content to create the ingredients for a vision—a coherent statement of the institution's best possibilities for the future. Academic professionals will yield some of their autonomy to serve an "absorbing errand" (Henry James, quoted in B. R. Clark 1987), a cause such as intellectual quality that requires common effort and successful institutionalization in order to be attained and sustained. The pull toward independence is always present, but it can be transcended by shared values that are precisely defined and that resonate with the authentic possibilities of creating a great academic organization. Although often buried under routine and distorted by conflict, it is the power and allure of exalted tasks like these that brought academic people into the profession in the first place. The task of leadership in academic communities is to reconcile structural conflict by mobilizing a commitment to shared intellectual and educational values and, as well, to the institutions that embody them (Morrill 2002).

NOTE

1. Several paragraphs in this chapter are an abbreviated, edited, and paraphrased version of an earlier discussion of these issues from a book that I wrote for the Association of Governing Boards of Universities and Colleges, *Strategic Leadership in Academic Affairs: Clarifying the Board's Responsibilities* (2002). The original impetus for my development of a theory of value conflict was a study of values and decision making in six institutions organized by the Society for Values in Higher Education (Morrill 1990). Parallel frameworks for analyzing issues of decision making among knowledge professionals can be found in Mintzberg (1979), B. R. Clark (1987), and Berquist (1992).

PART II

Preparing for Strategic Leadership

CHAPTER

Creating and Situating
an Integrative Strategy Process

I f a new approach to strategy is to prove successful, it has to be carefully situated within the models of thought and responsibility of educational communities, especially given what we have learned about the complexities and value conflicts of academic decision making. Strategy processes often yield less than they might, or they fail, because they have not been preceded by the hard work of clarifying assumptions about the use of strategy in collegiate settings (cf. Alfred et al. 2006). For academicians, the concepts and tools of strategic planning often resonate suspiciously with the language of marketing and commerce. Time invested in defining and translating the meaning of strategy is well spent.

In order to find the right place for it, this chapter will examine four broad themes that prepare for the work of strategy. By starting with a brief analysis of the evolution of strategic planning in higher education and the corporate world, I will trace several models of strategy and place in evidence emerging trends that implicate a method of strategic leadership. Then, I will explore some of the deeper issues in situating strategy by examining several conflicting paradigms that reveal the underlying tensions in contemporary academic decision making. Next I offer a detailed framework for an integrated strategy process that draws together methods and meanings that are often tacit or disconnected and that places identity and vision at the core of the approach. Finally, I will develop a brief typology of various patterns of strategic decision making to aid academic institutions in situating and assessing their own uses of strategy.

STRATEGY IN HIGHER EDUCATION
AND THE CORPORATE WORLD

By the end of the 1970s, it had become clear that the long cycle of growth and prosperity in American higher education was coming to a close. The end of the Vietnam War and the oil shocks of the 1970s ushered in a period of economic uncertainty punctuated by stagflation and soaring interest rates. Financial support for higher education from both state and private sources started to become grudging and erratic and increasingly tied to restricted use. Universities also began to see the first stirrings of more intrusive external control, both in federal regulation and in accountability to state governments and accrediting agencies.

Academic Strategy

In his 1983 book *Academic Strategy*, George Keller struck a vital chord for a large audience in describing how strategic planning could respond to these ominous changes in the environment. Long in use in the military and in corporations, strategic planning was just emerging in colleges and universities. Keller did not so much describe the details of the process as situate and articulate a new possibility at just the right moment.

Of course, universities had been involved in planning for many years and still are. Larger institutions had long created planning staffs to help manage their growth. Virtually every institution possessed a facilities master plan, and formal planning had been applied to finances, enrollment management, and human resources. In most cases, however, these forms of planning were one-dimensional forms of linear projection. The only variables in the equation were under the control of the institution itself. The motifs of contingency, of responsiveness to change, and of coming to terms with a turbulent environment had been largely absent.

At the other end of the spectrum, many institutions were accustomed to making decisions piecemeal by responding to internal and external political pressures and the dynamics of organizational culture. For them, however much data they collected and however many projections they made, decision making was largely driven by an opportunistic model fueled by growth and defined by the art of the possible (Keller 1983).

It was in contrast to "ad hocracy" and static models of linear thinking that strategic planning began to appear on campus, its methods and language largely borrowed from the world of business. Whatever form it took, strategic planning most importantly brought with it a new paradigm of self-understanding for academic institutions, whether recognized or not. Their identities were now coming to be seen as taking form at the point of intersection with the competitive and changing world around them. This new contextual model shifted the whole pattern of collegiate planning and decision making. At the heart of the new way of thinking was the presupposition that successful institutions would have to respond effectively to the driving forces of change and be in alignment with them. That basic assumption clashed rudely with the way colleges and universities had always thought about themselves as intellectual preserves committed to academic ideals for their own sake.

The Critique of Strategic Planning

Over the next two decades, triggered by the expectations of accreditors, state officials, governing boards, and foundations, strategic planning moved into a central place in the management processes of many campuses. As it took hold, collegiate strategic planning created an enormous diversity of positive and negative appraisals of its worth. Some campus leaders extolled its virtues and traced their institutions' viability back to "the plan." Others saw it as a massive waste of time that by nature produces nothing more than wish lists. R. Williams's vivid metaphor captures this sentiment: strategic planning "lies still and vapid like a tired old fox terrier on the couch. An occasional bark but no bite" (quoted in Dooris, Kelley, and Trainer 2004, 8). Frequently, too, strategic planning was and is still perceived as threatening established patterns of governance by taking away control away from the faculty or the administration (Rowley, Lujan, and Dolence 1997; Wilson 2006).

The diverse ways in which strategic planning is done more than match these clashing perceptions of its usefulness. Most practitioners of the art have learned that the famous SWOT (strengths, weaknesses, opportunities, threats) analysis is a de rigueur step in the process. The creation of some sort of statement of mission and vision, as well as a set of variously defined goals, appears to have become nearly universal (cf. Schmidtlein and Milton 1988–1989). As to process, strategic planning typically seeks to satisfy collegial norms by involving a cross-section of the academic community in its work. Beyond these formal common features, however, no orthodox version of strategic planning exists in higher education. The enormous variations in the way institutions do environmental scans, if they do them at all; set goals, if they really are goals; develop narratives, if they write them down; create financial models, if they use a model; or incorporate a vision, if they have one, touch upon many issues related to strategy in higher education.

Dooris, Kelley, and Trainer (2004) nimbly trace many of these characteristics and recent trends in strategic planning and management and conclude that its value depends on how skillfully it is practiced. They emphasize recent attempts to feature more flexible and creative models of planning as well as those that focus sharply on the implementation of plans. Keller (1997) also analyzes recent trends and underlines the importance of communication, while Peterson (1997) differentiates what he calls "contextual" or more proactive planning from other forms of strategy. Birnbaum (2001) chronicles and sharply criticizes various approaches to strategic planning in *Management Fads in Higher Education*, though he creates something of a straw man by identifying strategic planning with all forms of strategy. Rowley, Lujan, and Dolence (1997) also trace the many political pitfalls in planning in higher education as they review the literature and discuss their own travail in trying to implement a process at the University of Northern Colorado. Wilson (2006) does the same in describing a failed academic planning initiative at Cal Poly Pomona. In analyzing some of the weaknesses of strategic planning in the nonprofit world, especially from the governing board's perspective, Chait, Ryan, and Taylor (2005) note that many plans lack traction, pattern, realism, and input from the governing board. In addition, strategic plans often fail to contend with the pace of change and unforeseen outcomes.

One of the challenges in understanding the process is the use of the term "strategic planning" itself. The phrase necessarily brings to mind the rational activity of first formulating and then separately implementing a sequence of steps to achieve a projected goal. We plan a house by first designing it, and then execute the blueprints and specifications by coordinating the delivery of materials and the work of a variety of trades. If planning is truly strategic, however, it defines itself in terms of changing realities in the competitive environment. That is the very meaning of "strategic." This brings contingency, responsiveness, and the need for resourcefulness and creativity into the ways we both conceive and carry out strategies. The definition of strategic planning as a rigid series of linear steps and schedules invariably leads to frustration.

Although the word "planning" continues to be used to describe the strategy process in higher education, it is often stretched beyond its ordinary meaning and has come to function as a term of art or figure of speech, defined more by use than formal definition. In this text we often use the terms "strategic planning," "strategy," "strategy process," and "strategic decision making" interchangeably, though we believe the last three terms are preferable.

Given the wide variability in both its use and effectiveness it is time to take a fresh look at the possibilities for using the process of strategy in higher education (cf. Newman, Couturier, and Scurry 2004). After several decades, it has become a bit stale and perfunctory, or rigid and cumbersome. It often becomes politicized and unsure of itself. This is a logical moment to seek the renewal and reconceptualization of strategic planning and strategic management in terms of strategic leadership.

Evolving Concepts of Corporate Strategy

Many business leaders and students of management have also questioned the worth of strategic planning because of the rigidities to which it became subject in earlier decades. For a time, beginning in the 1960s, many large corporations created central planning systems that ran in parallel with operational management. An array of planners specified in advance every facet of the financial, marketing, sales, and production cycles of all products or services. Strategic planning systems took on a life of their own through the elaborate programming of sequences of events around rigid goals, actions, and timetables. Yet the detailed plans were often out of date even before they were completed, let alone implemented.

Projected events did not occur as anticipated or crises made the plans irrelevant (Mintzberg 1994).

Many of the problems of strategic planning as practiced in these ways have been explored in depth by Henry Mintzberg (1994) in *The Rise and Fall of Strategic Planning* and in other writings, such as the jointly authored work *Strategy Safari* (Mintzberg, Ahlstrand, and Lampel 1998). He claims that strategic planning rests on a series of fallacies including the beliefs that it is possible to predict the course of the future, that thinking (as the *formulation* of plans) can be detached from action (as the *implementation* of plans), and that formal systems of data collection and analytical thinking can replace the intuitive and synthesizing skills of human experience and intelligence. These flaws reduce to one grand fallacy: "Because analysis is not synthesis, strategic planning has never been strategy making.... [It] should have been called strategic programming" (Mintzberg, Ahlstrand, Lampel 1998, 77).

The excesses of programmatic planning do not, of course, undercut the more basic notions of strategy as strategic thinking and decision making. Mintzberg and his associates identify a large variety of "schools," or approaches to strategy, including strategic planning and its variants. One of these schools emphasizes strategy as the analytical positioning of products in a market, and another as a cultural process of collective decision making. Others see it as a method of negotiation for power, and yet others as establishing a vision. Some methods understand strategy primarily to be a form of cognition, or, alternatively, as a way to enact a process of organizational transformation (Mintzberg, Ahlstrand, and Lampel 1998).

Mintzberg gives considerable attention in various contexts to "emergent" strategy as a form of learning. In emergent strategy, what we plan to do is not a function of what we rationally calculate in advance, but what we discover we are already doing. Our strategy may be born of a combination of both formal analysis and intuitive understanding of promising directions that emerge in the normal course of business (Mintzberg, Ahlstrand, and Lampel 1998). The notions that strategy is discovered as much as it is invented, that it emerges from practice as much as it is designed, and that it is grasped by intuition along with reason are all eminently relevant in the world of thought and in the practices of universities, especially as places that house many autonomous spheres of activity.

New Directions in Strategy: Integration and Leadership

What seems odd in Mintzberg's analysis is the designation of separate schools for what often appear simply to be different aspects of a potentially integrative approach to the strategy process. Perhaps for the sake of debate, distinctions are hardened into differences that could easily be reconciled, especially in the sphere of practice. After elaborating on the schools and critiques of them throughout a lengthy study, Mintzberg and his coauthors tacitly acknowledge this as they outline an integrative approach to strategy development: "Strategy formation is judgmental designing, intuitive visioning, and emergent learning: it is about transformation as well as perpetuation; it must involve individual cognition and social interaction, cooperation as well as conflict; it has to include analyzing before and programming after as well as negotiating during; and all of this must be in response to what can be a demanding environment" (1998, 372–73).

Using different terminology, but covering much of the same intellectual ground as Mintzberg, Richard Alfred classifies various approaches to strategic management with an eye toward synthesizing their meaning for higher education. He claims that the common strategic theme is the achievement of competitive advantage in the marketplace through the creation of differentiated and sustainable value for stakeholders. "Advantage is the end goal of any and all perspectives on strategy" (Alfred et al. 2006, 83).

This language seems apt but presents challenges when we try to translate it into the thought world of higher education. The work of translation hinges on the meaning of "value," and the point of reference in terms of which worth is established. In corporate strategy, the creation of shareholder value is a primary goal, as defined by shareholder economic returns and the relationship between supply and demand for the company's shares in the financial market. The company gains advantage when it creates economic value for customers by providing high-quality products and services at the right price. In higher education, however, the meaning of these terms changes. Words like "quality" and "excellence" become the primary terms used to refer to the intrinsic forms of value created in the discovery and transmission of knowledge. Educational value is not in the first instance determined by market forces but is an end in itself, a basic intellectual and social good. "Advantage" remains a useful concept for thinking about the strategies of academic organizations, but its relationship to educational value is complicated by the enormous range of different types of educational institutions, with their dramatically different programs, sponsorships, purposes, and prices. As a result, it becomes clear that higher education is a peculiar marketplace: "the relationship between price, product and demand is different for different purchasers in different parts of the higher education market" (Zemsky, Wegner, and Massy 2005, 35). When academic reputation is the prime value in a market segment, there is little price discipline; but when convenience or credentials define value, price becomes more influential (Alfred et al. 2006; Zemsky, Wegner, and Massy, 2005).

Recent interpretations of strategy in higher education show that it continues to evolve both in theory and practice, often in the quest for more integrative models. Peterson has outlined a method of contextual planning to serve as a more proactive, integrative, and meaning-oriented process than strategic planning. Using the term "strategic leadership" only parenthetically, he offers interpretations that are broadly parallel to some of those suggested in this book, though he focuses more on very broad macro-level changes in the system or "industry" of higher education (Peterson 1997). Ellen Earle Chaffee and Sarah Williams Jacobson (1997) have discussed a new approach to planning focused on vision and the effort to change institutional cultures that makes it, in effect, a central method of leadership. They advocate "a transformational kind of planning, meaning that planning itself is an instrument through which organizations and their cultures can change and grow" (1997, 235). In "Enhancing the Leadership Factor in Planning," Anna Neumann and R. Sam Larson focus explicitly on the need for planning to become a tool of leadership as "the act of conceptualizing alternative ways of thinking about our organizations" (1997, 196). When leadership is not defined in linear and hierarchical terms, planning can be rooted in a "process of institution wide conversation and interpretation" that crosses administrative and faculty boundaries and that focuses on current activities as the sources of a vision for the future (Neumann and Larson 1997, 199). In all three cases, students of leadership and management in higher education are making both implicit and explicit connections between strategy and leadership as a process of change and motivation.

SITUATING THE WORK OF STRATEGY: THINKING ABOUT STRATEGIC THINKING

We have examined several of the major constraints, complexities, and fundamental conflicts in the way academic organizations understand leadership and construct their systems of values and academic decision making. Given what we have learned about both academic culture and the suppositions and methods of strategy, it is clear that a lot of preliminary work is required to bring two quite different ways of thinking together. To be successful, the work of strategy has to be situated both conceptually and practically in the academic thought-world and the culture of each institution. To do so, it helps to find the roots of several of the conflicts and confusions that we have explored in our analysis.

STRATEGY AND MODELS OF ACADEMIC REALITY

Max DePree opens a chapter in his masterful little book, *Leadership Is an Art*, with the declarative sentence "The first responsibility of a leader is to define reality" (1989, 7). The "reality" he has in mind has nothing to do with production quotas or corporate politics, but everything to do with values, beliefs, and people. In one of the most influential books on management theory of the 1990s, *The Fifth Discipline*, Peter Senge (1990) offers conclusions that parallel DePree's claim. He targets the powerful influence of what he calls "mental models," the hidden patterns and assumptions behind our thinking that shape the interpretations and decisions we make in organizational life. The attitudes and assumptions can apply to many different types of judgments, from a vision statement to ways of interpreting numbers. We may hear a comment or two about a situation or a person, or perhaps read some figures, and unconsciously interpret the issues in terms of a fixed pattern of thought, or a mental model. So, when asked about declining applications in admissions, we may respond that "numbers are off everywhere," using a pattern of fixed thinking that blocks our ability to reach other explanations, perhaps out of a mind-set shaped by defensiveness or arrogance. The "learning organization" about which Senge writes is one that has found ways to think about its own thinking, to penetrate fixed sets of assumptions with self-awareness, conceptual openness, and continuing inquiry about its own effectiveness. Again, it is the definition of reality that is crucial and that decisively connects to issues of strategy and leadership (Senge 1990).

We have seen that institutions of higher learning have complex layers within their identities, including value systems that are split at the root between academic and organizational commitments. These systems of values are interwoven with narratives of identity, patterns of belief, and ways of constructing reality that filter experience as to what counts as relevant, true, and worthwhile—thus the tasks of strategic self-discovery, decision making, and leadership encounter paradigms that precede them. Through our models of thought and judgment, we pick out and privilege the features of our experience that are consistent with what we value and tell in our stories, all within an integrated and layered process of sense making. These deep paradigms are often unconscious and unquestioned assumptions of thought that shape the whole landscape of judgment and decision making in academic organizations. They provide the hidden criteria for the ways we think about mission and vision. They define as well the deep standards of moral legitimacy for the exercise of authority and the criteria for evaluating performance and programs. All these presuppositions are expressed through the intricacies of each individual's and institution's enacted culture and thought world, so the web of local reality is dense and complex.

Academic leaders and planners who understand paradigms and their connectedness with values and narratives will be far better equipped to introduce strategy as a discipline of change and sense making into a world where it is often not welcomed or appreciated. They will be able to encourage thinking about strategic thinking, and a process of continuous learning about the true terms of collegiate reality as preliminary steps in a productive approach to strategic decision making.

One way to begin to find a place for strategy is through the analysis of several images that display different patterns of thinking about the purposes of higher education. We shall offer three such images, each of which connects a set of assumptions, values, and narratives to construct a paradigm or model of reality. The models are stylized and fanciful versions of types of educational organizations and are presented largely as narratives. Even with their whimsy, they are intended to capture values and beliefs that are widely influential in both traditional and contemporary higher education. Many of the current debates about the purpose, worth, and future of higher education in a competitive global marketplace echo in these sketches. Let us turn first to an examination of the paradigms of the academy, the corporate university, and the educational shopping mall. Subsequently we shall explore more conceptually the motif of the responsive and responsible university, or, more precisely, the paradigm of responsibility.

The Academy

As a young faculty member representing my colleagues, I found myself discussing a serious financial problem with the governing board. I insistently and righteously emphasized that the academic program should be exempt from any proposed cuts, especially the loss of faculty positions. As the conversation began to turn sour, the board chairman offered a gentle but pointed rejoinder that still echoes in my thoughts: "It seems that the faculty wants the board to build a little white picket fence around the campus to protect it from danger and evil. We are not able to do that."

The imagery of the white picket fence brings to mind a whole set of associations and symbols for one of the traditional visions of the academy as a protected domain, a place apart from the getting and spending of the world, one that serves fundamental values in which the good is rational inquiry. Behind the imagery, one finds a powerful paradigm. Even if it is mythic, it is of the structural variety that touches deep sources of meaning because it describes the purposes of academic communities. As we enter it, the academy seems to be a timeless place with immutable purposes. We see teachers engrossed in study for the joy of it, or engaged in deep conversations with one another or with students. They are elaborating ideas in elegant detail. Everyone assumes that rational inquiry and discourse will produce virtue and wisdom, though its usefulness in the wider world is of little concern. Even when they are highly skeptical of all received truths and are energetically engaged in deconstructing every idea and text that they encounter, the academicians believe that their own ideas are good for their own sake. People enter and leave the academy as they choose; it charges no fees, and no one is compensated. Since no accrediting society has yet tracked it down, nothing is measured, except by the standards of rigor and originality. If anyone uses the word "strategy," it is to refer to warfare. As the generations succeed one another, some teachers begin to worry about the place. A number of little white fences have come to dot the landscape to discourage people from venturing out of their intellectual domains and to keep away students who are not serious about the conversations, or who are looking for jobs.

The Corporate University

For reasons that no one can remember, the academy experiences a series of cultural revolutions and it disappears. In its place there is now a vast university on a campus with sweeping lawns and towering buildings filled with laboratories, classrooms, studios, and offices, all stacked with books of policies and procedures and filled with endless rows of computers. Thousands of students and teachers and legions of staff members are rushing to and fro or circling the campus in their automobiles, looking for a place to park. Different schools, colleges, programs, centers, and institutes are everywhere. Each of them is expected to secure revenues by seeking gifts, enlarging enrollment, raising prices, cutting costs, and pursuing contracts for research and professional services with government and business. Some of the newer contracts are especially promising because they may lead to the university's ownership of start-up companies or licensing of processes, with the prospect of large cash flows. A large new sports stadium is expected to be another source of revenue, though many shudder at its cost and fear the influence of business sponsorship that it entails. Clearly, an entrepreneurial model of choice animates the university.

With all these developments, people wonder often and aloud whether the institution itself has not become another kind of industry—University, Inc. Has it become a creature of the market, a corporation producing entertainment and knowledge for anyone who will pay for it? To many, the university has reached the point of compromising its deepest values of open inquiry to serve the proprietary needs of its research customers. Its purposes seem splintered and incoherent, and its values expedient and vulgar.[1] It seems no longer sure how to think about itself and its purposes. Strategies and plans are everywhere, but they reflect a wild variety of aims and pursuits that have no center. These very questions show that the paradigm of the academy, in spite of its mysterious disappearance, continues to serve as the touchstone for the values and beliefs of many of its university descendants. The golden age lingers in memory and in hope.

The Educational Shopping Mall

There is no ambiguity about the language and values in the paradigm of the educational shopping mall, for they are borrowed unabashedly from the world of commerce. Its conceptual scaffolding is structured by the logic of strategy, markets, customers, pricing, and branding. The primal assumption in the mall is that a successful organization finds its niche in the market by attracting and satisfying customers. Strategic planning is a discipline of management that guides the process of branding and marketing. Whether the customers ever experience the academy's love of knowledge for its own sake is of little consequence as long as they are satisfied and keep coming. Here value is contingent and instrumental and is measured by the calculating logic of marginal benefit to the consumer.

The imagery that accompanies this pattern of pragmatic presuppositions depicts education as a form of commerce. In our mind's eye we see a mall with students choosing from among the educational equivalents of boutiques, specialty shops, and department stores. Charging markedly different prices, the stores advertise with catchy slogans such as "Learn more, pay less" and "Useful education for today's world." The taglines are based on extensive market research that shows that customers want job training and are increasingly inclined to bargain over prices. They also want the stores to be open at all hours, meeting the needs of the customers, not the teachers. The mall offers programs and credentials that can be completed in short periods of time to fit the busy lives of the students, most of whom work full-time and have family obligations. As a result, customers complain loudly if too much is expected of them, so little is.

All the stores are nicely decorated and have ready access to the best in modern information technology, and some have an exceptional array of Internet, audio-visual, and telecommunications capabilities, including online courses with good courseware. In one large store all the offerings are online and are supported by extensive Internet materials and other information resources and study guides, so no teachers are on the site.

Everyone agrees that the mall is an exciting place because people of all ages and social backgrounds are coming to the educational stores. Although many of the customers stay only a short time, most claim that they intend to return later and often. To cover their costs, the stores only offer popular and practical programs that require modest investments in part-time teachers' salaries and that avoid overhead expenses for laboratories, libraries, arts facilities, and the like. As a result, the stores do not sponsor or expect any faculty research, and majors in the basic disciplines of the arts and sciences are not offered.

These three fanciful accounts of education in the academy, the corporate university, and the mall paint pictures with clashing colors. Yet even as images and fables, they reveal contending paradigms of thinking and valuing that are shaping the future of higher education. Each of them builds its system of value around a different point of reference. As leaders and planners approach the work of strategy in a college or university, they are well advised to consider how the institution thinks about and enacts the meaning of its own enterprise. If the strategy process fails to address beliefs at this fundamental level, it will lose much of its potential to gain commitment, credibility, and influence, especially as a tool of leadership.

The Responsive and Responsible University

As we have seen before, and as glaringly evidenced in the three models, strategic thinking in colleges and universities has to reconcile two conflicting approaches to reality. It must simultaneously honor a commitment to intrinsic academic values and to organizational viability. Zemsky, Wegner, and Massy (2005) call this being "mission-centered" and "market-smart." This may be, but we need a variety of conceptual resources to resolve the value conflicts in these two phrases. If we are to achieve a durable reconciliation of these mind-sets, the solution has to respect each part of the equation. Without doing so, we will end up considering higher education as either an isolated world of contemplation or a marketplace of commerce, not ideas. To effect the reconciliation requires many things, including appropriate ways of thinking about institutional identity.

Strategic thinking itself presupposes that an academic organization's identity is situated, not abstract; responsive, not fixed. A responsive and responsible institution takes its specific form at its point of interaction with the wider world. It brings its fundamental intellectual values into specific formative relationships with particular circumstances, and influence flows in both directions. Just as an individual's identity is constituted by an integration of basic elements of the self with the circumstances of time and place, so do the academic values of colleges and universities both influence and carry the imprint of the various social purposes and practical realities that differentiate them. The paradigm of responsibility (or response-ability, as the capacity to anticipate, create, and respond) provides the most hospitable pattern of assumptions for the work of strategy.

Colleges draw life from their values and purposes as well as from the constituencies and social institutions that sponsor them, whether these are government, alumni, foundations, local communities and businesses, or donors and board members. Countless colleges are the product of religious denominations, and they variously bear the marks of that relationship in their identities as they cope with various forms of change. Most universities are creatures of state governments, perhaps designed in the land-grant tradition to teach the "mechanical and practical arts," to give priority in admission to state residents, and to serve the agricultural and business enterprises of the state through teaching and research, all in the context of a shifting economic and social environment.

To respond effectively and congruently to the diverse fields of forces in which they live and to which they must respond, leaders as agents must first interpret the strategic issue at hand and ask, "What is going on?" They do this typically in dialogue with others and through the use of a wide variety of ways of thinking and knowing, from empirical analysis to storytelling. As agents, we respond both through our interpretation of the action on us and in anticipation of the response to our action, and "all of this is in a continuing community of agents" (Niebuhr 196, 66). The paradigm of responsibility takes us beyond the ideas of legal and moral accountability and suggests the notion of response-ability as open, creative, and anticipatory responses to the challenges and opportunities that the world sends our way (cf. Niebuhr 1963; Puka 2005).

As a paradigm, responsibility tries to find an integrated, authentic, and fitting response to the stream of life in which it finds itself. It does not dismiss instrumental values, as the classical academic model is prone to do, but tries to make sense of them in a continuing pattern of interpretation and responsiveness. Nor does it reduce its sense of value to commercial norms, as happens in the educational shopping mall. Unlike the corporate university, with its fractured identity, responsibility seeks integrity and authenticity through dialogue and interaction with the world around it. The paradigm of responsibility is pluralistic, with many valid patterns and syntheses of values, not relativistic, where any value is as valid as any other. The task of responsible leadership is to integrate values by staying riveted on both the guiding purposes of the organization and the meaning of change.

Contextual Academic Identity

Strategic planning programs often spin their wheels because they lack the concepts and the language to interpret the integral strategic identity of the institution. As a result, they shuttle back and forth between being mission centered on some issues and market smart on others. Where the challenge of conceptual presuppositions becomes most difficult is with regard to the strategic understanding of the academic program itself. The natural academic tendency is to enhance quality and improve programs through the elaboration of the evolving professional canon of each discipline, the addition of more specialties and brighter students being the surest way to add value and to bring a department to a new level of excellence. This natural pattern of thought is not wrong, and often it is appropriate. The problem is that it is frequently misplaced, for it lacks vital connection to the strategic possibilities of the institution or of the academic field itself.

A responsive and responsible university situates its academic programs in other ways by differentiating its competencies and purposes contextually. Just like the institution itself, academic programs have a situated identity. As such, they consist of a repertoire of academic resources and capabilities by which the college or university responds uniquely to a demanding and changing environment. More than just various sets of course offerings, however complete or sophisticated, the academic program represents as well a series of organizational and faculty competencies in the design and implementation of programs, and in differentiated approaches to teaching, student learning, and research.

To see academic offerings and the talents of faculty in this strategic light is to open oneself up to contextual ways of thinking about educational value. From the strategic perspective, connections to the larger purposes and worth of education come more quickly into view, linkages in self-understanding create novel possibilities, and the sense of shared communal enterprise is made visible and vital. The distinctiveness of the institution emerges from the way its organizational body combines with its academic soul to create a unique identity.

A FRAMEWORK FOR AN INTEGRATED STRATEGY PROCESS

In the framework that follows, our goal is to suggest the essential components of an integrated strategy process that bears the imprint of the paradigm of responsibility. Nothing especially elaborate or innovative is contained in the steps that are presented here, and they are not offered as the definitive or orthodox version of strategy. Decision makers who have experience with strategic planning will find it familiar, but those who do not can use it as a point of reference for part 3. We should note that this model suggests a more comprehensive and integrative approach to strategy than most of the textbook models. It does so by placing values and vision at the core of the process and by making quantitative strategic indicators, financial issues, and the tasks of implementation explicit parts of the work of strategy itself. As we shall see time and again, everything relates to everything else in both conceiving and enacting strategy, so it is systemic, especially as a tool of leadership.

The proposed centrality of identity and vision in the work of strategy may seem obvious, but many institutions fail to capitalize on its significance as a way to transform the process into a vehicle for strategic leadership. As I have been at pains to indicate in both the preceding argument and the following sections, strategy has to be placed within the appropriate conceptual framework for the power of identity and vision to take hold. They have to connect with the values, narratives, and possibilities of a place in order to be authentic and motivating. In precise terms, a vision is a narrative of aspiration. It announces meanings that are to be lived, not just contemplated, so the cognitive form of a vision is the same as that of a narrative. The shift from management to leadership also turns precisely on the ability of a strategy to create a shared sense of the future that motivates a community to make commitments, set priorities, and take actions. If strategy is about purpose and vision, then it has to be a form of leadership.

Interpreting the Work of Strategy

Those who are familiar with effective strategy programs know that the suggested relationship to leadership is often quite real, though not explicit or systematic. Successful efforts to set new directions in colleges and universities can often be traced to the deliberations and discoveries of a strategic plan, or to the less formal but very real influences of a consistent pattern of strategic thinking. Intentional strategic change may come about as much as a result of the process as the content of strategic planning when it serves as a touchstone for effective dialogue and decision making among campus constituencies (cf. Birnbaum 1988, 1992, 2001).

Of course, strategic planning often does not succeed in these ways for a variety of reasons. Our interest is in finding, articulating, and systematizing the characteristics of effective, though often implicit, syntheses of strategy and leadership. In doing so, we start with strategy as a given set of both tacit orientations and explicit practices and try to draw out their implications for leadership by placing them into a larger conceptual framework. We will be guided by the model of engaging relational leadership as we do so. As in much academic work, our aim is to discover meanings and possibilities that are hidden in familiar activities, in continuing conversations, and in emergent practices by interpreting them in a new light. If we are successful in tracing the contours of what can become a formal process and discipline, then it can be used consciously, systematically, and effectively in many different contexts throughout an academic organization.

As the workings of the method are systematized and communicated, it creates the basis for a coherent process of decision making that involves each of the groups participating in the governance system. When strategy processes are influential and effective, they function in a variety of ways: as a form of learning that uses cognitive methods, as a way to transform the organization by creating a collaborative vision of quality, as the positioning of the organization and its services in its competitive environment, and as a vehicle for leadership and management (cf. Dooris, Kelley, and Trainer 2004). In a word, the process is integrative both conceptually and procedurally. At its best, strategic leadership will be incorporated into the ongoing collaborative work of each level and unit of the university as it becomes a center of leadership, initiative, and strategic decision making.

Drawing again on the relational model of leadership, we become sensitive to dimensions of strategic leadership that we otherwise might not see. An effective strategy process can itself embody a sense of collegiality and procedural fairness that creates trust and mutual commitment among and between participants and the formal leaders of the process and of the organization (cf. Kezar 2004; Tyler 2005). When it is projected against the needs and values of human beings, we can understand how the work of strategy becomes leadership as it establishes background conditions that empower and motivate participants.

When practiced systematically as an applied discipline, the strategy process is inherently integrative. It connects the internal and external contexts as well as heritage with change, plans with actions, and needs for resources with a rationale for attaining and using them. It integrates planning with budgeting, data with meaning, and goals with measurements. As used here, strategy is an integrative and collaborative process of sense making and direction-setting that designs and implements initiatives, goals and actions based on an analysis of organizational strengths and weaknesses, and the threats and opportunities of the wider context. It creates a vision of the best possibilities to create educational value and institutional advantage for the future. The framework presents a comprehensive model of strategy that includes both the activities to prepare for the process and its major steps and procedures. As I shall try to show in the following chapters, when transacted through a method of engaging leadership, the content becomes integrated, the method flexible, and the implementation systematic. Each institution will find ways to customize the process to fit its needs, touching lightly on some steps under some circumstances, and emphasizing others as appropriate. In some cases, the environmental scan may be a dominant feature of the work, while in others it will be the analysis of identity and vision that will be central. On some occasions the academic program will receive the predominant focus, while at other times it may be financial issues that are the preoccupation. Strategy is intended to serve the institution, not the reverse. In all cases, institutions will choose carefully the number of strategic initiatives and projects to develop in each of the intensive phases of planning lest the process become overwhelming. The framework can serve as a preliminary checklist to sort out topics that deserve attention in an upcoming round of planning. Each entry should bring to mind the issues, policies, and programs that are or could be of strategic significance in that area.

An Integrative Strategy Process
1. Situating the Strategy Process
   Strategy and Models of Thought: Thinking about Strategic Thinking
   Strategic Diagnostics: The Elements of Strategy

2. Designing the Mechanisms and Tools of Strategy
   Strategic Governance, Strategic Leadership, and Strategic Management
   Role and Responsibilities of a Strategic Planning Council

Role of the President, other Officers and the Governing Board

Preparing for the Work of the Strategy Council: Dialogue and Process

Strategic Indicators: The Metrics of Identity, Performance, and Aspiration

3. Identity, Mission, and Vision

Narratives of Identity: Story and Values

Mission

Envisioning

Vision

4. External Environmental Scan

Driving Forces and Trends: PEEST (Political, Economic, Educational, Social, and Technological)

Scenarios

5. Internal Scan

Organizational Problems and Opportunities

Governance and Decision-Making Systems

6. Strategic Position

Strengths, Weaknesses, Opportunities, Threats (SWOT)

Core Competencies

7. Strategic Initiatives/Imperatives

Selecting Strategies: Key Strategic Programs and Projects

Academic Programs

General Education

International Education

Teaching and Learning

Faculty

Staff

Diversity

Research

Institutes and Centers

Academic Services

Technology

Libraries and Collections

Admissions/Enrollment/Retention

Cultural and Intellectual Climate

      Student Life

      Residential Programs

      Athletics

      Facilities and Equipment

      Fund-raising

      Alumni Relations

      Communications and Marketing

      Government and Community Relations

8. Goals

   Content

   Measurement

   Accountability

   Deadlines

9. Actions

   Establishing and Communicating Agendas for Implementation

10. Financial Model and Resources

   Using a Financial Model: Costing the Goals and Actions

   Financial Equilibrium

   Setting Priorities

   Connecting Planning and Budgeting

   Tuition Policy

   Financial Aid and Discount Policy

   Capital Funds and Other Sources

   Using Existing Assets

   State and Federal Subsidies

11. Implementation: Systemic Strategic Management

   Communication

   Implementation

   Assessment

   Momentum

SITUATING THE ELEMENTS OF STRATEGY

As leaders introduce a strategy process to a campus, they learn that it requires more than the involvement of a few staff members who know the techniques of strategic planning. If it is to be productive, it cannot just be dropped from on high into the work of an organization. The initiators of the process need to understand the way strategy has operated within the decision-making history, politics, and culture of the institution and to explain how they anticipate the work will be carried out. For most of the faculty and staff, strategy will be identified with whatever positive or unhappy experiences the campus has had with strategic planning in the past. Discussing and distinguishing the characteristics of the strategy process with campus decision-making bodies is a crucial part of the work of situating strategy. Every campus has a governance system that is variously codified in bylaws, documents, and agreements negotiated over the years. It is folly to ignore campus protocols and expectations for governance in designing the details of a strategy process.

A complex process never works by itself but draws on the energies of many people in many different ways. The work of strategy pulls on ideas, proposals, and conversations that occur all across the campus or in the unit using the process. Yet there are designated administrative officers and faculty members who will do the work of leading and coordinating the process and producing its products, starting with the president or chief administrative officer of a unit. The concepts and methods proposed in this book are addressed first to those who will define, describe, initiate, and answer for the process, and next to those will participate in it in various ways. In the initial stages of communicating about the work of strategy, it is essential to have a sense of how people will be involved, as explained in the next chapter.

Elements of Strategy

The literature and my own experience as a practitioner and consultant demonstrate that the work of strategy tends to sort itself out along a spectrum of approaches characterized by different purposes and conceptual models, as well as by various degrees of systematization and comprehensiveness. As a way to prepare for the tasks of strategy, we suggest analyzing it within a diagnostic framework. The categories help those responsible for the process clarify their intentions as they set and communicate goals for what they hope to achieve (cf. Chaffee 1991).

Tactical Thinking and Tacit Strategy

Although it has been in ascendancy for two decades, some institutions do not rely significantly on strategy formally or otherwise, so they can be said to have a tactical orientation. One typical pre-strategic practice involves decision making that reacts to issues, problems, and crises more than it anticipates them. The model of choice is more political and extemporized than purposeful. Substantial tactical skill and insight may be in evidence, but it is difficult to discern the design of a strategy. In contexts like these, individuals often complain that they have little sense of where the institution is headed, as it responds to a continuing series of problems and crises. Often an ad hoc orientation reflects the unavoidable realties of an environment that is filled with turbulence, as when budget crises overwhelm the plans of an institution, or other crises befall an organization. At other times, the avoidance of strategic planning can be traced to the reluctance of administrators and faculty members to cede authority and influence to a process that they distrust and that might take directions that they cannot control (Rowley, Lujan, and Dolence 1997).

Experience also shows that there are a number of institutions that cluster around the position of tacit strategy. Although they do not use a formal method of planning, they nonetheless demonstrate a tacit pattern of coherent strategic thinking and decision making. It may well be rooted in a vivid sense of institutional story that gives direction to the work of the organization. Often smaller institutions or academic units of larger ones have highly differentiated purposes and values that are driven by a vision or by a saga of distinctive achievement.

The problems with tacit strategy are many, including the difficulty that it presents in responding systematically to change in the environment or within the institution itself. If a strategy is not explicit, it becomes less useful in providing an orientation for coherent decision making throughout the institution and over time. It fails as well to provide the basis for systematically communicating goals and priorities to the continuing stream of new faculty and staff members and students who join the institution.

Strategic Planning

As we enter the area of strategic planning, we find ourselves in the most populated sector of the spectrum. Although, as we have learned, the method cannot be defined with precision in higher education, as a concept it separates the design of goals from their implementation. Although the conceptual gap is often closed through the way it is practiced, many times it remains a method of projection.

In many cases the approach involves an episodic or periodic planning process, often triggered by a change in the presidency, an accreditation review, or the preparation for a capital campaign. Typically a special committee or commission with membership from many constituencies is appointed to prepare a plan, and the group ceases to exist after it has issued its report. If the moment is right and the report receives strong backing from the governing board, the administration, and a critical mass of faculty, the strategic plan can have a decisive influence.

Strategic planning can also be practiced as a continuous discipline in which plans are constantly under review or development, and goals are revised periodically and distributed widely across the campus. As a continuous discipline, it becomes much more likely that planning will be more than the projection of goals, because they will be regularly proposed as items for implementation. Conceptually, though, a gap still exists between the formulation and implementation of goals.

Strategic Management

At this position along the spectrum, strategic planning has become institution-alized by forging connections with the organization's operational systems of deci-sion making. The goals of strategy are made into administrative responsibilities and combined with continuous methods of evaluation that are fed back into the system of strategic management. As institutions have experienced the frustra-tion of planning as a form of projection, the profile of strategic management has sharpened in the last decade.[2]

In many institutions there is an uneven and segmented pattern to the tasks of strategic management. Some offices and programs ignore or sidestep the process and fail to develop methods for ensuring that goals are satisfied. The full integra-tion of the strategy into the management system occurs as key administrative leaders develop control systems and protocols to integrate operational and stra-tegic decision making.

Strategic Leadership

Among institutions that use strategy consistently and continuously, it often functions as a vehicle of reciprocal leadership—as an interactive direction-setting process, not just as a system of control. In this position on the spec-trum, the strategy process focuses clearly and authentically on a vision for the future. Strategic leadership is often relatively centralized and dependent on the commitment of the president, other top officers, and the effectiveness of a central committee or council. Strategic leadership occurs as a continuous process that drives the institution's systems of evaluation, decision making, and communica-tion at all levels, including the work of the governing board.

In a few institutions, strategic leadership appears to be embedded in parts or all of the organization as a cultural and organizational disposition, not only as a set of formal procedures of deliberation. When this occurs, a position has been reached that shows itself in the distribution of leadership throughout the organization. New ideas surface in many places, initiatives are taken by a large range of groups and individuals, and the differences between leaders and followers becomes hard to define, since they are always changing places. Those with authority follow those with the most compelling ideas and lead by mobilizing people and resources around the best possibilities. The story and the vision have been widely internal-ized, and leadership is a transparent process and presence in the ways decisions are made and executed.

Even as hypotheses, these positions offer a set of reference points for charting an institution's experience and its goals for the tasks of strategy. As a college or university decides to inaugurate or to refashion a strategy program, it benefits significantly from situating its approach and defining its intentions. It should ask itself two basic questions: How have we used the strategy process in the past? How should we use it now? Those who lead the process need to know what they intend and what they expect: of the process, of themselves, and of those who will give it their time and energy. Whatever the opportunities for the use of strategy, many of which may be limited by circumstance, a careful consideration of the organizational dynamics and models of thought that define the context makes the prospects for success far more likely.

NOTES

1. There is a growing literature on the commercialization of higher education and its challenge to academic values. See Bok (2003); Geiger (2004); Kirp (2003); Newman, Couturier, and Scurry (2004); and Zemsky, Wegner, and Massy (2005).

2. The recent literature on strategic planning shows the clear shift in focus from planning to implementation. Compare Dooris, Kelley, and Trainer (2004) and Rowley and Sherman (2001). A widely read book by Bryson (1995) on planning for the nonprofit sector makes these points, emphasizing that the book is as much about action or management as it is about planning.

CHAPTER 5

Strategic Governance: Designing the Mechanisms and Tools of Strategy

W e have set in place some of the conceptual and practical foundations on which strategy rests as a form of leadership. Yet these resources by themselves are not sufficient to the task. Strategic leadership has to be inscribed in a college or university's systems of governance, in the ways it makes daily decisions and collects and uses information about itself, and in its culture as a set of traditions, expectations, and relationships. It will involve various decision-making bodies such as commissions, committees, teams, and task forces to do its work. Unless strategic practice is handled legitimately and effectively, the possibilities of strategic leadership will not be realized. In this chapter I examine governance mechanisms for doing the work of strategy and several important methods and tools, such as strategic indicators.

FRAGMENTATION AND COMPLEXITY IN COLLEGIATE DECISION MAKING

As we turn toward the design of the decision-making vehicles for strategy, we must confront again the complexities of governance in higher education. As we have seen, while the administrative tasks of a college or a university are organized hierarchically, academic work occurs collegially. The two systems operate separately as systems of management and of governance within the same institution. One of the central purposes of strategic leadership is to integrate these segmented systems of authority.

We have also examined how the intricate components of shared governance live in fragile balance with one another, resulting frequently in serious disputes about both the content and the canons of academic decision making. The persistent clumsiness and occasional dysfunction of the system should not, however, lead us to think that academic organizations could somehow circumvent or dismantle the collegial model. Academic expertise has to drive the core mission of the organization.

From the perspective of strategic leadership, the fundamental problem is not shared academic governance, but the way it is typically practiced. Strategically, its central weaknesses are its structural fragmentation and its complexity. The issue is not so much what the system sometimes fails to do, but what it cannot do as normally constructed. Both classical and current studies focus on these perennial problems (Duryea 1991; Tierney 2004; Tierney and Lechuga 2004).

Since it lacks mechanisms of integrative decision making, shared governance as normally practiced is not able to address systematically and coherently the whole institution and the demands on it. Whereas the strategic identity of a college or university is lodged in a pattern of interconnected relationships with the wider world, the mechanisms of shared governance deal with issues through fractured and time-consuming processes of decision making. The issues are sliced into pieces and handed out to different faculty and administrative committees. One group deals with general education, another with retention, others with educational policies, another with teaching and learning, and yet others with financial aid, the budget, and so on. Increasingly, too, important decisions are made at the margin or outside of the faculty governance system in research institutes, centers, and programs that control substantial resources but may only be loosely tied to the academic core of the institution (Mallon 2004). The strategic whole is hidden by partial points of view and complicated procedures. The normal mechanisms of academic decision making frustrate rather than enable effective leadership.

With horizontal fragmentation comes vertical complexity. Decisions about academic matters travel slowly up and down a cumbersome series of reviews that include departments, divisions, schools, colleges, and the university, with an array of committees and academic officers involved in the process. Operational decisions often run smoothly in the system. Yet when issues of strategic and academic change have to be confronted, the system is not able to respond coherently or quickly because its systems of decision making are splintered, cumbersome, and time consuming.

CASE STUDY: RETENTION AND GENERAL EDUCATION AT FLAGSHIP UNIVERSITY

Let us illustrate the issues of academic decision making with a case study that draws directly from my own experience in several contexts. Flagship University is a prominent comprehensive university of 24,000 students that offers a full array of undergraduate and graduate degrees and sponsors a large number of successful programs, institutes, and centers in basic and applied research. Through a recently completed study, the university has learned that its attrition rate among first- and second-year students is significantly higher than is predicted by the academic abilities of the study body. As a large and sophisticated institution, the university uses a talented staff in its office of planning and budget to regularly analyze important issues of this kind. Data from departing and continuing students have been collected and analyzed, and a report has been sent to all the relevant offices.

The report suggests that the new general education program has a negative effect on student retention. Students believe the program repeats work from high school, offers too many lecture classes, and forces students to meet requirements in areas that do not interest them, chosen from too small a list. Because of the limited number of sections in several fields, students often have to delay enrollment, sometimes in courses that are prerequisites to a major or in areas where a delay may cause them to lose skills, such as foreign languages. High attrition after the first and second years seems to be correlated with a lack of personal involvement in the academic program.

When the various vice presidents receive the report, they make sure that it is put on the agenda for the weekly meeting of the president's executive staff, and that the president is briefed about it. The president and his senior colleagues are quite concerned about the report's findings, and the senior business officer notes the loss of tuition revenue and the state subsidy. At the staff meeting, the decision is made to ask the chairman of the faculty senate and of the senate's curriculum committee to read the report and consider its results. What ideas and recommendations can they offer?

The vice president for student affairs notes several references in the report to problems in life in the student residences, binge drinking, and complaints that the fraternity and sorority pledging practices consume inordinate amounts of time for first-year students, contributing to the high rate of attrition. He discusses the issues with his staff and asks for ideas.

The report is on the agenda at the next meeting of the senate's curriculum committee. Several faculty members with background in statistics take issue with the report's methods and conclusions. Others show genuine concern but comment on the political delicacy and complexity of the issue. The new general education program reflects an exquisite political compromise that added a variety of new courses to internationalize and diversify the offerings. It also achieved a good balance in enrollment among many departments. To avoid delving into all these issues again, the committee decides to refer the report to the dean of arts and sciences. The committee expresses its concern that departments in the arts and sciences are not receiving enough support to develop the new program as planned, and they recommend to the president, provost, and dean of arts and sciences that additional resources be found to remedy these deficiencies.

When the dean of arts and sciences receives the senate committee's report, she holds a series of meetings with department chairs and requests that key departments discuss the issue. The results of these sessions are inconclusive because the meetings raise many issues and problems that are not directly related to the problem of high attrition. Many of the tensions within departments over the content and methods of the general education courses surface, and there are numerous complaints that there are not enough financial resources to do justice to the new program.

When the staff of the vice president for students completes their meetings, they suggest a program to link first-year courses with new residential hall programs that would involve the faculty members who teach general education courses. They recommend that funds be found to support the new initiative. They send their report to the vice president, who forwards it to the dean of arts and sciences, the provost, and the president.

Reading about the senate committee's response, and studying the other reports, the president meets with the dean of arts and sciences, the vice president for students, and the provost. He learns that several departments and the curriculum committee in arts and sciences are still studying the problem, which leads to a blunt expression of his rising frustration: "We have a very important problem with retention linked to a core academic program, and no one is ready to do anything about it. Everyone wants to shuffle the issue off to someone else and throw money at it. I never liked the new general education program, anyway, because it was too much of a political compromise. I said so at the time, but no one wanted to listen. How can we get a purchase on this issue and do something about it?"

Decision Making at Flagship

This case illustrates many things, one of which is that the institution's problems began long before its high attrition rate. These problems are lodged in the way the university makes decisions. It does not have a way to define and to address educational and strategic issues that transcend a series of segmented decision-making systems. The best it can do is to try to build linkages after the fact. Its governance system is functioning properly, and procedures are being followed. No one is protesting about arbitrary decisions or a failure to consult or communicate. The operational systems are also working. Studies are being completed, meetings are being held, and actions that move up and down the governance system are being proposed.

The problem is that the university shows a deficient ability to anticipate strategic issues and their interconnection. In this case, the senate committee is trying to address curricular and retention issues from a university-wide perspective but does not have the expertise, authority, time, or resources to pursue its agenda to completion. The dean, department chairs, and faculty in arts and sciences all come to the problem from different directions with multiple interests, so the discussion generates a complex mixture of conflicts over professional and academic issues, priorities, and resources that bring to mind the garbage-can model of decision making. Administrative officers such as the provost and vice president for students have the authority needed to review the issues, but not to implement any proposals that require faculty action. The problem behind the problem is that the university lacks a coherent strategic understanding of itself as an integrated system. Nor does it have a decision-making mechanism to set agendas, define priorities, and allocate resources that respond to the most pressing issues that are shaping its future.

Marginalized Faculty and Administrative Roles

We see again in this case many of the structural and organizational realities that make leadership in colleges and universities so difficult. The neat separation between "academic" and "administrative" issues has become increasingly artificial. In this example, the problems with general education trigger lower enrollment, increase demands and costs in admissions, and cause a drop in tuition revenues. Countless other problems ripple through the organization from this source. Yet because general education is considered to be an academic problem, it is studied in isolation rather than as part of an organizational system.

The president is frustrated as an academic leader, as his complaint made clear. He has studied many successful general education programs and is a respected educator. Yet he is also aware that good ideas about academic programs and practices often count for little. On his campus, like most, academic matters are decided by groups and committees that live in a world with their own rules, expectations, and proprieties. Even with so much at stake for the institution, he feels marginalized.

Yet this case and many like it reveal something else. The forces that are shaping the wider society and higher education do not pause to differentiate themselves around the disjointed decision-making protocols of academic organizations. Powerful sweeping realities like technological innovation, market forces, demographic shifts, social change, economic cycles, internationalization, and political trends happen as they will. As these changes have swept through the halls of higher learning in the last twenty-five years, the identities of colleges and universities have become ever more contextual. The outside world has insistently shaped the inside world. As we have seen in the images and models that we explored earlier, some educational institutions increasingly mimic the market-driven realities of corporate decision making. Among other things, these trends have created a new depth and density of administrative decision making. Increasingly specialized and professionalized, it has by force of necessity assumed responsibilities that were once the faculty's.

In many spheres, including the initiation of new academic units and institutes, the implementation of governmental regulations, the planning of facilities, and the management of financial resources, administrative decision making is dominant. Often to their relief, faculty members on most campuses—although there are exceptions—no longer play a decisive role in policies on student life or in decisions related to admissions and financial aid, especially since the latter are now dominated by marketing plans and computer models. Just as academic administrators and trustees often feel frustrated by their inability to move the academic agenda, so do many faculty members feel marginalized in their organizational roles. Yet they cannot easily find ways to change the situation, except through the commitment of more time and energy, which they are reluctant to make. The changing world has taken much of the university away from them (Burgan, Weisbuch, and Lowry 1999; Hamilton 1999).

STRATEGIC GOVERNANCE

The frustrations that that exist on both sides of the administrative and academic divide cannot be resolved simply with ever-more precise clarifications of the responsibilities of shared governance. The need is for new ways of thinking and new mechanisms of decision making. I have suggested some elements of an integrated conceptual framework for strategic leadership and now intend to offer ideas for new forms of strategic governance.

Over the past several decades, it has become increasingly clear that organizational decision making occurs in three fundamental forms, all intertwined in practice. We can differentiate these levels as governance, management, and strategy. The role of governance is to define and delegate formal responsibility and authority within the organization, which are derived from the legal powers and fiduciary responsibilities vested in the governing board. Yet the formal governance system can only work through the multiple systems of decision making and management that are delegated to the administrative and academic operating systems of the institution. In turn, however, the operational and governance systems cannot function effectively unless there is a strategic link between them. The strategy system, whether formal or tacit, sets goals and priorities and allocates resources in the name of an overall direction for the future. At all three levels, leadership is currently understood largely in terms of the authority vested in positions and the knowledge and skills required to exercise formal responsibilities. Leadership as an engaging relational process of mobilizing meaning and commitment to common purposes is not a defining characteristic of the formal academic decision-making system.

In making campus visits for accreditation, visiting teams conclude that important strategic decisions about programs, policies, facilities, and budgets are usually dominated by whatever component of the governance system is most influential in the local institutional culture. In research universities and small colleges, one or more faculty committees or advisory councils sometimes tacitly take up pieces of the strategy portfolio, working in various ways with administrative leaders. They often do so by tradition as much as by formal delegation of authority. Or, most commonly, as at Flagship, there is no ongoing integrative strategic process of leadership or governance to respond to problems that cut across several domains—which is precisely the nature of most organizational problems. Although strategic decision making appears in a variety of forms in higher education, it is not a central, defining, and structural feature of the system of shared governance.

Given these broad challenges, the development of closer and clearer connections among strategic governance, strategic leadership, and strategic management is of decisive importance. Strategic leadership as a method and discipline offers a way to integrate the mechanisms of governance and management to respond effectively to the hard realities of the world.

In this context, strategic governance refers to the development of the deliberative bodies, processes, and procedures that are required to carry out a continuing process of strategic decision making as part of a larger governance system. The issues rise to the level of governance because the strategy process and its vehicles require formal definition, legitimacy, and authority. As the institution's highest governing authority, the governing board will ultimately be called upon to endorse a formal strategy process on the recommendation of the president after collaboration with the faculty and administration.

STRATEGY COUNCILS

Given the collaborative norms and forms of decision making in higher education, one of the central questions about strategic governance focuses on the nature of the deliberative body that will lead the strategy process. In *Strategic Governance*, Schuster, Smith, Corak, and Yamada (1994) trace the issues related to institution-wide planning committees and councils at eight universities.

In doing so, they are responding to an idea expressed by George Keller (1983) in *Academic Strategy* that a "Joint Big Decision Committee" of senior faculty and administrators is an effective vehicle for strategic planning. Schuster and his colleagues found that one of the goals in the creation of each of the committees they studied was to provide a basis for engaging the big strategic issues facing the institution, although they were strikingly different in composition, purpose, and effectiveness. Even though none of the eight institutions used the exact term, and most of them did not consistently do comprehensive strategic planning, the authors chose the generic term "Strategic Planning Council" (SPC) to designate the role of these committees and to capture their apparent intent. Although the aim of these SPCs was purportedly to provide a venue for faculty and staff participation in important fiscal and planning issues, a continuing focus on strategic matters is often hard to find in their activities. In spite of this, such bodies often came to meet other important institutional needs and were appreciated for the work that they did. In half of the eight cases studied, members of the campus community and participants in the process gave a positive or highly positive appraisal of the SPC's work. In the other half of the institutions, the evaluation was decidedly mixed and, in two instances, strongly negative. In three institutions the SPC eventually went out of business or substantially changed its form, typically with the arrival of a new president (Schuster, Smith, Corak, and Yamada 1994).

Schuster and his colleagues analyze four primary factors that they believe will contribute to the effectiveness of SPCs as vehicles for strategic governance: (1) the SPC should demonstrate that it does not intend to circumvent or replace existing forms of academic governance or administrative authority; (2) the SPC must focus on the genuine strategic issues facing the institution, and not be drawn into debates and controversies about operational issues or budgetary details; (3) the SPC must be conscientious and consistent in communicating with the campus community about its work and recommendations; (4) the president and other university leaders should be fully engaged in the enterprise and balance the work of the SPC with the responsibilities of other university officials and decision-making bodies.

Case Studies in Strategic Governance

As one reviews the literature and the practice of strategic planning in a variety of settings, it is clear that institutions continue to struggle with the nature of the governing body or bodies that can best develop an authentic strategic agenda. Larry Shinn describes some of the issues and conflicts in strategic planning and faculty governance at liberal arts colleges (Shinn 2004). Many colleges and universities now have the formal equivalent of SPCs, though their roles and responsibilities vary widely, as we have seen. They operate with differing powers and duties along a spectrum of institutional centralization and decentralization. Leaders and participants often report a central advisory or steering committee to be particularly useful (Dooris, Kelley, and Trainer 2004; Steeples 1988).

One of Burton Clark's (1998) central findings in his influential study of five entrepreneurial European universities was the presence of a strategic "steering core" in each of the institutions. Clark notes elsewhere that these central groups are committed to effective planning, to allocating resources as investments to gain the best returns, and to creating "a desirable and sustainable institutional character" (1997, xiv). In sum, there must be effective forms of strategic thinking occurring throughout the organization, but most especially at its core.

The University of Northern Colorado

In a riveting irony, a prominent work on collegiate planning describes how the faculty senate and the academic deans at the authors' own institution, the University of Northern Colorado, never fully accepted the institution's strategic planning process (Rowley, Lujan, and Dolence 1997). Aspects of the process were nonetheless implemented through the work of the SPC and the president's authority. Based on their controversial experiences with governance rules and protocols, and study of the issues, the authors offer extensive counsel and object lessons about how and why to establish an effective SPC.

Brown University

Revealing both the diversity and similarity of governance issues at different universities, Brown University offers a parallel yet different model of strategic decision making. Brown has recently established a new faculty committee and revised an existing one to advise the president on academic and financial priorities. The Academic Priorities Committee is an effort to strengthen the voice of the faculty in advising the president on the strategic use of educational resources. A parallel

University Resources Committee will make recommendations on the full range of financial and budgetary issues facing the university. There is no central SPC or its equivalent (Savage 2003).

A number of questions present themselves in this case as well. How and when do the deliberations of the faculty committee on academic program priorities become integrated with other strategic goals and priorities of the university? The faculty voice on academic programs and priorities is central but must ultimately be connected to the institution's larger strategic needs and its financial capabilities. It would ring louder were it heard continuously around the central table of integrative strategic decision making within an SPC, rather than in separate advisory committees.

An Effective Steering Core for Strategy

The challenge for each college and university is to forge local pathways and mechanisms that create effective informal and formal linkages across various domains of strategic decision making. Lacking a systematic way to integrate an institution's strategic possibilities with its ongoing academic decisions, the process can easily become splintered, duplicative, and frustrating, as we have seen at Flagship. It works in fits and starts, sometimes wasting time and energy on academic projects and plans that may lead nowhere because they are not related to broader educational issues and other priorities and resources.

All these studies and cases reveal that the establishment of an effective vehicle for strategic governance and leadership has become an inescapable and pressing issue for colleges and universities. The time has long since come to renew and reconfigure the mechanisms of collaborative decision making to deal coherently with strategic change. Although governance is the live rail of campus politics, educational leaders who do not have the will or wisdom to build sturdy vehicles for strategy may never safely reach their destinations.

GUIDELINES FOR CREATING A STRATEGY COUNCIL

We can use the Flagship experience and findings from the literature and case studies to offer guidelines for the creation of a strategy council. The analysis and recommendations take the form of a hypothetical report issued from a blue-ribbon commission appointed by the governing board on the president's recommendation. The report systematically reflects the problems and issues in strategic governance that have to be addressed in creating an SPC. It directly reflects my own work in several institutions and the literature on the topic.

Report of the Flagship Commission

Powers and Responsibilities

A Strategic Planning Council should be duly constituted and empowered by the governing board on the president's recommendation to develop and monitor the implementation of an integrated and continuous strategy process for the university. The SPC will communicate periodically with the campus community about its work and will issue reports and studies that define the challenges and opportunities that the institution faces in the wider environment. The SPC will propose strategies, programs, goals, and priorities that fulfill the university's mission and that define its vision for the future.

The SPC will normally discharge its responsibilities through the periodic creation of various subcommittees and task forces with joint faculty, staff, student, and board membership, as appropriate to the issue, to address a broad range of institutional policies and programs. Based on the analysis of information and opinion and the use of strategic indicators, surveys, roundtables, open meetings, and its own deliberations, each task group will communicate its findings and recommendations to the SPC. Functioning in the role of steering committee, the SPC will meet with each subgroup to receive its report and discuss its findings. The SPC will draw specifically from each set of recommendations in preparing its own report but is not bound by the interpretations, language, or conclusions of the subgroups.

In addition to developing an institution-wide plan every few years, the SPC will assist the institution's executive and academic leaders to ensure that strategy and planning activities are in place in each of the institution's major academic and administrative units. Although these processes should reflect the central priorities of institution-wide strategies, they will focus on the specific strategic issues that different units must address. The findings, concerns, and priorities displayed in the various units and divisions will help to shape and define subsequent rounds of the institution-wide strategy process.

After the completion of an intensive cycle of strategy development and the publication of a strategy report, the SPC will help to monitor and review the goals established during the process. The SPC and/or relevant administrative officers will issue periodic public reports and make presentations to faculty and staff bodies on progress in reaching strategic goals, and on the reasons for any new or revised goals. Meetings of the governing board and of its committees will be organized around the vision and goals of the university's strategy.

The SPC will be an institution-wide body that reports to the president; in turn, the president will recommend strategies, goals, and priorities to the governing board. Since it deals with issues concerning finance, facilities, educational programs, and administrative policies that involve both faculty and administrative authority, it is neither a faculty nor an administrative committee, but a university-wide council. The reports or recommendations issued by the SPC do not enact programs or policies that require legislative action by the various faculties, the faculty senate, or other university governing bodies. Rather, it will define strategic issues and priorities within a broad internal and external context. Through the endorsement of the governing board, its work will serve as a mechanism for integrative and collaborative leadership by setting an agenda for the university's future.

While the content of strategy documents is not subject to the legislative control of the faculty or of faculty or staff committees, the SPC will function in the context of Flagship's traditions of collaborative decision making and shared governance. As a result, the SPC will present its major periodic strategy plans to the faculty senate for consideration and endorsement. Although the SPC owns its reports, the deliberations of the faculty senate, other faculty councils, and key administrators provide a testing ground for the strategies as they move to the governing board. Should the faculty senate vote for changes in the the SPC's recommendations and priorities, the SPC will deliberate on the issue and then either alter its report or include any negative faculty action as a dissent to be noted in the report.

When the SPC's goals and priorities are ultimately adopted by the governing board, then various faculty committees and administrative groups and officers will be expected to consider the enactment of new academic or administrative programs that have been featured in the plan. The SPC will analyze and present the proposed changes in the context of integrated strategic priorities. As a result, the process will not circumvent the normal academic system of decision making, since legislative authority for academic programs will remain with the faculty.

Planning and Budgeting

The SPC can also play a vital role in the critical process of connecting strategy with operating budgets on a continuous basis. The commission is aware that one of the constant challenges in college and university decision making is relating strategic goals to the tactical realities that often drive the annual budgeting process. The SPC, in particular, will be in a position to assist in shaping the broad parameters and priorities of each budget cycle and relating it to the goals of the strategic plan and to the financial model that is included in the strategy process. Thus, the SPC will review and deliberate annually on the key components of the university's revenues and expenses. It will be able to recommend to the president the amount of funding available for new positions and programs, or the way spending should be restrained or reduced to reflect strategic priorities.

The commission believes that the SPC would best carry out some aspects of these financial responsibilities through a standing subcommittee of faculty and administrative officers. The subcommittee would entertain proposals or set broad criteria for new expenditures for programs and personnel and do the same if reductions are necessary, based on information received from the various academic and administrative units. After receiving recommendations from the subcommittee and the SPC, the president will make the final decisions on the budget.

Leadership and Membership

The SPC's leadership and membership will contribute critically to its effectiveness, which will require it to be relatively small in size, as the literature suggests. The university's president and chief academic and business officers will be continuing members, and two other executives will be chosen by the president to serve renewable rotating three-year terms. Five faculty members—no more than two from the same unit—will be nominated by the faculty membership committee after consultation with the chief academic officer, and elected by the senate. Three deans will be rotating members: one will be from one of the two largest schools, and the two others will be chosen by the president in consultation with the dean's council. The SPC will require staff support from the director and another member of the planning and research staff. Total membership, excluding staff support, should not exceed sixteen members, including one undergraduate and one graduate student serving two-year terms.

Since the SPC is a continuing body, the issue of its leadership is of critical significance. Persons who assume the position of chairperson should have both substantial academic or administrative authority, as well as considerable talents in integrative thinking and in communication. Since the SPC is to work at the nexus of governance, strategy, leadership, and management, the chairperson should be able to conceptualize skillfully the institution's identity and vision, as well as possess the authority to help ensure that goals and priorities are implemented. Most members of the commission believe that the SPC would best be chaired by the provost, or by the vice president for planning and administration. Some members have argued that the SPC should be under the leadership of the president as chair or as co-chair, since that office has the most influential role in forging links between the different levels of decision making.

President's Role

The commission unanimously believes that whether as chairperson, co-chair, or an ex-officio member, the president must make the work of the SPC a defining responsibility of presidential duties. This means attending meetings, working intimately with the chairperson, shepherding reports and recommendations through the institution and on to the board, and ensuring the implementation of approved projects. Many times the president will contribute decisively to the SPC's deliberations, especially on issues of mission and vision and the most pressing strategic challenges and opportunities. The task of collective university leadership will find one of its core mechanisms in the work of an effective SPC.

Questions about Strategic Governance

Any recommendations with the scope of the Flagship commission's report may stir some measure of controversy on many campuses, less on others. They will have to be discussed, debated, and negotiated in various campus forums, venues, and decision-making bodies. The issues to be debated can be clarified by series of questions that can be used to test the Flagship report as well as the designs that other campuses may develop to address the issues of effective strategic governance.

- How does the SPC relate to the work of existing faculty bodies and administrative committees and officers?

- Is a strategy process a familiar method of campus decision making?
- Will the role of the SPC be consistent with the formal policies, rules, and documents that define the system of shared governance?
- Will the SPC create another layer of authority in a system that may already be too complex?
- Does the proposed SPC help to integrate the institution's fragmented systems of decision making and serve as a vehicle for collaborative leadership?
- Have the appropriate groups had, or will they have, a chance to express their views and influence the provisions of the report before it is acted on by the governing board?
- Are its membership and other operating assumptions and responsibilities appropriate?
- Can the SPC effectively guide a complex process to completion in a reasonable period of time?
- Will the institution be able to implement the goals that the strategy process establishes?
- Will the organization be able to create a continuous loop of quality improvement by linking assessment to the development and implementation of strategy?

There is a series of other questions and issues about the effectiveness of an SPC that go beyond the formal issues of governance and authority. From a cultural perspective, an SPC needs to serve as a vehicle to bring talented people with good ideas from across campus into productive relationships with one another in teams, subcommittees, and study groups. One dimension of strategic leadership is for those with authority to bring those who have innovative and promising ideas into fruitful relationships with one another. Good leaders are followers of good ideas. A central role of an SPC is to draw upon, encourage, and strategically connect the best educational and administrative practices that are emerging in different parts of the organization.

Analysis of the Flagship Case

As we take our leave of Flagship, we are left with a number of impressions and conclusions. The work of strategy ultimately can be effectively translated into the methods of leadership and the governance processes of institutions of higher learning. When this occurs, it can make a decisive contribution to collaborative and integrative leadership. An SPC, regardless of what it is called, offers a critical point of reference to achieve effective strategic leadership. Although the proposed model will not fit every circumstance, the burden shifts to those who would not choose to pursue its possibilities. At the very least, the question that must be answered is, if it is not to be a strategy council, then what should it be? When this question has been answered and the debates have ended, the focus shifts to decisions that reside in the authority of the governing board.

THE ROLE OF THE GOVERNING BOARD

The responsibilities of the governing board for strategy and strategic leadership have often been neglected. Although board members may or may not be represented formally on an SPC—it depends on circumstances—the governing board is an essential participant in the total strategy process. Beyond whatever involvement board members may have by reason of talent or interest in some aspects of the work of strategy, the board's active endorsement of strategic governance is essential to the total process. The authority and prestige of the board needs to be evident in the creation and oversight of the strategy process, and in its active consideration of the reports and plans that come to the board for endorsement and final approval.

The governing board should consider the creation of an SPC as essential to effective decision making and of leadership in the university. The board's authority in these areas is often peculiarly absent. As a consequence, faculty and administration often churn in conflict over the fine points of shared governance while fundamental strategic issues are handled episodically and incoherently. How can the board's ultimate legal authority and fiduciary responsibility have any meaning unless it is actively involved in shaping the institution's capabilities to respond effectively to the world around it? What could be more relevant than the board's direct involvement in a consideration of the mechanisms that shape the institution's mission and identity and its strategic position and vision? There may be times when the board can legitimately be active or even proactive in addressing the strategic governance process. If there is unresolved conflict about the effectiveness of the strategy process or the role of a group like an SPC, the board can and should address the issues to ensure that the methods of strategic decision making are effective and coherent. As Chait, Holland, and Taylor put it in their study of the characteristics of effective governing boards, "competent boards cultivate and concentrate on processes that sharpen institutional priorities and assure a strategic approach to the organization's future" (1993, 95).

One of the board's critical roles is to make sure that the processes of decision making in the institution are functioning in a constitutional, balanced, and effective manner. It does not interfere in the decisions on programs and personnel but ensures that good policies and processes are in place to make them. When it sees deficiencies or recurrent problems such as fragmentation, dysfunctional conflict, or loss of a strategic focus, it has a reason to be concerned and to raise the issue. Without denying a proper place for each element in the governance process, it can seek to connect them all in a coherent framework through a process of strategic thinking and leadership.

The way the board fulfills this strategic role will vary enormously by context. In many situations, the board will be a repository of wisdom about the organization's narrative of identity and can be a testing ground for an emerging vision (cf. Chait, Ryan, and Taylor 2005). The mission and vision of the organization are inalienable leadership responsibilities of a governing board, and its active initiative and participation in consideration of these topics are essential. Many board members also have much to offer in the development of an environmental scan, the analysis of financial position, the development of marketing programs, and the assessment of the institution's strengths and vulnerabilities. Along with the president, they see the institution as a whole. Some boards have their own committees that focus on long-range planning and broad strategic issues. In other cases individual board members have a special role in strategic planning based on their professional expertise, for example, participating in, chairing, or co-chairing a task force or a major new planning initiative.

However it comes to them, the board should consider and endorse a strategic plan through an active process of review, often in a special meeting or retreat. As we shall see below, once adopted, the strategy gives the agenda of each board and committee meeting a new pertinence and purposefulness. Questions can be raised and answered with reference to an established strategic vision, set of goals, and metrics, as part of a continuing strategic review, assessment, and dialogue. As the institution's final legal authority, the board's symbolic and real involvement provides an aura of seriousness to the dimension of accountability in the process of strategic leadership (Morrill 2002).

To summarize, the board's role in strategic governance and leadership includes the following (Morrill 2002):

- It ensures that an effective strategy process is in place and adopts those governance provisions that may be required to enable it.
- It supports and participates in the process as appropriate.
- It receives the plan that results from the strategy process and considers it for adoption.
- It holds the president accountable for implementing the goals of the strategy.
- It receives data, reports, and information that enable it to monitor, assess, and ensure accountability for the implementation of the strategy.

ORGANIZING THE WORK OF THE SPC

In discussing the possibilities of an SPC, we have considered a major organizational vehicle that can spearhead one facet of the process of strategic leadership. Before we analyze the components of the strategy process, it is worth attending to some of the essential steps that should be taken to prepare a strategy council to do its work effectively, always keeping in mind its contribution to leadership. Based on his work with hundreds of executives at MIT, Peter Senge (1990) reminds us that one of the fundamental tasks of leadership is to design decision-making systems that work, not simply operate them once they have been built. Nowhere is leadership through authority more critical than in the painstaking work that is required to build the right methods and vehicles for the tasks of strategy.

Faculty Involvement

The need to prepare faculty and staff for involvement in a strategy process is obvious in a number of ways. A third or a half of the strategy council may be faculty members who typically have neither studied management nor been involved in formal strategy processes. They may also have a distaste for some of its methods and language. Most importantly, faculty members already have full-time jobs that consume much of their time. Strategy development is not business as usual, and it periodically consumes more time than a typical committee, especially for those in leadership roles. Given these very real challenges, leaders have to ask themselves how faculty participation in the process can be most worthwhile. Surely if faculty members are asked to chair a major task force, they need ample staff support and time to make it possible. Their other responsibilities may have to be adjusted temporarily. Intensive faculty involvement in the strategy process may also be enabled by carving out a week at the end or before the beginning of a semester for concentrated work on strategy.

Orientation to the Strategy Process

One of the fatal blows to a strategy program is to begin without an orientation to the procedures, timetables, expectations, and organization of the process. Especially as a committee or council is about to begin an intensive cycle of planning, it is essential that ground rules be made explicit and that participants be given the tools they need to make a contribution to the deliberations.

In most cases, the preparation should involve a one- or two-day retreat, for which new members receive a special orientation. In particular, the leaders and staff of the process do well to prepare a notebook and or Web site with articles on current issues facing higher education; key information from documents of the institution; excerpts from prior plans, including mission and vision statements; and materials that convey a sense of institutional history, identity, and distinctiveness. Participants should also receive a fact book or similar materials that contain important quantitative data about the institution, including a full set of strategic indicators. A presentation on the significance of the data, especially of the financial information, should be part of the retreat.

In considering the process and content of planning, the issue of financial constraints and opportunities should be addressed forthrightly. If an institution faces tough financial times, it makes sense to build that fact into expectations from the outset. The strategy effort may, in fact, have to focus on creating equitable procedures for reallocating resources. If new resources are available, the SPC and its various subgroups need to know the institution's broad financial capabilities. Limits should not be so tight as to discourage high ambition and creativity, but it is ultimately self-defeating to create high expectations that can only be disappointed.

Role and Responsibilities of the SPC

The SPC serves as a steering committee for the process both organizationally as well as with regard to the larger questions of strategy and leadership. In most cases, the total process will benefit from an early focus by the SPC on the crucial fourfold strategic elements of identity, mission, vision, and position. At this juncture, it becomes clear that an open, effective, and continuing dialogue between the president and the council is critical. Out of the shared understanding of these defining perspectives, the work of strategy will become effective in galvanizing commitment to shared strategic goals across the campus. The participants in subcommittees and task forces will find that their work becomes much more focused and productive if they can orient themselves to an authentic narrative of identity and aspiration, even if it is preliminary.

If the council anticipates working in task forces and subcommittees, as is usually the case, it should be made clear how the SPC hopes to divide the responsibilities of each group in meaningful ways. Typically one of the members of the SPC will either chair or co-chair subcommittees, so all its members need to be aware of the responsibilities that await them. The selection of topics requires a lot of analysis and discussion, and there will need to be some negotiation about how various topics will be treated, since many issues will fit into several contexts. As we emphasize later, only a limited number of issues can be treated in each intensive planning cycle, so careful thought about managing the work of each subgroup is essential.

This is also the time to begin to sketch the length and characteristics of the report that is to be expected from each group. The art and science of preparing situation analyses, developing goals, and assigning responsibility for them should be explored in order to develop common purposes, formats, and patterns of presentation. Anticipating that usually only two or three people write the first draft of committee reports will bring realism into the discussion. As suggested in the Flagship SPC case, it is also important to establish the protocols for the various subgroups to work with the SPC and to clarify what happens to their reports and recommendations once they are submitted. They should expect that their ideas will be taken seriously but be subject to significant reformulation in the final decisions and reports of the SPC.

Group Process

The various subcommittees as well as the SPC itself will also want to consider the dynamics of constructive group work and relationships. How can group interaction be productive and positive, encouraging people to make contributions to deliberations? How will the group become an effective collaborative team based on dialogue, not endless disputes? How will the leadership and facilitation of group processes occur? The notion that the group is a team, not simply a committee, is a useful starting point to answer these questions. Team members should be chosen not simply through position but because of their ability to think about the larger organization and the broad issues that it faces. They should know the campus and how to get things done, be widely respected, and have the time and commitment to bring to the work of strategy and change (Eckel, Green, Hill, and Mallon 1999). To be effective, teams should have a clear and compelling sense of direction; function as a group, not as individuals; use the right processes; and get help through coaching when they need it (Hackman 2005). Bensimon and Neumann (2000) offer a cognitive perspective in analyzing effective presidential teams that applies to strategy teams as well. A team is a collective sense maker—"that is, its members are collectively involved in perceiving, analyzing, learning, and thinking" about the organization's future (Bensimon and Neumann 2000, 249; cf. Bolman and Deal 2003).

Perhaps with the help of a carefully chosen consultant, the members of a strategy group will benefit from exploring ways to develop joint skills in problem solving and strategic thinking. In *The Fifth Discipline*, Senge (1990) discusses ways to foster teams' skills in the art of dialogue, as distinguished from debate or argumentation. He gives the example of a company that invites key executives to attend a retreat to discuss the final steps in developing a strategic plan. The president asks participants to practice the art of dialogue by following these ground rules:

1. Suspension of assumptions. Typically people take a position and defend it, holding to it. Others take up opposite positions and polarization results. In this session, we would like to examine some of our assumptions underlying our direction and strategy and not seek to defend them.

2. Acting as colleagues. We are asking everyone to leave his or her position at the door....

3. Spirit of inquiry. We would like to have people begin to explore the thinking behind their views, the deeper assumptions they may hold, and the evidence they have that leads them to these views. So it will be fair to begin to ask others questions such as "What leads you to say or believe this?" (Senge 1990, 259).

A focus on group dynamics is not especially common in academic decision making, perhaps since so much of the work is driven by professional expertise. Yet when strategic thinking is in play, the idea of dialogue as the suspension of assumptions and authority makes a valuable contribution to the structuring of collaborative work.

Although in my experience many faculty members do not take well to the exercises and group work that consultants use in other organizations, it is worth the SPC's effort to consider professional assistance with the right kind of questionnaires, discussion protocols, and processes to get issues related to mission, vision, and other complex subjects on the table. A good tactic is to test proposed procedures with several members of the SPC before they are used widely. An excellent source for ideas and techniques is found in *Strategic Planning for Public and Nonprofit Organizations*, by John Bryson (1995), and in guides that accompany it.

The support of the total strategy process by adequate staffing, some of which should be provided by individuals well schooled in the discipline of planning, is also essential. The SPC or its subgroups may want to conduct interviews, do surveys, or hold opens meetings and roundtables, and staff support will be essential in organizing these. There is always a heavy amount of staff work involved in coordinating the work of subcommittees and task forces with one another, and with the SPC as the steering committee. Successful strategy programs rest on the pillar of effective staff work. A strategy process is a good context in which to give greater visibility and influence to the work of planning officers, not just as staff specialists in planning, but as strategic leaders. There is good reason to make strategy and planning one of the formal responsibilities of a vice president or director who has the influence and skills to carry out its demanding duties effectively.

More important than any of these suggestions is the commitment of the leaders of the SPC to focus systematically on the preliminary effort to create a productive process that is consistent with the ways in which their institution does its best work. The process itself should be more satisfying than frustrating, and membership on the SPC should be viewed as a prestigious and welcome assignment.

USING STRATEGIC INDICATORS: THE METRICS OF IDENTITY, PERFORMANCE, AND ASPIRATION

Another prerequisite for strategy to be productive is a set of data to serve as the institution's key strategic indicators. Although by no means developed simply to aid the SPC, it becomes a basic and invaluable tool in the deliberations and work of the group. At this date, most institutions have created data profiles that they regularly publish in fact books or issue on Web sites. If they do not, they should. Transparency concerning important information builds credibility for the strategy process and fosters a shared understanding of the institution's relative position. Since the requirements of accreditation include institutional research and assessment, accessible collections of quantifiable information have become a norm of good practice. Their use in deliberations concerning strategy is essential and can be potentially decisive in defining an institution's identity and charting its future.

More often than not, however, the data that institutions collect are not presented in ways that are strategically useful. Information is frequently provided in lists or sets of numbers that have no clear strategic significance. The goal of the data should be to convey the meaning of the organization's evolving position in the world, not to overwhelm the reader with operational details (Morrill 2000).

Metrics of Identity

If carefully chosen and properly defined, a consistent set of strategic indicators displays an institution's distinctive capacities and characteristics in relation to its context. As Collins (2001, 2005) reminds us, great institutions develop metrics that penetrate to the core of what they do best; they display their distinguishing abilities, especially in terms of their ability to generate and control their resources. The story and identity of a place are revealed in its numbers as much as in its values; or, better, the distinctive values and capacities of a college or university are embedded in its strategic data and can be read in them (cf. Shulman 2007). Stories of identity are not created or related in a vacuum, and they must reflect the factual realities of the institution as much as its memories and hopes. The rigorous analysis of data is an excellent example of the integrative thinking that is essential in a discipline of strategic leadership. The integration of the meaning of values and facts, narratives and numbers, and metaphoric language and quantification is a defining feature of strategic thinking. Quantitative reasoning—such as regression analyses to isolate and examine key strategic issues—becomes the way to test the relationship of different variables in the data. It is highly instructive, for instance, to study the relationship between retention rates and SAT scores among a group of similar institutions. There may be much to ponder strategically from the results.

If quantitative indicators are to serve their purpose in strategic decision making, they need to be carefully selected for their ability to reveal the institution's strategic identity and position. Various books and guides that discuss strategic indicators provide helpful background to inform the strategy process. Generally, these texts recommend that indicators be developed around a number of critical decision areas such as financial affairs, admissions and enrollment, institutional advancement, human resources, academic affairs, student affairs, athletics, and facilities (Frances, Huxel, Meyerson, and Park 1987; Taylor and Massy 1996; Taylor, Meyerson, Morrell, and Park 1991).

Were one to follow all their suggestions, the number of potential indicators would be impossible for a planning council to review meaningfully. In most cases the central planning group will want to work with no more than about fifty strategic indicators as its primary and continuing benchmarks. Top administrators will regularly review twice that many, while a governing board would typically receive twenty-five to thirty dashboard indicators (like the vital gauges on the dashboard of a car) to give them an immediate sense of institutional position. Although a research and planning staff would want to track a large number of indicators, the work of strategy always seeks to focus its attention on data that tell a story. The aim is to find strategic meaning in the indicators, and the task of institutional leaders is to manage those meanings.

Key Strategic Indicators

Even with the benefit of good handbooks and sources, there is no shortcut to the work that each institution must do to define its own system of strategic measurements. The following list is but one possibility designed for a small college inspired by and derived from an excellent dashboard used at Juniata College, and graciously provided by President Thomas Kepple. It presents an enormous amount of strategic information in very economical fashion and has the advantage of including many proportionate measures and trend lines as well as strategic goals and comparative data. In doing so, it is able to address issues of identity, performance, and aspiration in one place. Without doubt, much of the information simply opens a strategic conversation that will require many other statistical analyses and fuller sources of information as it proceeds. It also should be noted that I have added a section on academic indicators, which are often missing from key indicators, simply to emphasize the issue of strategic academic assessment.

Based on this example, it is clear that an institution's sense of identity shapes the development of the indicators, and vice versa. We learn what matters to a place when we see the indicators by which it chooses to measure itself. Some of the choices are inescapable because they define universal strategic issues concerning financial resources and the realities of admissions and enrollment. They convey information about both the social and economic forces at work in the wider world and the institution's position in relationship to them.

Whatever set is chosen, the validity and usefulness of the measures are always a function of the care with which they are defined in response to the strategic opportunities and challenges of the institution. If we are to learn anything significant for effective strategic decision making, the data have to be collected and analyzed carefully, consistently, and systematically. To define a retention rate, for example, is no simple matter, for it depends upon a complex model of classifying complicated patterns in student enrollment and eventual graduation or departure, all of which vary significantly among various types of colleges and universities and the units within them. Getting good numbers to address the specific strategic questions that we should pose to ourselves is a foundational task of strategy itself. There was a time, for instance, when all we needed to know was the percentage of students on need-based aid. In today's world that figure alone has little strategic significance. It takes both imagination and rigor to get it right.

Proportionate Measures

One of the first things to be noted in table 5.1 is the use of relative and proportional measures (i.e., ratios and percentages and per-student and per-capita indicators.) By combining two variables in the calculation, the institution is able to develop indicators that pick out the significance of its special characteristics of size and mission, position and performance. Analyzing financial position in absolute terms without reference to the size and characteristics of the institution is an incomplete and misleading process. Financial information that is useful strategically is always based on ratios and percentages, now a standard aspect of the financial self-analysis of revenue and expense and assets and liabilities, as we shall discuss in chapter 10. As we shall see, proportionate measures are also easily compared to the norms of the higher education industry at large, so the data reveal an institution's strategic position relative to the competition and wider economic realities.

Table 5.1

	College Trends				Comparison Group		
	Current Value	% Change +/–	Ten-Year High/Low	Strategic Goals	Peer Median	College Position % Median	Peer High/ Low
			High Low				High Low
Enrollment							
Fall FTEs							
% Men/Women							
% International							
% Minority							
Five-Year Gradu- ation Rate							
Admissions							
Applications							
% Applications Accepted							
% Enrolled (Yield)							
Number Enrolled Middle 50% SAT							
Total % Tuition Discount							
Entering Class % Discount							
Unfunded % Discount							
Entering Class Unfunded % Discount							
Average Aid Package							
Average Grant Aid College Funds/Stu- dents							
% on Institu- tional Aid							
Faculty							
Average Faculty Salary							

(Continued)

Table 5.1
(Continued)

	College Trends				Comparison Group		
	Current Value	% Change +/–	Ten-Year High/Low	Strategic Goals	Peer Median	College Position % Median	Peer High/ Low
			High Low				High Low
% International Faculty							
% Minority Faculty							
Student/Faculty Ratio							
Development							
Total Gifts + Grants (Nongovern- ment)							
% Alumni Con- tributions							
Total Individual Gifts							
Sponsoring Organization Gifts							
Total Corporate and Foundation							
Bequests and Trusts							
Total Gift Receipts/ Students							
Endowment							
Total Endow- ment							
Additions to Endowment							
Endowment/ Students							
Revenues and Expenditures							

(Continued)

Table 5.1
(Continued)

	College Trends				Comparison Group		
	Current Value	% Change +/−	Ten-Year High/Low	Strategic Goals	Peer Median	College Position % Median	Peer High/ Low
			High Low				High Low
Tuition and Room-and-Board Charges							
Tuition % of Revenue							
Endowment % of Revenue							
Unrestricted Annual Gifts/ Revenue							
Educational and General Expenses per Student							
Assets and Liabilities							
Change in Total Net Assets							
Net Assets / Net Liabilities							
Change in Operating Fund Unrestructed Net Assets							
Unrestricted Net Balances/ Annual Budget							
% Debt to Unrestricted Net Assets							
Debt Payments % Operating Funds							
Academic Indicators							

(Continued)

Table 5.1
(Continued)

	College Trends				Comparison Group		
	Current Value	% Change +/–	Ten-Year High/Low	Strategic Goals	Peer Median	College Position % Median	Peer High/ Low
			High Low				High Low
% Graduates Entering Grad School One Year after Graduating							
% Graduates Entering Grad School Five Years after Graduating							
% Graduates Employed Six Months after Graduating							
Pass Rates (CPA and other exams)							
% Programs with Outcome Assessment Processes							
Average/Percentile Scores GRE, MCAT, LSAT							
Selected Outcomes Assessment Measures (NSSE, CLA, etc.)							

In many cases the data will also be presented in trend lines, since the results for any given year often are not strategically significant, while recurring patterns reveal clear and decisive meanings. Accelerating or decelerating rates of change in the trends are of special significance since they often signal problems or opportunities with crucial strategic consequences. In sum, relative measures are aptly suited to disclose strategic meaning because they can reveal the organization's distinctive characteristics in terms of its place in the world around it (Morrill 2000).

Comparative Measures

Another crucial characteristic of proportionate measures is that they enable meaningful comparisons with other institutions, as our illustrative set of indicators reveals. Most colleges and universities collect data from a group of comparable institutions, use a consortium like the Higher Education Data Service, or rely on the IPEDS service of the U.S. Department of Education, sometimes assisted by a national organization with a data service like the Association of Governing Boards of Universities and Colleges. Both the selection of the comparison group and the definition of the information that is gathered are crucial strategic tasks. The analysis of a thoughtfully chosen set of definitions and characteristics has to set the stage for constructing comparisons.

The use of comparative data can lead to the development of common benchmarks in which certain measures come to be associated with a best practice and thereby take on the character of a norm. Yet even when a normative measure is not achieved, institutions can still discover much about their identities and their strategic position through analytical comparisons. Like individuals, institutions discover themselves through the optic of an external point of view, by seeing themselves as they themselves are seen.

An institution that examines its tuition policy, for example, may be at a loss as to why a financially and academically similar institution in its comparison group has an 18 percent higher tuition charge. Both institutions have large endowments and share similar cost and revenue structures. A detailed comparative analysis provides the answer: almost all the discrepancy in tuition pricing is explained by different tuition discount levels, 30 percent in one and 45 percent in the other. The strategic implications of the finding can be decisive in shaping financial aid policy, admissions strategies, and tuition pricing, hence total resource levels for the future.

Comparative analysis can also reveal differences in resource patterns that have powerful implications for the way an institution defines its vision for the future. An examination, for example, of five- and ten-year trends in fundraising from various sources (alumni, foundations, corporations, individuals, etc.) will help to define the likely horizon for the next cycle of projects and goals, especially in private institutions. When colleges and universities compare their development numbers on a per-student basis, they may find that a direct competitor enjoys a major advantage, which widens as time passes. This insight can produce a variety of results, including a more realistic or nuanced set of aspirations or bold initiatives to stir a sleeping constituency to action. As the findings of *Good to Great* make clear, the ability of organizations to confront "brutal truths" about themselves is a key to their success.

Indicators and Assessment

Strategic indicators play a central role in another fundamental sphere of organizational decision making, the assessment of performance. Much of the data that define an organization's identity also reveal the effectiveness of its work in reaching the goals that it sets for itself. To be sure, evaluation requires it own systems and subsystems of measurement, much of which will have an operational focus. Institutions have many more sources of data and measures of results than will ever appear in a single collection of key strategic indicators. In an effective strategic leadership process, though, mechanisms are created to relate the continuing results of institution-wide assessment to the fulfillment of the organization's purposes and strategic goals. Knowing the contours of institutional identity, strategic leaders at many levels of the institution are able to interpret results in terms of their broader significance. By seeing the task of strategic leadership to include a continuing integrative interpretation of information on performance, the institution's managers and leaders set off a chain reaction of strategic inquiry and decision making throughout the organization.

Often the data produced through assessment, especially in core academic activities, require a substantial amount of interpretation and professional judgment to be properly understood. The data serve more as proxies or indices than as direct evaluations. When, for example, it is learned that 35 percent of graduating students move directly to graduate study in a given year, as many questions are raised as are answers given. Much more needs to be known before this information takes on genuine significance. What is the trend in graduate study over a five- to ten-year period, and how do these results compare? What are the regional and national trends in similar institutions? Which institutions are accepting the graduates, and with what rates of admission? What scholarships, fellowships, and other awards have been received? How do the graduates fare in their future studies and in their careers? How do the data relate to prior strategic goals, or to ones to be developed for the future? The indicators are important but fragmentary forms of information. They give rise to questions, to further inquiries, and to the exercise of professional judgment. As the data are drawn up into strategic thinking and continuous self-improvement, they have much to contribute. If, on the other hand, they are used as independent variables to rank order the achievement of institutions, they represent a dubious if not mischievous enterprise.

Indicators and Strategic Goals

As is presupposed in these comments, strategic indicators can also be crucial in the process of establishing measurable goals as benchmarks for the aspirations defined in a strategic plan. In many cases indicators that are gathered annually become a logical point of reference for setting goals for the future, especially in those aspects of the enterprise that are easily measured. The goals of a strategic plan in areas such as finance, admissions, and fund-raising should obviously be based on a careful analysis of prior trend lines and not represent an eruption of wishful thinking that has no quantitative foundation. If the institution has a history of good assessment practices in the academic sphere, then its strategic goals can also be based on demonstrable results and prior evaluations.

When a basic set of indicators is combined with other sources of information and assessment in a continuing process of scrutiny and analysis, the institution creates a powerful strategic engine. It takes control of a valuable form of quantified self-knowledge that combines with and certifies the images, values, and metaphors that define its identity and its vision. The integrative knowing that it achieves leads to effective, coherent decision making. The groups and individuals involved in the total process of institutional leadership and management now share common points of reference. As goals are met, new and more elevated ones can be set. Where they are not, changes in operations can lead to improvements. The faculty, administrative, and trustee participants in strategic decision making now have a common language with which to communicate. They may speak in different accents and dialects, but they understand one another. The indicators they use together do not produce rankings among institutions, as many want to force them to do. Rather, they reveal the distinctiveness of the institution and its success in reaching the goals it sets for itself. When used this way, indicators become part of an unbroken process of strategic sense making, decision making, and action, and the same disciplinary processes are at work. Since its aim is to move the institution toward its chosen future, the insights and decisions are inscribed into a process and discipline of strategic leadership.

As essential as they are, the work of strategy as leadership requires more than just effective procedures and good preparation. Finally, the methods and the content of strategy have to be adequate to the tasks of collaborative leadership. We now turn to a detailed consideration of the components of a strategy process that is oriented to the challenges and possibilities of leadership.

PART III

Practicing Strategic Leadership

CHAPTER

Integral Strategy: Narratives and Identity in Strategic Leadership

We have defined the broad organizational context in which strategy will do its work and examined some of the tools and concepts that it needs to become an integrated process of leadership. Ultimately, though, strategic leadership is indispensably a matter of practice. It must enact its designs and use its tools. Part III will focus on the practices of a systematic and integrated strategy process. The current chapter opens with a sketch of the elements of strategic leadership as a summary and a prospectus. Then, we turn to the core of our conceptual model by focusing on both the significance and the use of narratives of identity in strategic leadership.

INTEGRATING STRATEGY AND LEADERSHIP

We are proposing the formulation of a collaborative process and discipline of strategic leadership. It pretends to be neither a science nor a discrete method of discovering knowledge. Rather, it is an integrative and applied discipline of decision making. Although different from them, it has parallels with other disciplines of decision making such as management, which aims to integrate knowledge with decisions and actions. It also has clear similarities with fields like the creative and performing arts and applied psychology. These practical fields use rigorous concepts and systematic methods to engage with human agency and experience, which they intend to influence and enrich but cannot fully objectify and control. As an integrative discipline, strategic leadership relies on interdisciplinary knowledge and insights about leadership and human experience and uses a variety of methods of empirical and conceptual inquiry. As an applied discipline, it uses systematic methods in developing strategies, making decisions, and taking actions. Inherently collaborative, strategic leadership engages participants in group processes and makes decisions through an intentional and structured series of deliberations.

As will become clear, the connections between strategy and leadership require careful elaboration. In effect, each of the concepts includes criteria that will set the terms for its relationship in strategic leadership. Since leadership engages humans at deep levels of their experience and motivation, strategy will have to begin there. The idea of integral strategy takes us to organizational self-definition through narratives as the starting-point for strategy. Leadership petitions strategic management to find its depths and broaden its vision. The idea of "integral" strategy also tries to capture the notion that strategic leadership has to be persistently reflective about its own models of thought and judgment. To be adequate to the task, it also must look toward both its connections to legitimate systems of authority and its linkages to methods of implementation.

The integration of strategy and leadership involves a series of explicit expectations from the side of strategy as well. The strategy process asks that leadership commit itself to a set of orderly steps and procedures, and to diverse forms of knowledge, analysis, and measurement. Strategy and leadership offer each other disciplined ways of understanding problems and making decisions, and interrelated processes that can mobilize the people and the resources of an organization.

The Prerequisites of Strategic Leadership

We have drawn together several streams of reflection on leadership, decision making, and values in order to set the course for a process of strategic leadership. One way to appropriate the fruits of this labor is by elucidating a set of prerequisites or conditions that must be satisfied for strategic leadership to be an effective practice in the decision-making world of the academy. Given what we have learned, what tests does strategic leadership have to satisfy? I offer here a series of initial propositions that will be developed, illustrated, and discussed throughout subsequent sections of the text. By offering these motifs here, I hope to provide the reader with both a recapitulation of key findings to date and an outline of the argument and proposed practices that will unfold throughout the text. Strategic leadership is:

- **Integral:** It begins at the level of human agency, values, and paradigms.
- **Sense making:** It relies on narrative to make sense of experience and give meaning to the future.
- **Motivational:** It mobilizes energy and commitment.
- **Applied:** It takes form in decisions and choices.
- **Collaborative:** It uses collegial deliberative methods.
- **Systemic:** It connects separate decision-making systems within the organization.
- **Data driven:** It depends on good metrics and strategic indicators.

- **Integrative:** It integrates different forms of data and knowledge into insights and decisions.
- **Embedded:** It depends on distributed leadership throughout the organization.
- **Action oriented:** It requires effective systems of implementation.

THE BIRTH OF STRATEGY: THE POWER OF NARRATIVES

Discussions with college administrators about strategic planning quickly reveal how differently people think about the process. The conversation may start as a discussion of the meaning of a vision for a college to be the best in its class, or it might come to focus on the organization's distinctive competencies and its responses to a threatening environment. Frequently the most energy about strategy surrounds questions of financial resources and the college's market position in enrollment, especially its net tuition income after discounts for financial aid and scholarships.

All these issues may be critically important, but in themselves they are strategies of management, not of leadership. How can the strategic focus be shifted to leadership? How can the language of strategy be translated into the idiom of leadership? The answer begins by locating the foundation of strategy in the organization's unique identity, as revealed in its narrative of identity, its story. For our purposes, narrative is the form that stories take as they tell of events that unfold through time and create dramatic tension around conflicts and challenges and their resolution (H. Gardner, 2004). Narratives are the *way* we tell, and story *what* we tell, so often the two are one and the same. Narratives of identity are one type of story that give an account of an organization's or a society's unique characteristics. This point of departure moves strategy to a deeper plane of self-analysis and self-understanding, where we begin to see that it has to do with sense making and sense giving, and so with leadership.

For the past several generations, the modern imagination has been drawn to the importance of narrative in understanding human experience. Most contemporary fields in the humanities and social sciences have been fascinated, even preoccupied, with the significance of narratives. The literature on the topic in each discipline is so vast that it represents the shape of the modern sensibility.[1] Far from being seen as simply fanciful inventions, stories are narratives of the meaning of events as persons and groups live them rather than objectify them. Thus we find that case histories and case studies, original historical texts and documents, myths and sagas, songs and dances, paintings and sculpture, biographies and autobiographies, letters and diaries, and novels, poetry, and plays are powerful sources of revelation of the meaning of the human project. As Roland Barthes, one of the most influential theorists on narratives, puts it, "under this almost infinite number of forms, the narrative is present at all times, in all places, in all societies:... there does not exist, and never has existed, a people without narratives" (quoted in Polkinghorne 1988, 14).

Stories as people live them or imagine them give us access to the participant's sense of meaning, to human interiority as the individual's or the group's lived forms of self-awareness. Through the meaning of the events that they recount, narratives display values and commitments that matter decisively to people, often with an unqualified sense of importance. Objectified external analyses typically lose sight of the richness and ambiguity of human intention and motivation, and the drama of personal meaning in both ordinary and extraordinary events. Objectification cuts the vital nerve of connection to the self's or the group's investment in these events, their *caring* about them. Stories, on the other hand, convey the sense *of meaning and of mattering* with which persons live their lives. Neil Postman captures precisely these motifs: "Our genius lies in our capacity to make meaning through the creation of narratives that give point to our labors, exalt our history, elucidate the present, and give direction to our future" (quoted in Connor 2004, 10).

Stories capture and convey the dynamic of values as the internalized norms of self-enactment. After reminding us that humans are always in the pursuit of what they take to be good, Charles Taylor notes that as we "determine the direction of our lives, we must inescapably understand our lives in narrative form, as a 'quest'" (1989, 51–52).

Narratives as a Distinctive Form of Cognition

Human intelligence grasps the truths of stories, identifies with them, and remembers them in ways that cannot be matched by abstractions. Ask any teacher or speaker what people remember in their talks. Stories appear to constitute a distinctive cognitive form. "This appears to be so pervasively true that many scholars have suggested that the human mind is first and foremost a vehicle for storytelling," claims Dan McAdams (1993, 28). Just as there are structures to knowledge, so too there are forms and patterns in the search for meaning in our lives. The noted psychologist Jerome Bruner argues that the mind apprehends the world by way of two different cognitive forms, each with its own radically different methods of verification. The "paradigmatic" mode is logical, empirical, and analytical, while the "narrative mode" is concerned with wants, needs, and goals, "the vicissitudes of human intention" in time (Bruner, quoted in McAdams 1993, 29). Stories convey the shared meanings of human striving, the intensity of conflict, and the unpredictability of experience. In our finitude, nothing is guaranteed, so we are forever finding and losing our path, often in unexpected ways. Stories are adequate to this inherent tension and uncertainty of human existence in time since they illuminate the changing meanings of who we are and what we intend to become (Ricoeur 1984–1986). As Bruner puts it, "Through narrative we construct, reconstruct and in some ways reinvent yesterday and tomorrow.... Memory and imagination supply and consume each other's wares" (2002, 93).

Organizational, Cultural, and Religious Stories

Although works of imaginative literature are significant and powerful forms of narrative, our attention will be focused on organizational stories. The importance of narratives has been fully appreciated by students of contemporary organizational culture. We agree with Polkinghorne: "The narrative is a basic form of coherence for an organization's realm of meaning, just as it is for an individual's" (1988, 123). As we saw in chapter 1, along with norms, values, rituals, and symbols, stories play a decisive role in shaping the leadership of organizations. Important aspects of institutional identity can only be communicated in narrative form. The consuming devotion and passionate vision of the founders and leaders of organizations are passed from generation to generation and group to group as stories that define the present, not just the past. Two of the most popular and influential management books of the 1980s and 1990s, *In Search of Excellence*, by Peters and Waterman (1982), and *The Fifth Discipline*, by Senge (1990), reflect a deep sensitivity to the significance of institutional values and narratives. In the *Leader's Guide to Storytelling*, Stephen Denning (2005) charts the many ways in which business organizations do, can, and should rely on stories in accomplishing many of the tasks of leadership. Stories appear to be the epitome of organizational sense making in Weick's understanding of the concept. Stories ground identity with reflections that select the meaning of past events and are enacted and shared with others as a plausible way to understand ongoing experience (Weick 1991, 1995).

Nowhere is the centrality of narratives clearer than in religious traditions. Judaism, Christianity, and Islam recount narratives about how the divine has appeared in certain people, places, and events. Jesus of Nazareth taught primarily through stories and parables and by narrating the impending events that would usher in God's Kingdom. Narrative is the basic biblical voice (Borg 1994). Even in the more conceptual texts of classical Buddhism and Hinduism, stories are nonetheless abundant and indispensable, as in the Hindu devotional text the Bhagavad Gita. The crucial significance of story for leadership is foreshadowed in the ways that religious leaders such as prophets, teachers, and saviors communicate and embody narratives about ultimate meaning.

Collegiate Stories

As it is for other organizations and institutions, so it is for colleges and universities. Stories fill the campus air. The tales of greater and lesser campus comedies and tragedies of intellectual toil and fulfillment, of academic reward and failure, of intimacy and conflict, are constantly given voice. They always begin in one of the basic forms of narrative with "Remember the time ... ?" From playing fields to the laboratory, in offices, classrooms, and studios, from the stage to the library, every institution creates a wealth of stories in which it displays itself and its values. The prominent alumni are extolled, legendary leaders are honored, distinguished professors are celebrated, and great coaches and teams are remembered. Some academic programs and achievements come to take on iconic status and become normative legacies and markers of identity. All the smaller and larger stories can be drawn together and interpreted as part of an inclusive narrative, for they reveal common beliefs, meanings, commitments, and values that reflect a unique identity.

Narratives are never told as raw facts or antiseptic histories, but as the tales of participants. They are always shaped by the drama and tension of conflict: success and failure, triumph and defeat, achievement and frustration, loyalty and betrayal (cf. Denning 2005; Toma, Dubrow, and Hartley 2005).

The story as a narrative of identity displays the unique characteristics that set the institution apart, and in which it takes pride. The place is recognizable in the fragments of its story because they share in a narrative that makes sense of the parts with reference to a larger whole and temporal sequence. Narratives also reach out for larger stories, so each college interprets and reinterprets itself as participating in the comprehensive narrative of certain traditions, norms, and practices of liberal and professional education and the values of scholarly discovery. Postman again helps us to understand the connection between local stories and master narratives of education because they share a story "that tells of origins and envisions a future, a story that constructs ideals, prescribes rules of conduct, provides a source of authority, and, above all gives a sense of continuity and purpose" (Postman, quoted in Connor 2004, 10). The story, then, is far more than a history, although it is revealed in history. It lives in multiple recollections, but it is defined in shared memory and in common meanings and values. Although not free from conflicting understandings, its common meanings as a story of identity and its bearing on the future as a narrative of aspiration can be coherently interpreted and widely affirmed.

Collegiate Sagas

The power of the generic idea of story has been applied to the study of higher education in a variety of ways, so it can be illustrated in several forms. In *The Distinctive College: Antioch, Reed, and Swarthmore,* the distinguished sociologist of higher education Burton Clark (1970) used the notion of organizational saga to capture the power of the cultural dimensions of experience in formal organizations. As such, a "saga is a collective understanding of a unique accomplishment based on historical exploits of a formal organization, offering strong normative bonds within and outside the organization. Believers give loyalty to the organization and take pride and identity from it" (B. R. Clark 1991, 46). The concept of saga can be taken as a strong form of what we have called story.

Each of the three colleges in Clark's study illustrates different patterns of a saga, although they share many common features. At Reed in 1920, a young president created a new college in the Northwest of the United States to be a pure academic community that prized nonconformity. Antioch, on the other hand, was an old institution in slow decline before Arthur Morgan became its president in 1919. Under this bold and charismatic president, the college introduced a novel plan to alternate periods of study and work as part of general education. At Swarthmore, a strong Quaker college responded to the leadership of its gifted and magnetic president, Frank Aydelotte, to create an honors program inspired by the Oxford model.

Although not all institutional stories have the depth and salience of sagas, they all display the characteristics of narratives of identity. Whether it is present in strong or weak forms, the institutional story is the starting point for strategy. Those institutions that cannot take possession of their life stories will find the work of strategy and leadership frustrated at every turn. As the Association of Governing Boards of Universities and Colleges' 2006 report on the college presidency, *The Leadership Imperative*, puts it, "Only by embracing and building on...the institutional saga...can a president span successfully the full range of leadership responsibilities" (12) as one element of what the report calls integral leadership. The story, as we shall see, enriches institutional self-definition through statements of identity, mission, vision, and position, and, as a result, it fuels leadership as a reciprocal process.

THE STORY OF CENTRE COLLEGE

The story of Centre College, a small liberal arts college founded by the Presbyterians in Danville, Kentucky, in 1819, can illustrate something of the significance of narratives as they inform the strategy processes of an institution.

In the late summer of 1983, Rick Nahm, the vice president of Centre College, called the president. He said excitedly, "We have passed 67 percent participation in alumni giving for last year. I am checking with Dartmouth and Williams, but I think that we have beaten them. We will have the best record in the country."

The Centre story, as described in the strategic plan then being completed, tells of a tiny college, 725 students at the time, with an exclusive commitment to education in the arts and sciences, and a disproportionate influence in Kentucky and the mid-South region of the country. The only small college in the state to house a chapter of Phi Beta Kappa, it has a remarkable legacy of preparing the state's and the nation's leaders. Centre serves as a beacon of excellence and a source of pride in a region that has always lacked resources for education. At the turn of the twentieth century, Woodrow Wilson, then president of Princeton, commented about the challenges of measuring educational quality. Discussing and questioning the proportion of alumni who achieve distinction as a measure, he said, "There is a little college down in Kentucky which in sixty years has graduated more men who have acquired prominence than has Princeton in her 150 years" (quoted in Trollinger 2003, 13). What Wilson questioned became part of Centre's story of disproportionate influence, singleness of purpose, leadership, loyalty, and achievement. By that time, Centre had awarded diplomas to dozens of state and federal legislators, two vice presidents of the United States, and several Kentucky governors and had established a tradition of producing leaders for the ministry, the bench, and the bar. The "great dissenter," John Marshall Harlan, the Supreme Court justice who rejected the doctrine of separate but equal in *Plessey v. Ferguson* in 1896, was a Centre alumnus. Later, another alumnus, Fred Vinson, would serve as chief justice of the Supreme Court from 1946 to 1953.

The next year, the alumni-giving victory became complete. Dartmouth distributed a green-and-white button for alumni that read, "Go Big Green, Beat Centre." Not since Centre beat Harvard in football 6–0 in the upset of the century in 1921 had the story of a metaphoric David and Goliath become so vivid. Not long afterward, many of the goals of an ambitious strategic plan were fulfilled: enrollment grew by one hundred students, new facilities were built and older ones renovated, salaries were substantially increased, and a capital campaign reached its $40 million goal a year ahead of schedule. The power of Centre's story was decisively revealed in 1985 when the Olin Foundation awarded Centre its annual grant for the complete financing of a new physical science building. In its contacts with the college, the foundation marveled at the loyalty of Centre alumni and noted the college's heritage of leadership in its region. Driven by strategic planning, Centre's record of financial and academic achievement has steadily continued to progress since that time.

Although the Centre story has some especially rich motifs, it is representative of the narratives of identity that can be told in virtually every institution of higher education. As we have suggested, narratives do what all good stories do, which is to capture important insights, values, lessons, and truths about identity in accounts that reach us as agents rather than as observers of life. Stories touch us as persons, reaching both our minds and our emotions. They use the language of metaphors, images, and symbols and turns of phrase pulled from everyday life that interpret the drama of experience in ways that empirical description cannot. In their empirical study of the use of metaphors in planning and leadership at the University of Minnesota, Simsek and Louis(1994) describe similar characteristics of symbolic and metaphoric language. In their study of twenty widely diverse colleges and universities that have higher patterns of student engagement in learning and graduation rates than comparable institutions, Kuh, Kinzie, Schuh, Whitt, and their associates (2005) show the deep educational significance of campus culture, symbol, and story. Each campus has a connected set of strong symbolic meanings and owns a powerful narrative of achievement and identity. Stories draw us in as participants as we identify through imagination and memory with the narrative of our community's identity.

We should not go on to conclude that all is consistent, successful, and cheerful in stories of identity, for disruption and conflict bring trying challenges to places and may even tear them apart. These chapters, too, are part of the story. The Civil War tore a hole in the heart of Centre College, dividing families, students, faculty, alumni, and the Danville community into two hostile camps, and the Presbyterians into two churches. It led to the founding of a competing university fifty miles away. The wounds required almost a century to heal, and the college suffered as a result. In the early 1960s the college had to put the ugly legacy of racial segregation behind it, and through decisive presidential leadership by Thomas Spragens, it did so with conviction and moral purposefulness.

FINDING, TELLING, AND TRANSLATING THE STORY

As we seek to know and tell our stories, it becomes clear that there are many individuals, programs, traditions, rituals, documents, and cultural norms and values around which stories collect. Often a specific program or a set of practices will continue to exercise influence indefinitely because they have taken on definitive or iconic status, perhaps as part of a saga as described by Clark or as an element of identity that continues to have meaning. Those who wish to discover and give voice to an institution's narrative of identity will do well to consider these various practices and beliefs. They offer clues about the larger story, and they can be discovered through a disciplined and integrative reading of the institution as a text.

Clark's discussion of saga and our analysis of story reveal that there are different layers and levels of meaning in narratives. As a consequence, different forms of inquiry must be used to understand their significance. As we have seen, they always begin in the concrete, in specific events, particular relationships, actual places, and real people. These particulars are then drawn together into accounts that use language in various ways to describe a sequence of events and outcomes, following an infinite variety of plotlines. Often the stories circulate as smaller or larger fragments, while in some contexts their content is widely shared and understood. Although organizational stories cannot be invented, they can be discovered and brought to awareness. In doing so, we may find explanations for all sorts of issues and peculiarities of an organization that have eluded us. More importantly, we may be able to take fuller possession of our circumstances and our future as we become more purposeful in understanding and telling our story. As we seek to know and to articulate an institution's story, it becomes important to look for the characteristic patterns, themes, values, markers, and motifs that they contain, for stories have been created around and through them. They include the following:

- **Precipitating events:** the founding, a transforming gift, a dramatic occurrence, a bold new direction, encompassing change, a crisis survived
- **Transforming leaders:** individuals such as presidents, board members, or faculty and staff whose leadership and vision created a distinctive and enduring change in the organization
- **Salient personalities:** individuals whose passions, accomplishments, and endearing eccentricities mark the experience of the community
- **Generative programs:** distinctive educational programs that define the organization's practices and self-consciousness in a normative way
- **Markers of distinction:** the accomplishments of the institution, faculty, staff, students, and alumni that stand out for their special quality and level of achievement in all forms of teaching, research, service, athletics, and leadership
- **Markers of distinctiveness:** those elements that are experienced as setting the institution apart, including a special mission, a religious commitment, a particular location, unusual programs, powerful administrative and academic competencies, a distinctive campus, special service to a community or profession, or a relationship with a particular constituency
- **Features of the culture:** the traditions, rituals, practices, values, norms, and patterns of relationship and forms of community that distinguish an institution as a human and intellectual community

- **Larger meanings:** the ways that the story represents and embodies the larger purposes and values of education in the search for knowledge, in human transformation, and in service to society, sharing thereby in the larger narratives of the purposes of education

One important source for stories of identity is the voices of the campus and of key constituencies. Telling the story depends first on listening for it and hearing it in the narratives of others. When the time is right, the leader begins to tell the story as she has systematized, interpreted, and perhaps transformed it, reflecting all the while what has been learned from listening. In the process, she will discover how much people appreciate hearing the story, even when they know it well. They find it energizing to hear it told in a new way, many times hearing elements of it they knew but could never quite state. The listeners feel affirmed because it is their story, one in which they have participated and to which they have contributed.

One of the ways to listen carefully is with the help of a formal process. The following set of questions (O'Toole 1981, 129–30, used by permission of the author) provides one example of a way to open a dialogue about identity. It has a light touch but can yield helpful insights to be explored in greater depth in other contexts.

QUESTIONNAIRE

PORTRAIT OF A COLLEGE OR UNIVERSITY

1. Age

   Apart from the actual chronological age of the college, how would you characterize the institution?

   _____ (1)   An infant   _____ (6)   A young adult

   _____ (2)   A toddler   _____ (7)   An adult

   _____ (3)   Prepubescent   _____ (8)   Middle aged

   _____ (4)   An adolescent   _____ (9)   Old

   _____ (5)   A suspended adolescent _____ (10) Senile

2. Health

   Apart from the financial health of the organization, how would you characterize the state of health here?

   _____ (1)   Robust   _____ (6)   Intermittently feverish

   _____ (2)   Sound   _____ (7)   Declining

   _____ (3)   Better than can be expected,   _____ (8)   Infirm
               given institution's age

_____ (4)   Improving   _____ (9)   Paralyzed

_____ (5)   Convalescing   ___ (10)   Call the morgue

3. Key Events

    a. Describe the three most important pivotal events that have occurred since the founding of the institution.

       (1) _____

       _____

       _____

       (2) _____

       _____

       _____

       (3) _____

       _____

       _____

    b. What is the best thing that has occurred here over the past two years?

    _____

    _____

    _____

    Why?

    _____

    _____

    _____

    c. What is the worst thing that has occurred here over the past two years?

    _____

    _____

    _____

    Why?

    _____

    _____

    _____

4. Competencies

    a. What distinctive competencies does this institution possess?

    _____

    _____

    _____

b. What competencies does it need to develop?

_____

_____

_____

Why?

_____

_____

_____

5. Characteristics

   a. What five short descriptive phrases or adjectives best describe the institution?

   1. _____

   2. _____

   3. _____

   4. _____

   5. _____

   b. Circle the phrase or word you would most like to change.

   c. Underscore the phrase or word you would most like to preserve.

   d. What is the typical image that outsiders (in higher education and in the community) have of the institution?

   _____

   _____

   _____

   _____

   e. What do you think the institution should be ten years from now?

   _____

   _____

   _____

   _____

Translating the Story into Themes and Values

Connecting the threads in an institution's narrative represents an important dimension of strategic thinking. It brings the benefits of systematic reflection to issues of identity, the strategic significance of which is often ignored. Yet another stage of analysis is required to create a full narrative of identity to serve as the foundation for strategy. As we have suggested, it is important to translate the story into a set of distinctive concepts, themes, meanings, purposes, and values. In doing so, we create a set of conceptual touchstones to which participants in the work of strategy can repair as they seek to capture and elucidate the bearing of the institution's sense of itself for the future.

Strategic leadership uses the power of a systematic method in its work as a discipline. Yet the method comes with cautions. If we do not keep the story connected to concrete events, it will lose its power to energize and motivate the participants in a community. Abstractions are necessary, for without them we could not communicate widely, create policies and systems, and relate our educational responsibilities to the wider society. Yet abstractions draw their vitality from the currents of life out of which they have emerged and through which they must be continuously renewed. In studying strategic plans and related documents, one finds a large series of concepts and values that institutions use to describe themselves and their purposes. To illustrate with a consistent example, we can turn again to Centre College, for its current leaders have recently thought and written self-consciously about the values that define the Centre story. For one member of the faculty and leader in the planning process, the common thread in the many forms and memories of the Centre experience is "a combination of high expectations and high commitment, of ambition and affirmation, or rigor and reward. It's tough love" (Wyatt 2003, 7). As one chemistry professor used to put it, "At Centre the collar fits a little tighter." Students experience the college as an intimate educational community of intense relationships and high expectations that showcases a student's multiple talents in the classroom, around the campus, on the playing field, and on stage. Other leaders at Centre, including its current and preceding presidents, have reached for words such as "transformation," "empowerment," "education of mind and body," and "leadership" to describe the educational purposes of the college. In exploring these elements of the larger story of liberal education, the college's own story is enriched.

Our emphasis on narratives prompts the question of how they are to be related to the practice of strategy within a formal process. Is the institutional story a lengthy chapter in a strategic plan, or is it found in one or more summary statements, or is it not part of the strategy document at all? How does the story function in the formal strategy process?

IDENTITY STATEMENTS

Because institutional circumstances and stories are so different, there are many answers to these questions. Yet despite the variety, it is clear that strategic leadership depends upon effective ways for the connection to be made, for values and insights derived from the story to be present explicitly in the strategy process. To accomplish this, we propose that strategy documents should include a brief section on institutional identity, unless the task has already been accomplished in other easily available documents. The identity statement should synthesize and summarize the institution's story, thereby constituting with mission, vision, and, eventually, position a fourfold self-definition. Although an identity statement typically does not have a linear relationship to the decision-making process, it provides a coherent interpretive framework for the development of the other aspects of the self-definition and priorities of the plan. By offering participants in the process a set of shared reference points, values, images, and metaphors, it sets a common course for their work. By reflecting the experiences, beliefs, and contributions of the wider campus community, it provides an important resource for leadership as an interactive process of influence.

The length and character of narratives and identity statements will vary widely to reflect institutional needs, characteristics, and circumstances. If an institution already has a heightened consciousness of its story, it may only need a paragraph or two to communicate its identity. In other cases, a college might need several pages or more to capture its defining epochal moments, themes, characteristics, and core values. If there has been little thought given to the institution's narrative of identity, or if strategy is a new process to the campus, the section will be longer. Institutions that have undergone substantial change or that contemplate doing so can use an identity statement to interpret their changing story to their constituencies. They can reflect their sensitivities to the challenges of change, show authentic continuities of purpose and values, and rally support for the challenges and opportunities that lie ahead.

Core Values

Similarly, a set of core values should be defined and stated as a thematic expression of the institution's identity and in some cases may be that statement. Based on our earlier analysis of values, this means inquiring into what really matters to a place—as expressed in its history, its priorities, its budgets, its facilities, its policies and programs, and its culture and relationships. What is privileged and what is secondary? What is enduring and what is passing? What would people sacrifice in the name of what greater good? What are the authorities and norms that do and should drive choices? If a good cross-section of a campus is asked to pick out a limited number of truly characteristic values in answer to these kinds of questions, the institution's profile of values begins to emerge. When a value is proposed to be central and fundamental, it can be queried repeatedly with the question "Why?" until people give good explanations of its relevance and reach deeper levels of identity. Core values can never be just a set of abstract nouns but should be characterized and explained with reference to events, programs, and practices that give the values texture, authenticity, and credibility as the lived norms of the organization's story (cf. Sevier 2000).

In his study of five entrepreneurial universities in Europe, Clark (1998) describes the evolution of the University of Twente in the Netherlands as a successful and innovative technological university over a thirty-year period after its founding in 1964. We can use the interesting analysis of its core values as an illustration of a statement of identity.

The university has become:

- **The two-core university:** by offering an unusual combination of programs in both applied science and applied social science
- **The campus university:** by creating a beautiful verdant campus with a self-sufficient living and learning environment, distinctive in the Dutch context
- **The responsible university:** through its commitment to the development of its region both economically and culturally
- **The university without frontiers:** by means of its international character in both teaching and research
- **The focused university:** by providing in-depth study in a number of fields
- **The flexible university:** by using a variety of methods of governance and decision making, and creating various streams of funding to achieve its goals

The Critique of Stories

Often stories take on mythic status and become miniature paradigms that work like magnets drawing everything toward them (cf. Simsek and Louis 2000). It can then become nearly impossible to get behind the myth to see events in fresh and novel ways. As a result, it often falls to new leaders or to crises to do the hard work of demythologizing the stories of a community that have hardened into orthodoxy or have become defensive and stale. The task of criticism is a part of strategic leadership.

Both for good and ill, not everyone in an academic community interprets the story in the same way or embraces the one they know. In every organization, there are different accounts about what the founders meant and did, and the true content of the place's values. Some of the story may be flawed and include memories of exclusion and discrimination that need to be brought to awareness and addressed. Yet even when there are defects and discord, to position strategy within a narrative of identity is to give it a point of departure that creates a sense of common enterprise. Differences in values are often disagreements over their specific content, not their intent, so they can be resolved through dialogue and deliberation about the authentic meaning of educational quality. The story will enrich the strategic conversation and debate, deepen involvement in the process, create more coherent insights, and build credibility. It will, most importantly, define and illuminate the shared commitments that are needed to transcend the structural tensions in academic decision making and to define an inviting trajectory for the future.

STORY AND LEADERSHIP

Our effort to find the roots of strategy within narratives has also given us a clear glimpse of the relationship between story and leadership. Consistent with our earlier characterizations, it has become clear that some of the essential tasks of leadership are to know, to tell, to enact, and to embody the organization's story. This perspective allows us to penetrate into the dynamics of leadership as an engaging reciprocal process. Leaders show exceptional sensitivity to narratives of identity because they reveal the central beliefs, needs, desires, and values of their followers. As they learn the story of the group they represent, leaders come to understand what matters, what motivates, and what triggers action (cf. Denning 2005). They know the way the story of their group shows human experience unfolding through commitments to that which has decisive importance in the lives of its members and in the life of the leader.

National Identity: Lincoln at Gettysburg

To see narrative at work in leadership, we can do no better than to examine a familiar story of national identity. When Abraham Lincoln speaks at Gettysburg on November 19, 1863, in the middle of a terrible civil war, he evokes America's past, but he does not give a neutral historical account of its founding. Rather, he makes his comments in the framework of a narrative of identity. A historian examining the same events might highlight the political circumstances in which independence was achieved, emphasizing the economic interests of the founders and France's desire to aid a fledgling nation to foil its ancient enemy, Great Britain. In a philosophical account, the Declaration of Independence might be characterized as a derivative document, one that lifts ideas from a variety of Enlightenment thinkers and makes exalted but dubious claims about human equality that contradict common experience. We can call these external or outer histories. Yet as Lincoln steps to the podium on Cemetery Hill, he speaks as an agent in a historical drama to other participants in it by offering an inner history, which takes the form of a narrative (Niebuhr 1941). Thus, he can say to his countrymen that "our forefathers brought forth on this continent a new nation conceived in liberty and dedicated to the proposition that all men are created equal." He evokes the shared memories and collective commitments of a national community by using metaphoric images of birth and telling a story about truths on which the founders, "our forefathers," staked their lives and their reputations. He goes on to say that the devotion to human freedom has been communicated most powerfully not by words but through the acts and deeds of "those who gave the last full measure of their devotion" to preserve it. In closing, Lincoln repeatedly calls on the "high resolve" of his countrymen. They must act to ensure that those who have fallen in battle will not have died in vain. All of Lincoln's central themes at Gettysburg and in other speeches involve active forms of sense making and sense giving and require engagement from his listeners. In his second inaugural, he calls on the nation to attend to the ravages of war and to "bind up wounds," "to care for" the widow and the orphan, and "to achieve and cherish a just and lasting peace" (quoted in Goethals 2005). Lincoln's narration of events is a summons to responsibility and a call to action for those who claim the American story as their own. Stories matter.

Leading Minds

This example of story as a vehicle for leadership can be multiplied many times over and has been made the subject of studies from many perspectives. George Goethals (2005) finds strong echoes of the theme in Freud's comments on the power of ideas over leaders. In his important book on leadership, *Leading Minds: An Anatomy of Leadership*, Howard Gardner (1995) offers a cognitive theory of leadership, emphasizing the leader's ability to discern and articulate the group's story. The notion of leading by knowing, of course, supports our thesis that there is a disciplinary component to leadership. Yet the cognition in question is complex, for it involves strong elements of emotion as well as reason (H. Gardner 1995). Perhaps put more aptly, it is a form of cognition that is enacted in the choice of authentic values, and that must provide evidence of their authenticity.

Gardner (1995) pursues his thesis through a series of brief monographs of eleven prominent leaders, including both direct and indirect leaders. Among others, he studies Margaret Thatcher, Robert Maynard Hutchins, George C. Marshall, Pope John XXIII, Eleanor Roosevelt, Martin Luther King, and Mahatma Gandhi. In doing so, he uses a broader characterization of story than we do here, calling them "*invented accounts* in any symbol system," yet he focuses primarily on the way these leaders used narratives of identity in their exercise of leadership (H. Gardner 1995, 42).

A Narrative of Freedom and Justice: Eleanor Roosevelt

Several of Gardner's studies focus on leaders who exercised extraordinary influence on society although they did not occupy formal positions of high authority, for example, Gandhi, King, and Eleanor Roosevelt, each of whom also crossed racial, cultural, or gender boundaries. A patrician by birth and by marriage to one of the commanding figures of the twentieth century, Eleanor Roosevelt began to find her own independent voice and influence in her middle years. She and other female leaders demonstrate that narrative leadership is not bound by gender, especially since it emphasizes elements of personal experience and relational knowledge in which many women find their voice (Gilligan 1982). As Roosevelt started to participate actively in political organizations and causes, she developed and communicated simply and clearly the message that women should assume independent roles of leadership in public life. Her story came to include the call for greater social justice for all citizens, and she wrote, argued, and spoke tirelessly in public and private forums for civil rights for blacks and for women. Although her ideas were often controversial, she found ways to differentiate her role to avoid political problems for her husband while constantly trying to influence him. She was for years one of the most influential women in the world in her own right. In time her story became a global one as she championed human rights for the dispossessed in her role as a member of the American delegation to the United Nations. Many of the social and cultural revolutions of the 1960s and after were first articulated, brought to national awareness, and championed by Eleanor Roosevelt as she lived the story that she told (H. Gardner 1995). A summary of Gardner's thesis captures well the significance of story in leadership:

> Using the linguistic as well as nonlinguistic resources at their disposal, leaders attempt to communicate, and to convince others, of a particular view, a clear vision of life. The term *story* is the best way to convey the point. I argue that the story is a basic human cognitive form; the artful creation and articulation of stories constitutes a fundamental part of the leader's vocation. Stories speak to both parts of the human mind—its reason and emotion. And I suggest, further, that it is stories of identity—narratives that help individuals think about and feel who they are, where they come from, and where they are headed—that constitute the single most powerful weapon in the leader's literary arsenal. (1995, 42–43)

The Embodiment of Stories

The power of story should not tempt us to conclude that it wholly explains the role of the leader. In particular, leaders must live, or, as Gardner says, embody, their story as well as tell it if it is to be effective as a vessel of leadership. Thus, storytelling as a discipline of thought is supported by an even more rigorous discipline of personal commitment. As Gardner puts it, "It is a stroke of leadership genius when stories and embodiments appear to fuse—when...[in the words of Yeats] one cannot tell the dancer from the dance" (1995, 37). Mahatma Gandhi and Martin Luther King preached the power of nonviolent resistance based on deep ethical and spiritual principles and stood firm against the blows that resistance to power unleashed. General George C. Marshall believed in integrity as a military virtue and put his own career on the line by always speaking the truth to those in power, including President Roosevelt. Robert Maynard Hutchins believed deeply in the power of rational thought and the study of the great books and debated passionately and worked endlessly to instill his ideas at the University of Chicago and elsewhere. By embodying the values he claimed, he permanently shaped the curricular debate at the university. Followers are deeply suspicious if leaders fail to show in their lives the values they articulate; the "walk" must always accompany the "talk." If it does not, then judgments of hypocrisy or deceitfulness quickly surface, destroying the leader's credibility and influence for all but a few diehards.

I believe that the leader's embodiment of the story brings to light another dimension of leadership that is not always in evidence. We usually attend to the power of the story to motivate followers and neglect its strong influence on the leader. Embodiment empowers leaders as well as followers. It taps into deep levels of intrinsic motivation because it reaches the leader's values and personal identity. As the story is clarified, understood, and embraced by the leader, it becomes a source of energy that drives commitment and creates self-confidence. As leaders deepen their self-awareness and convey their commitment to the story, they find increasing respect and loyalty from their followers, so the engaging power of leadership takes on a new depth of meaning. The authenticity of the mutual commitment builds trust and elevates performance (W. L. Gardner et al. 2005).

Forms of Leadership: Visionary and Ordinary, Transactional, and Transforming

The examples that we have chosen to illustrate the power of story might lead us to conclude that it is only leaders on the main stage of history—the Lincolns, Kings, Gandhis, Roosevelts, Marshalls, and their peers—to whom the theory applies. Howard Gardner refers to individuals of this stature as "visionary" or "innovative" leaders, since they often renew familiar stories or see the world in bold new ways. Yet "ordinary" leaders also draw on the motivating power of stories, although their influence may not be as profound or their narratives as original.

These typologies, and the categories of transforming and transactional leadership, are helpful for sorting out the different dimensions and dynamics of leadership but are not easy to apply to concrete cases or individuals with precision or consistency. At times the leadership of great presidents like Franklin Delano Roosevelt appears innovative and even visionary, while at others he is much more of a traditional backroom politician. Lincoln had an extraordinary moral vision of the American union but was inconsistent in responding to the glaring evil of slavery. So, one should be circumspect in applying unqualified labels to individual leaders and the nature of the story, especially in professional organizations like universities. Loosening the hold of fixed categories also allows us to consider the broader uses of story in the everyday work of organizations. As they respond to a changing world and plan their futures, universities and colleges need the resources provided by their narratives of identity for the work of strategy and leadership, whether their stories are visionary or transactional, transformational or ordinary.

NARRATIVES IN THE LEADERSHIP OF COLLEGES AND UNIVERSITIES

I have provided a number of glimpses into the ways that collegiate narratives inform and orient the processes of leadership in colleges and universities and have reviewed methods to disclose and to articulate institutional stories. We now can turn to a more explicit discussion of the use of narratives in collegiate leadership processes, especially related to strategy, and will return to the theme on a more practical level in other sections of the book.

Legacy and Leadership

Whenever one finds college leaders wrestling with their strategic responsibilities, the issues of change and legacy are often at the center of their concerns. Any analysis of collegiate strategic plans shows the dual emphasis, although sometimes the language used to describe the conflict is formulaic. In *Presidential Essays: Success Stories* (Splete 2000), a collection of essays focusing on issues of strategic change by the presidents of thirteen small colleges and universities, one can see clearly the tension between tradition and innovation. Especially as the presidents deal with broader strategic questions, rather than circumscribed innovations in management, the need to relate change to the organization's story is consistently evident. In the words of one president, "Perhaps most important to bringing [the university] community on board with our vision is a continuing commitment to link the accomplishments of the present with the traditions of the past" (Argnese 2000, 13). Or, as put by another, "It was very important to respect tradition even as dramatic change was being undertaken because that tradition was a major source of the college's pride and identity" (Barazzone 2000, 22).

In a similar way, a collection of twenty-four commentaries on the presidency by the heads of many large and complex institutions presents similar themes about legacy and change as they focus on the moral dimensions of leadership (D. G. Brown 2006). The presidents describe the tasks of leadership, especially during crises, in many ways, but they often mention the critical importance of knowing intimately the values and culture of the organization. Presidents should be teachers who are always looking below the surface of events to find the currents that are shaping the future of the university and the larger society. In finding the right symbols and metaphors, they are able to tell their organization's story to create a "bridge from where we are to where we might be" (Penley 2006, 180).

These examples of the significance of narratives in leadership find support in large-scale empirical studies. Birnbaum (1992) concludes that presidents who are judged to be exemplary by their key constituencies (faculty, staff, and trustees) are distinguished by their strong interpretive skills, their ability to embody the institution's values and to affirm its strengths. They are able to relate their leadership to the norms and values of the organization's culture "by articulating a vision of the college…that captures what others believe but have been unable to express" (Birnbaum 1992, 154).

The University of Minnesota

To add further definition to this point, Simsek and Louis (2000) and Simsek (2000) have shown the centrality of narratives, metaphors, myths, and paradigms in charting what they see as transformational change at one of America's largest land-grant universities.

By the early 1980s several planning processes and state budget cuts had made it clear that the University of Minnesota's constant and unfocused growth was stretching it beyond its resources and compromising its quality. Teaching loads were rising, open admissions were the norm in many programs, and resources for research and graduate study were in relative decline. In offering his own interpretation of these developments, the interim (and later) president Kenneth Keller proposed a strategy called Commitment to Focus. It suggested the development of clear priorities, a better balance in undergraduate and graduate enrollments, more coordination at the central level, and an emphasis on quality rather than size. The proposed changes received both criticism and support since they represented a deep shift in the institution's image of itself (Simsek and Louis 2000).

In analyzing these developments over time among faculty members, Simsek and Louis (2000) found evidence for a shift in the paradigms, myths, and metaphors by which the faculty made sense of their experience in the organization. The use of concrete metaphorical language rather than conceptual abstractions often made it easier for people to express their ideas about change. The university's earlier period had produced dominant images of large unwieldy animals like elephants, or wildly growing vegetation. Images for the later period include that of the lion, and metaphors that show a greater sense of being focused, directed, and smaller in size.

Simsek and Louis see a shift in the basic paradigm for the organization itself from "entrepreneurial populism" to "managed populism." The older story of the university being all things to all people was transformed into a model emphasizing more central direction, smaller size, and an ability to make differentiated judgments about program quality and funding. In terms of the traditional paradigm of populism, the change was dramatic. Based on their study and their theoretical assumptions, Simsek and Louis conclude that real organizational change requires "leadership strategies that emphasize [the] interpretation of organizational values and meaning." Further, "Leaders must become effective story-tellers rather than commander-in-chief" (1994, 562). The implications for strategic leadership are clear. A vision cannot be imposed from the top but may emerge as a consequence of a strategy process that explores competing paradigms, values, and myths that make sense of the experience of members of the organization.

The University of Richmond

By the late 1960s, the financial future of the University of Richmond was in doubt. This small, largely undergraduate private university with some 3,500 students, founded by Virginia Baptists in 1830, had served long and well to provide educational quality and opportunity for local and state residents. As the new decade of the 1970s was dawning, however, competitive challenges were mounting, especially as Virginia provided new funding for its prestigious public institutions and opened the Virginia Commonwealth University on the University of Richmond's doorstep.

During this period the university had an endowment of $6 million, and faculty salaries were at the fortieth percentile. Empty residence-hall rooms were being used for faculty offices. The food services failed a health inspection, two dormitories had to add fire escapes or close, and the campus heating system was on its last legs. With only two hundred seats, the library did not meet accreditation standards, and the science labs were equivalent to those of local high schools. President George Modlin suggested to the trustees that only a miracle, or a merger into the state system, could save the university from financial collapse (Heilman 2005).

Some three decades later, a compelling story of transformation has unfolded at the University of Richmond. The endowment and other investments are over $1.5 billion, and total assets are near $2 billion. Faculty salaries by rank are over the ninetieth percentile for small universities, and the faculty-to-student ratio is under one to ten. Residences are filled to overflowing, applications average 6,000 for 750 undergraduate places, board scores have increased from 1,000 to 1,300, and the School of Law has become highly selective. The stunning campus is filled with an ever-enlarging collection of state-of-the-art facilities and new educational programs. There are substantial plant and operating reserves, and there is no deferred maintenance. Faculty and student achievements continue to hit ever-higher benchmarks.

What happened? Among many things, one of the university's graduates, E. Claiborne Robins, stepped forward in 1969 to make a commitment of $50 million ($240 million today), the largest gift at that time ever made by a living individual to a college or university. Over the next twenty-five years, Robins and his family would give another $125 million in gifts and bequests. Through his leadership, others, including the Jepson and Weinstein families, joined in providing multimillion-dollar contributions.

When I arrived as president of the university in 1988, many of these transformations had occurred through the energetic leadership of President Bruce Heilman, and they continued under the ambitious goals of my successor, William Cooper. I found a robust pulse of opportunity and an aspiration for national leadership shared by many of the faculty, staff, and trustees. A proposed new school to study leadership funded by alumnus Robert Jepson with a $20 million gift symbolized the sense of momentum. But I also found deep and perplexing forms of resentment over changes in the university during the transformation. Troubling notes of discord existed in large segments of the alumni body and among some of the senior faculty and a few of the trustees. For many, the measures of success brought little satisfaction, and every board meeting would bring the question "How many of the applicants are from Virginia?"

As I reflected on the era of transformation, I concluded that the university's story of identity had become fractured, and with it, the meaning of its achievements. An institution that had been in financial distress had become rich. A place that had enrolled more than 80 percent of its students from Virginia now enrolled the same percentage from out of state, mainly from the Northeast. An institution founded and governed by Virginia Baptists became independent, and the coordinate academic structure of Westhampton College for women and Richmond College for men had evolved into residential programs.

One of the ways that I tried to confront these issues was by hearing, learning, and articulating the university's narrative. My aim was to attend to the sense of loss felt by many graduates and then to place the university's identity in a larger strategic context. My goal as a leader was to enlist their understanding and commitment to the university's ambitious vision of national leadership.

I argued in different places and ways that the story of the place remained whole and vibrant, with more continuity than discontinuity. and pride in its achievements more appropriate than resentment. To demonstrate that continuity, I tried to distill the main themes and values in the university's story. The powerful sense of place that defined the Richmond experience through its exquisite wooded collegiate gothic campus was unchanged even as new facilities were continually added and renovated. A sense of community, civility, and service prevailed, inspired in part by the spiritual heritage of the campus, and by the example of superior levels of commitment by the faculty and staff. A continuity of purpose and practice was unmistakable in the commitment of the faculty to engaged learning through an ever-enlarging set of opportunities for student research and other forms of active and collaborative learning. Education as the transformation of human powers and possibilities, enabled by the faculty's intense investment in students and their own scholarship, remained the touchstone of Richmond's mission. The structural condition for the story remained the same, a small collegiate university with the intimacy and style of a college and the reach of a university. Student learning was at the absolute center of the collegiate experience, even as the university's complexity was manifest in Division I athletics; schools of arts and sciences, business, law, leadership and continuing studies; a large array of interdisciplinary programs; and an extensive program in international education. A sense of the connectedness of the different educational threads in the Richmond experience remained a constant theme and goal. I also argued that, above all, a sense of possibility in the commitment to pursue and the ability to achieve the highest academic aspirations had long been a part of the university's self-understanding and its vision of the future.

The momentous but implausible decision in 1910 to relocate the campus from near downtown represented the touchstone of the narrative to display the consistency of the vision of possibility. The site for the campus was inauspicious, an abandoned amusement park with a small lake surrounded by barren hills in a remote part of the city. The college had only modest resources to undertake the construction of a new campus and to create Westhampton College for women, but it decided to borrow the money that it needed—an exceptional risk for the time and place. In a compelling symbol of high aspiration, President Boatwright secured the services of the distinguished Boston architectural firm of Cram, Goodhue and Ferguson, designers of the Princeton chapel and graduate quadrangle. The board accepted the proposal to design the buildings in the collegiate gothic style and to configure separate colleges on the model of Oxford and Cambridge. For a Baptist College in the South to find its architects in the North, to counter the prevailing tradition of Georgian campus design with high-church architecture, and to start a woman's college that would come to have rigorous academic standards were other earnests of a compelling vision taking shape within otherwise traditional forms.

It is difficult to gauge the success of this effort to tell the Richmond story as a form of strategic leadership with any assurance of showing causal connections. The ability to reach the goals of two demanding strategic plans and a major capital campaign may indeed be associated with the motivating power of the story, and the campus climate for decision making remained focused and highly constructive. Direct evidence for a changed perspective by alumni leaders about the university's national horizon of aspiration was quite persuasive at the time, and the resentment over change seemed to abate. But those changes may have been driven by other events, and there is no easy way to prove the relationships.

Nonetheless, I and others became convinced that the legacy of the university was authentically defined by seeking academic distinction through a sense of possibility. The story set the conditions within which much of the university's achievements took place and through which its evolution made sense. The story worked its way into strategic plans, reports, speeches, fund-raising campaigns, and all the forms of governance and management. Most importantly, perhaps, it provided me as president and the leadership team with a sense of clarity, confidence, and conviction about what the place stood for and what it might become. The story became an authentic source of energy and purposefulness for the tasks of leadership. Studying epochal events carefully, encouraging dialogue about their meaning, interpreting their significance consistently, motivating others to affirm common values, and translating the story into plans and priorities are some of the elements of narrative leadership.

NARRATIVES IN THE DISCIPLINE OF STRATEGIC LEADERSHIP

The examples of narrative leadership that we have examined all have a theme of continuity and change, which is undoubtedly one of the central motifs in collegiate stories. Yet its recurrence should not lead us to think that narratives have no other plotlines. In other cases stories have to do with recounting the transformation of apparently negative characteristics into resoundingly positive results, describing national or global supremacy in applied or fundamental research, telling of a steady rise to greatness through an unchanging focus on student learning, narrating an institution's disproportionate influence relative to its size and resources, or telling of a singleness of purpose that does not change. As leadership unfolds through strategy, the story remains a touchstone of identity, a point of reference for sense making and sense giving, and a source of the integrative and systemic possibilities of the total process.

Identity and Mission

Perhaps the most common word in the lexicon of higher education for these matters of self-definition is "mission." "Identity" is, however, a larger concept and richer word than "mission," which is often misinterpreted as static. Identity encompasses culture as well as structure, meaning as well as purpose, motivation as well as accomplishment, and aspirations for the future in addition to past and current achievements. Identity is about uniqueness. In relating his experiences as a consultant in strategic management, Lawrence Ackerman emphasizes that finding identity is about "seeing through" all the layers of the organization—its organizational charts, numbers, earnings, staffing, and history—to find "the heart, mind, and soul of the company as a self-directing entity in the purest sense" (2000, 22). Mission remains an essential concept, but its meaning as active commitment to a purpose can be renewed and reclaimed when it grows out of identity. Each needs the other in leadership, although they are not the same thing.

Strategy as an Integrative Discipline

As we have now been able to see in a variety of different contexts, the discovery and narration of the content and meaning of the story depend in turn upon methods of reflection, analysis, and synthesis that are critical aspects of strategic leadership as an integrative and applied discipline. It takes a definable set of capacities and skills to understand and communicate the meaning of narratives. We associate many of these abilities with the humanities and some forms of the social sciences, especially as they come to terms with understanding human commitments and values. To find and articulate the larger human significance of the story depends on an appreciation of the way the imagination expresses itself in various types of language and systems of symbols. The written and spoken word is the primary but not exclusive way in which stories are known and communicated, so an understanding and command of language are powerful vehicles for leadership.

We have also learned that an institution's story is a subtext embodied in its programs and policies, structures and relationships, campus and resources, and in what has come to be called the culture of the organization. In order to be effective in shaping strategic decisions for the future, the cultural text needs to be brought to the surface and read explicitly. The discovery of the defining characteristics and values of the culture takes other kinds of intellectual skills, some of which we find on the applied sides of fields like anthropology, sociology, social psychology, and organizational behavior. Now the task becomes more analytical and less poetic, as a variety of methods of inquiry and forms of information have to be used to capture the organization's cultural and structural patterns of identity. The way the institution sees itself and does its work, sometimes through important rituals and practices, forms a backdrop for knowing and telling the story. As we have seen and shall see repeatedly, numerical strategic indicators represent another indispensable tool with which to grasp an institution's identity.

Story and Motivation

As a discipline of leadership, strategic inquiry has a special dimension that relates to the power of the story to inspire, to motivate, and to guide decisions. The story in leadership is more than a good tale or a set of propositions to engage the mind, for it addresses values that create a shared sense of commitment among its members. A narrative of identity involves the communication of beliefs to believers and of responsibilities to those who hold them. Although leaders must not ignore the facts or evade cogent arguments, their task is to go beyond external explanations to create interior meanings that address persons, including themselves, as participants in a community of commitment. In doing so, they seek to tell the story in language and embody it in actions that engage the lives of those they lead. Leaders relate stories that will give life to shared beliefs and release the power of values held in common. Stories, as we have seen, involve the inspiration of a vision and a summons to responsibility. So, first to know and then to tell the story are foundational aspects of an integrative discipline of leadership.

Normative Criteria for Stories

The place of narratives in leadership also has deep moral ambiguities and challenges that must be confronted, for history bears ample witness to the way that leaders manipulate and distort stories for their own purposes. Countless narratives of identity are exclusive and repressive. They can capture the imagination and draw humans into perpetual cycles of war, domination, and suffering. Stories can be products of an evil imagination and unleash ugly passions.

As we have learned in reviewing several examples of controversies over mission, the story has to be interrogated and evaluated by criteria and standards of evidence, as is the case with any cognitive inquiry or discipline. Not every story is good or true, and they must be tested in appropriate ways. The modern imagination has not found it easy to find tests for matters that have to do with values; yet it would be foolhardy to leave the most important commitments that humans ever make simply to the play of passion, preference, or circumstance. Whatever diffidence we entertain intellectually about the worth and objectivity of our master values and stories, we inescapably shape the actual content of our lives around values we take to be indubitable. We should be able to do more than just stammer or shrug our shoulders when it comes to giving an account of the stories and convictions by which we live.

These reflections may seem far from the narratives of colleges and universities, but they are connected to them in important ways if some of the tasks of leadership are to follow the methods of an applied discipline. As Howard Gardner (1995) indicates, every story encounters counter-stories that offer an alternative account of an organization's history, values, and purposes, so the credibility of collegiate stories depends on criteria and evidence. If a story is to be persuasive against its contenders, it must have support for its claims. If college leaders try to treat the story as a plaything of their egos by distorting the facts, erasing the legacy, or proclaiming an empty vision, the story will not be effective or credible as a vehicle for leadership.

This is not the place to develop a full analysis of the normative dimensions of stories of identity. Collegiate storytelling does not require as much, but it does benefit from being connected to the kinds of questions that ordinary experience carries with it to test its own commitments. Just as we hope to conceptualize and systematize a method of leadership that is already at work in a good strategy process, so it is worthwhile to examine briefly the ways that we bring normative expectations to the narratives of our organizations.

We should be assured that the stories of identity that we tell and are told are accurate and plausibly reflect the facts of history and the truth of circumstances. We know that legends and exaggeration are the stuff of stories, but we do not want to deceive in what we say or be deceived in what we hear. Stories must as well be authentic and reflect the meaning of events as they are owned and lived transparently by the participants. As we revise and reinterpret stories, we must provide evidence for our arguments and not manipulate the audience. Although not a matter of logic or deductive thinking, stories have to have an inner consistency to be persuasive and motivational. To be consistent, stories inspire action, not just talk; persistent goals rather than expedient ones; and steady focus rather than shifting enthusiasms. Coherence is another test for our narratives, for without it we cannot relate different aspects of the story to each other and see various themes as connected in a broader integration of values and beliefs. We also ask that our collegiate stories be comprehensive in relating the meaning of local commitments to the wider world of fundamental social and educational values, to important emerging realities, and to the cause of education as a form of human transformation, which has its own wider narrative. Parochial and defensive stories, or those that rigidly worship the past, are products of a flawed imagination that will not be adequate guides to the future. And so it goes. By consistently emphasizing questions that have normative force, we ask that our narratives present their credentials. A discipline of leadership has distinctive forms of evidence, but it has them nonetheless.

NOTE

1. It is beyond anyone's ability to be familiar with and document the massive literature on narratives and stories in various fields. Beyond the references in the chapter, I have been especially influenced by the work of H. Richard Niebuhr (1941, 1963), Paul Ricoeur (1984–1986), and Robert Coles (1989). For useful summaries, see Polkinghorne (1988) and Clandinin and Connelly (2000).

CHAPTER 7

Mission and Vision: The Heart of Strategic Leadership

If strategy is to become a form of leadership, we shall have to put in place a new set of criteria for its tasks. Leadership is demanding because it addresses human values and purposes, wants and needs. It changes the intention of strategic decision making and planning, even as it works within the same forms. In a leadership process, integrative thinking connects findings in new ways. Decision making becomes sensitive to symbolic meanings at the same time that it shapes a systematic agenda for action.

The articulation of a mission and vision is that moment in strategy when the dynamic of leadership inescapably takes center stage. Once these concepts enter the strategic dialogue, the logic of management necessarily cedes to the language of leadership. Leadership is asked to perform its distinctive role in mobilizing commitment to shared purposes and goals. Intimately linked to the definition of purpose or mission, the articulation of a vision is a requirement of strategy and a responsibility of leadership. It cannot simply be tacked onto a process of strategic management that otherwise would do business as usual. In spite of all the ambivalence that academic communities have about how authority should be exercised, they simultaneously insist on a clear sense of direction.

As we have seen and will find again, leadership answers to deep levels of human psychic need and expectation. So, strategy moves into deep waters when it navigates questions of mission and vision. Not only must mission and vision set an authentic direction that connects with the narrative of identity, but it must also develop the mechanisms through which the organization can attain its goals.

MISSION AND ITS FRUSTRATIONS

Most campuses regrettably identify their mission with the statements that have to be revised once a decade for regional or specialized accreditation. Unfortunately, anyone who has sat at the accreditation table for mission statements tries not to return for a second helping. The process is often lifeless, with dicing and splicing words and phrases the menu of the day. Or it is clear that the effort is largely political, with individuals trying to advance disciplinary, administrative, or other interests. Typically the process is not intimately related to the development of strategy but is pursued as a requirement of compliance. Conversations enriched by discussions of the key markers of strategic self-definition or the central goals of student learning or the social forces affecting education or the results of internal or external evaluations do not usually occur around this task (Meacham and Gaff 2006).

As a consequence, most mission statements are bland and vague. The accreditation panels, which must read dozens of them at a time, often joke about their sameness. When Newsom and Hayes (1990) asked institutions how they actually used their mission statements, they were unable to answer. They also discovered that when the names of the colleges and universities were disguised, the mission statements could not be identified by institution.

In an even more pointed critique of mission statements that reflects the political realities of competition for resources in state institutions, Gordon Davies says, "It is in no one's interest that mission be defined clearly.... The recruiting slogan of the U.S. Army, 'Be all that you can be,' is parodied in higher education as 'Get all that you can get'" (1986, 88).

Why are there such disincentives to clearly define the most fundamental feature of an organization, namely its purpose? The contexts of the effort provide one answer. Both accreditation and budget processes can distort the strategic significance of self-definition. In one case, the mentality of administrative compliance can stifle strategic thinking, while in the other, the tactics of budgetary gamesmanship makes it inopportune. Playing it safe with hallowed abstractions about teaching, research, and service keeps peace at home, and the accreditors and bureaucrats at a distance.

In substantive and strategic terms, of course, academic institutions cannot even begin to hide their purposes. They are manifest and unmistakable in the configurations of the tangible assets of a campus and in the intangible values and programs through which an institution differentiates itself. Although missions may be avowed only vaguely in words, they cannot be removed from deeds and actions. George Kuh and his associates (2005) suggest that institutions have two missions, one that is *espoused* in policies and print, and one that is *enacted* in campus life and culture. Institutions that seem to be especially powerful in reaching their goals for student learning are "alive" to their mission both conceptually and in everyday and strategic decisions (Kuh, Kinzie, Schuh, Whitt, et al. 2005).

Being all things to all people can be a ploy to gather resources or hide from hard choices, but it cannot be sustained as a purpose. In time such a standard will consume the organization that submits to it. Humans cannot live or think without specifiable purposes, at least not well. As Leslie and Fretwell suggest, "The freedom to be whatever the imagination suggests is also the freedom to be nothing in particular" (1996, 173).

MISSION AND STRATEGY

As colleges and universities have negotiated the challenges of the past several decades, the issue of purpose has been transformed into a constant strategic challenge. As we have seen in our analysis of various models of decision making from the academy to the corporate university, virtually every turn of the clock brings new forms of change in the social forces and market realities of the wider society. Coming to terms with change responsibly lends a new urgency to the old question of institutional mission.

Our earlier exploration of the ideas of story and identity provides the appropriate context for the explication of institutional mission as a primary point of reference for strategic leadership. The narrative of identity provides the depth and meaning, the texture and context, within which purposes have been enacted. As the institutional story is translated into the broad themes and values of its identity, so does identity disclose itself explicitly in a defined sense of purpose.

Not everything concerning the organization's identity—its unique life as a culture and its forms of community, its full range of memories and hopes, assets and achievements will be explicit in its purpose. In considering purpose, we focus more on why we exist, and less on the specifics of how we came to be. The emphasis is primarily on the content of what we do. The strategic discipline of leadership that explicates purpose is focused. It aims for precision in unfolding the distinctive values, aims, and capacities of the organization. In doing so, it engages the institution in continuing reflection on its self-definition as it differentiates itself within the wider world of higher education.

Although the discipline of purpose is sharply concentrated, it yields findings that are crucial for the exercise of leadership. The need to fulfill purposes is built into the nuclear structure of human inclination, so it comprises a central component of the sense making that participants seek in an organization and the sense giving that they ask of its leaders. In turn, purposefulness provides leaders with a powerful rallying point that creates energy and commitment to common goals (Hartley and Schall 2005). The sense of conviction, commitment, and calling that belong in the idea of mission can be recaptured and then released.

Developing a Mission Statement

Before a college or a university's mission can become a component in a process of strategic leadership, it first has to be raised to lucid awareness. The SPC or one of its subcommittees offers the most likely context for a continuous strategic conversation on mission. It brings leaders of the faculty and administration together around the same table. Whatever group or groups actually undertake the task, by whatever process, the following kinds of questions will help to bring an institution's mission to explicit form as a pattern of self-definition that places a claim on its members. To articulate a mission as lived, we must ask of ourselves (cf. Hunt, Oosting, Stevens, Loudon, and Migliore 1997; Sevier 2000):

- Where did we come from? (the issue of legacy, of the founders and the founding, of decisive events, and of notable leaders)
- What really matters to us? (the question of values)
- By whom are we governed? (the issue of sponsorship by state, church, profession, or independent board)
- Why do we exist? (the essence of the purposes we serve)
- What do we do? (the question of the range and type of the institution's educational programs and services)
- How do we do it? (the issue of the specific ways we create value and quality in executing teaching, research, and service programs)
- Whom do we serve? (the size and scope of our activity by types of programs, clientele, and geography)

Although they represent a place to start, serial answers to separate questions do not produce an effective sense of mission. Criteria that emphasize the differentiation of the institution should wind through the process of inquiry and self-definition, producing a coherent sense of purpose. For example, which of the proposed defining characteristics in the mission rise to a level of effective strategic differentiation? What are the things that set a place apart from others, that make it what it is? What special educational or administrative capacities does it possess? What particular economic, social, and political challenges define its past and its future? The notion of core competencies (which we explore in depth in the next chapter) asks us to look at the distinctive, creative capacities in an organization that may cut across departments and programs. Have any competencies risen to a level of consistent distinction, so that they have become legitimate defining characteristics of achievement and quality? In the language of business strategy, we ask how educational value is created and competitive advantage is achieved (Alfred et al. 2006).

The process of strategic differentiation has other criteria to guide it, including the test of effective measurement. As purposes are articulated, an organization must have some way of knowing that it does what it claims to do. The measurement need not be quantitative but can be substantive. The purpose of "student transformation" is not verifiable by quantification alone but may be evaluated by a large variety of other forms of analysis and assessment. So, as an institution considers its mission in a strategic context, it tests itself continually by asking, "In terms of what measure, indicator, or evidence can we advance this claim?"

The clear and coherent articulation of purpose in a strategy process is a critical task for many reasons. Among the most important is that it gives the organization a template for systematic strategic decision making. It provides the focus for the development of strategic initiatives and goals and for the establishment of financial priorities. Achieving strategic wisdom in effective financial decision making is critical in organizations like universities that are filled with talented and ambitious professionals. In such places, perceived needs and good ideas always outstrip available resources. A clear sense of purpose is a vital mechanism of good management.

Mission and Strategic Leadership

A compelling sense of strategic mission provides more than just an effective benchmark for decision making. It answers to deeper features of the human constitution and the need for meaning. If people sense that any choice is as good as any other, they soon become demoralized or confused. The loss of a sense of purpose or development of meaningless systems of control in bureaucracies, including academic ones, deadens people or makes them cynical or rebellious. On the other hand, when people are able to shape the purposes of their organizations and know why they are doing things, they become engaged. Lived purpose is a basic form of sense making that contributes to the growth and the empowerment of a person. As a consequence, the articulation of authentic purpose is a dimension of leadership, not just of management.

As people in all organizations know well, a sense of purposefulness not only empowers the individual; it also creates a sense of community (Senge 1990). Just as an individual flourishes by understanding her work as a calling, so does an academic organization empower itself by interpreting its life as a community, which is a consistent theme in the historic narrative of higher learning. Communities are created around many things—experiences, memories, values, and common space—but they are always defined by shared purposes that create a sense of common enterprise. Through awareness of a common mission, the members of a community forge a fundamental relationship to one another created by service to a common cause. The shared allegiance to the cause creates bonds between people that come with mutual obligations and expectations and express themselves in acts of reciprocal affirmation and correction.

In a time when market realities dominate higher education and its worth as a public good has been has been clouded, it is important to emphasize that it serves purposes that provide the foundations for a free society. One of the tasks of academic leadership is to lift up and affirm these powerful values as a source of commitment and inspiration. Though often perceived to be eternal skeptics, academic professionals are fundamentally motivated by a commitment to the power of knowledge and to the integrity that is required to pursue it. As Burton Clark puts it in his masterful study, *The Academic Life*, "In our cultural world the academy is still the place where devotion of knowledge remains most central, where it mot merely survives but has great power. Many academic men and women know that power.... In devotion to intellectual integrity, they find a demon who holds the fibers of their very lives" (1987, 275). To try to understand the mission of an institution without awareness of the depth of these values and beliefs is to miss a central motif in the institution's story of identity. When we see an institution's mission as the self-investment in worthy ends, then we see more clearly how strategic leadership draws on a rich well-spring of motivation and loyalty.

CASE STUDY: THE MISSION OF THE NEW AMERICAN COLLEGE

We have emphasized the importance of clarity of purpose for the tasks of leadership while knowing that most academic institutions produce mission statements that are vague or perfunctory. Rather than fill our text with lengthy examples of flawed mission statements pulled out of context, it will be more useful to describe an effort to reconceptualize mission that has made a telling difference for many of its participants.

Now formalized into an association of colleges and universities called the Associated New American Colleges (ANAC), the group began in the early 1990s as an informal but continuous dialogue among the chief academic officers of a set of small primarily undergraduate universities and comprehensive colleges offering a range of programs in liberal and professional education. (At the time, the institutions included the University of Redlands, the University of the Pacific, Trinity University, the University of Richmond, Ithaca College, Susquehanna University, North Central College, Hood College, and Valparaiso University.) The conversations began in frustration occasioned in part by classification and ranking systems that listed their institutions as an indeterminate "regional something else" that did not fit the primary and more prestigious categories of national liberal arts college or national university. There was no clear model of educational quality to which they could aspire, and their missions were portrayed and perceived negatively, as that which they were not or, as one of the deans put it, as the ugly duckling of higher education (cf. Berberet 2007).

In fascinating ways, the deans' conversations paralleled the concerns of the inimitable Ernest Boyer, whose uncanny ability to frame old issues in novel ways crystallized an emerging consensus in the deans' conversations. Boyer (1994) wrote about the need for a new kind of American institution of higher learning, one that was more engaged with the world, more practical in its vision of the power of education, and more spacious in its understanding of the different forms of faculty scholarship than traditional colleges and universities. In a word, Boyer portrayed an institution that would be definitively *integrative* in working across the boundaries between disciplines, the liberal arts and professional studies, undergraduate and graduate education, the campus and the wider world, and the classroom and campus life. In doing so, he coined the phrase the "New American College" to describe the institutional type he was describing.

The following paragraph describes many of the common features of the missions of its member institutions:

> ANAC…members make student learning primary within a traditional higher education commitment to teaching, research, and service. Most express dedication to education that is value-centered (often reflecting the church-related heritage many ANAC members have in common)....ANAC institutions acknowledge their comprehensive character and qualities of practice, integration, and application that reflect their identification with the New American College paradigm. These include the mission of educating diverse graduate and professional as well as liberal arts students; a commitment to service in their surrounding region; and the goal of developing applied competence as well as theoretical knowledge. (Associated New American 2004)

The effort to reconceptualize the mission of these institutions has been richly rewarding for many of the participants. The ANAC schools asked themselves what it meant to be a distinctive type of collegiate university and found that the theme of "connectedness" was especially suggestive in describing their strategic intent. In virtually every direction they turned, the theme of integration, of crossing intellectual and organizational boundaries, illuminated their strategic initiatives (Boyer 1994). It gave them confidence that the idea of a small undergraduate university was rich in possibility and could stand by itself as a model of quality. The mission of the new American college has inspired a number of dramatic success stories in which the academic and financial strength of the institutions has improved markedly (Berberet 2007).

Many of the ANAC schools discovered that a clear and authentic purpose brings a focus to all the work of strategy and surfaces issues that are truly *mission critical*. Mission then becomes a conceptual reference point that can be internalized throughout the institution and that brings coherence and continuity to the decision-making process. In essence, it provides the organization with purposefulness, an indispensable component of leadership. In charting turnarounds at some two dozen institutions, MacTaggart (2007a, 2007b) emphasizes that a revitalized sense of mission defined around new or transformed academic programs is the culminating stage of the process.

VISION AND LEADERSHIP: CONCEPTUAL FOUNDATIONS

The development of a vision for the future is part of the very meaning of the concept of strategy and provides an indissoluble connection to the theme of leadership. Yet for a variety of reasons, the power of a vision is often not captured in campus strategic plans. Sometimes the term is regarded as a trendy part of the jargon of pop management and resisted. Commonly, too, prior experience with a vision may stir campus resentment because it did not produce the ambitious changes that it promised (Keller 1997).

The basic idea of vision is not esoteric or fanciful but is the soul of strategy and of leadership. If, regarding identity, we inquire, "Who are we?" and concerning mission we wonder, "Why do we exist?" then in terms of vision, we ask, "To what do we aspire?" We use a metaphor of sight to refer to an institution's discernment of its best possibilities for the future. The dependence of strategy itself on vision is articulated well by Burt Nanus: "A good strategy may be indispensable in coordinating management decisions and preparing for contingencies, but a strategy has cohesion and legitimacy only in the context of a clearly articulated and widely shared vision of the future. A strategy is only as good as the vision that guides it, which is why purpose and intentions tend to be more powerful than plans in directing organizational behavior" (1992, 30). Without using the words, Nanus is describing the relationship of strategy to leadership. The presence of an effective vision in strategy is the condition that grounds and enables the process and discipline of strategic leadership. When all is said and done, one of the most extraordinary human capacities will drive the process, namely, the ability to imagine the future in order to create it. When the circumstances are right, humans can turn their images of the future into reality by committing skill, imagination, resolve, and resources to the task. Many of the central components of strategic leadership arise out of this extraordinary human ability.

The intellectual synthesis required to create a vision is complex and difficult. While being rigorous and analytical, strategic decisions must also be innovative and imaginative. To grasp possibilities that are not yet fully formed, strategic reflection, again, has to rely on stories as well as concepts, images, and metaphors, along with facts. Narratives of identity and aspiration both require a penetrating use of language. We speak of "greatness" or "eminence" or "distinction" and try to grasp and convey the emerging meaning of education in "cyberspace," of "engaged" learning, of "diversity," of "global education," and of education as "discovery" and "empowerment." Each concept conveys a complex set of meanings that strategic leadership must first explain and then enact through a set of strategies, goals, and actions. An effective vision is a quintessential form of sense making and sense giving that often takes a narrative form (cf. Gioia and Thomas 2000).

The Moral Significance of a Vision

To focus strategy in a vision is to learn again in a compelling way that leadership is about the human condition. It touches deep layers of human agency and motivation, of human limits and possibilities. A vision of the future reaches us as beings that live and move as temporal beings. Without images and patterns that make sense of our personal and collective memories, we would not be the selves we are, nor would we find meaning in our relationships and responsibilities. Because our time is limited, both in the tasks we assume and in the days of our lives, we experience the intensity of our finitude and seek achievements and meanings that will endure. Whether as individuals or as members of the smaller or larger communities in which we participate, we try to grasp the future through stories that provide images of hope and symbols of promise. For these reasons, we respond to leaders who offer an authentic vision of possibility for the future (Niebuhr 1963; Ricoeur 1984–1986).

Given this daunting context, what should be the content of a collegiate vision? The notion that they must be miniature epics, boldly creative, or stunningly unique is untrue. They are better known for their consequences. Visions provide authentic and worthy aspirations that affirm, inspire, and energize the community by unfolding the promise of its future. Their message should be vivid and memorable, and recognizable in everyday decisions. When claims are made about levels of attainment, it should be clear how the institution will substantiate them. When, for example, the word "excellence" or its parallel appears, the reader or listener should be able to say, "That means excellence in terms of these determinable characteristics and achievements."

Just as we found in discussing purpose, so it is as well that a vision contributes to a powerful sense of community. By definition a vision must be widely shared if it belongs to the organization and not just an individual. A shared vision stirs enthusiasm among a group of people and motivates commitment to common tasks, though it will never capture the imagination of everyone. In the process, connections are created among members of the community that reinforce the vision itself, contributing to a sense of direction and momentum. As the group executes the vision, a sense of pride and affirmation takes hold in the organization and in the contributions of each person. To fail the vision is to fail each other.

Not surprisingly, a vision creates these mutually reinforcing patterns because much of its basic content, especially in organizations like colleges and universities, comes from the ideas and experience of the group itself. To be sure, leaders at all levels contribute decisively to the vision, especially those at the top, which is why they are there. They give it systematic expression in various forms. Or they may enlarge and even transform it at various points in its development. Yet to be shared, it must originate and take root in the organization. Its lineage, in fact, is typically traced to authentic elements in the institution's story. As Peter Senge puts it, "Once people stop asking, 'What do we really want to create?' and begin proselytizing the 'official vision' the quality of relationships nourished through that conversation erodes. One of the deepest desires underlying shared visions is the desire to be connected, to a larger purpose *and* to one another" (1990, 230).

As a vehicle of strategic leadership, a vision taps the deep human drive to reach ever-higher levels of quality. A defining commitment to quality is palpable in the work of most academic professionals and, as we have seen, is woven into the person's sense of identity. Although the professional's drive for quality can easily become brittle and self-regarding, its presence as a powerful source of motivation is never absent. The search for personal fulfillment, academic excellence, and professional recognition becomes a reinforcing dynamic of achievement, what psychologists refer to as intrinsic motivation. Once the leadership process has been able to stir the human need to create something of lasting significance, then a large part of the leadership task has been accomplished.

As the process of strategic leadership gains momentum, people feel a genuine sense of empowerment and pride, and many new leaders step forward to meet their responsibilities. They lead themselves and others at the same time (cf. Ganz 2005; Messick 2005; Tyler 2005).

DEVELOPING A STRATEGIC VISION

We have seen something of the content and the deep significance of a vision for the strategy process as a form of collaborative leadership. As with mission, we must ask not only what a vision is, but also how it is created intentionally in a strategy process. Although there are no recipes, there are systematic practices and insights to be used as circumstances suggest and as the dynamics of a campus indicate.

As we have seen, similar to the development of purpose, the process of developing a vision is rooted in the institution's story and identity. In many ways, vision is the story told anew for the future, now as a narrative of aspiration. This may mean that the story is transformed through change and new ambitions, that it is reinterpreted and enlarged, and some chapters of it left behind. Yet in the examples we have seen, aspirations for the future draw forth the commanding master values and images of the past. They legitimize the vision in the eyes of the community and make it intelligible. As standards, values and images are open to new content. They are orientations to choice, not the changing content of choice. Effective leaders are always circumspect about which buildings, programs, or policies will have to be replaced to fulfill a vision because they may carry unexpected meanings in the institution's legacy. But some will have to go, and, if so, their loss can be regretted as a necessary sacrifice to a larger good and an authentic vision.

Illustrations

Whereas mission statements may require several paragraphs, visions can usually be stated in several lines, although their accompanying explanations can run many pages. To bring some concreteness to our discussion, it will be helpful to examine a handful of statements from a diverse group of institutions as they appear in mission statements, strategic plans, accreditation self-studies, and official publications. With the statements before us, we can analyze some of their patterns and parallels to shed light on their development.

> **The University of Connecticut** will be perceived and acknowledged as the outstanding public university in the nation—a world class university (2000).
>
> **Duke University** aspire[s] to become fully as good, over the next twenty years, as any of the leading private research universities in the country, with comparable breadth and depth, and deserved reputation for excellence in teaching, research, and wide-ranging contributions to society (2001).
>
> **Princeton University** strives to be both one of the leading research universities and the most outstanding undergraduate college in the world (2000).

Carnegie Mellon will be a leader among educational institutions by building on its traditions of innovation, problem solving and interdisciplinary collaboration to meet the changing needs of society (1998).

Sweet Briar College has determined that to claim its pre-eminence as a woman's college for the 21st century, the College's faculty and staff will demonstrate that intellectual and professional endeavors will permeate our students' lives (2004).

Centre College aspires to be a national model of consequence for institutions of its size and type—the very small coeducational liberal arts college (Morrill 1988).

Williams College take[s] it as our commitment to be the exemplary liberal arts college, nothing less (1997).

Pfeiffer University will be recognized as the model church-related institution preparing servant leaders for lifelong learning (2001).

Rhodes College aspires to graduate students with a life-long passion for learning, a compassion for others, and the ability to translate academic study and personal concern into effective leadership and action in their communities and the world (2003).

The University of North Carolina at Greensboro is a leading student-centered university, linking the Piedmont Triad to the world through learning, discovery, and service (1998).

The University of Richmond is embarking on a mission to create an institution that is second to none, better than any and different from all … by transforming bright minds into great achievers (2003b).

Juniata College [is] a learning community dedicated to provide the highest quality education in the liberal arts and sciences and to empower our graduates to lead fulfilling and useful lives in a global setting (2001).

Roanoke College intends to [be] one of this nation's premier liberal arts colleges (1993).

Virginia Commonwealth University (building on its position of leadership among *urban* research universities) aspires to be an innovative leader among the nation's major research universities (1997).

Baylor University, within the course of a decade, intends to enter the top tier of American universities while reaffirming and deepening its distinctive Christian mission (2002).

The Vision to Be the Best

As one analyzes these statements, a number of common patterns become evident. One of these is the effort to seize on the language of superlatives, particularly the phrase "the best." The language may vary and include words and phrases such as "the preeminent" or "the outstanding," but the meaning is the same and refers to the highest level of achievement. In a slight variation on the theme, vision statements sometimes use the logic of equivalence by stating positively that the institution will be "as good as any," or negatively, by claiming that none will be any better. The necessary implication, of course, is that there are other institutions that are just as good.

As ambitious and inflated as they often sound, the claims about being the best and its variants show signs of realism because they are almost always differentiated by institutional mission and type. The references are about becoming the best liberal arts college, or the model of quality for the very small coeducational liberal arts college or the private research university. Many smaller and midsize private universities explicitly refer to their dual aspirations as undergraduate colleges and graduate research universities.

Although vision statements are brief, they typically differentiate themselves by recounting aspects of their narrative in the texts that surround them. So, Rhodes College (2003) describes its path toward excellence and its place among the top tier of liberal arts colleges by describing the influence of President Charles Diehl, who boldly moved the campus to Memphis in 1925 and suggested that "The good is ever the enemy of the best." To be the best and in the top tier may be mutually exclusive logically, but they show the way narrative and metaphor shape statements of vision.

For years the University of Connecticut has had a mission and vision to be "a great state university" and, since 1994, to be the nation's "outstanding public university." During the past ten years, the vision has served as a rallying cry to turn the dilapidated campus, once called "a neglected embarrassment" by the local newspaper, into a showplace worthy of its high aspirations (MacTaggart, 2007b). A staggering $2.8 billion has been invested in remaking the campus and creating fifty-three new buildings, as well as making dramatic improvements in applications, selectivity, funded research, and other strategic indicators. The ambitious vision has taken on local significance by triggering the will of the university and the government to take the lead in meeting the educational and economic needs of the people of Connecticut (MacTaggart 2007b).

Many of the sample statements that we have listed represent another common way to frame a vision statement, which is the goal to be "among the best," a claim that involves a large number of variant phrases such as "in the top tier," "among the top ten," or simply "to be a leader." In setting such a goal, the aim is to draw a circle of shared reputation around a group of top performers that includes or will eventually include the institution. The vision may acknowledge tacitly that the purpose of its strategy is to reach a level of quality that it does not now have or it may affirm its ambition to maintain its current position within a leadership group of peers (cf. Gioia and Thomas 2000). Again, the aspiration is differentiated by mission and by the taxonomy of institutional types that consists of such variables as national and regional, public and private, undergraduate and graduate, and liberal arts and professional.

The Vision to Do the Best

A quite different approach to constructing a vision involves the aspiration to reach a high level of achievement in designated educational programs, methods, and outcomes. The emphasis shifts from seeking to be the best to doing the best.

From a strategic point of view, the question becomes, "At what do we or could we excel?" Or we ask, "In what distinctive ways do we create educational value?" Put more pointedly, "For what do we want to be known?" Thus we find references on our list to creating a "passion for learning," educating "servant leaders," or "empowering students." The language of aspiration is still in evidence: terms like "highest quality" are typically used to describe the desired level of performance.

Characteristics of Vision Statements

When understood in the context of strategic leadership, how effective is the language of "the best" and its surrogates? Does it succeed in providing an academic community with a worthy and inspiring shared vision of its future? Although its ultimate effectiveness as an instrument of leadership will always be highly contextual—the aim is to reach and motivate engaged participants, not the general public—there are some clear characteristics and criteria about visions that use superlatives.

It appears that at least one of the goals of a vision is to stimulate the instincts of people to create a reputation and results that are superior to those of others, namely the competition (Gioia and Thomas 2000). The normally polite but very real rivalry to attract the most talented faculty and students, and the most resources, is driven in part by an ambition that will make an institution equal to or better than competitors and be perceived that way. Even a cursory reading of strategic plans shows clearly the presence of this competitive impulse. As much as one might want to do so, one cannot ignore the reality that competitiveness is an integral part of strategic thinking and a source of motivation.

But competitiveness sinks into a negative spiral of distortion if the ambitions to be the best are not redeemed by the aspiration to reach levels of quality that are substantive and worthwhile in themselves. If the vision is to motivate people to seek ever-higher levels of quality as a matter of fulfillment, it has to meet a variety of criteria. It must articulate the values and authentic aspirations of a given institution with its own history, profile, and possibilities. For these reasons, the effort to define that niche or space within which an organization can excel or exercise leadership is a fruitful endeavor. Differentiation is a way to capture the specific promise and possibility of an institution. The goal is to find and to state the precise structure of the highest form of quality and value creation that a particular institution is able to attain. A differentiated vision reveals the distinctive forms of quality that are possible, thus opening the way to levels of commitment that otherwise might remain untouched.

If a vision is to contribute to the tasks of leadership, it must be not only ambitious but plausible. In being inspirational, it will define attractive possibilities, and in being realistic, it will be seen as attainable over a period of time. The key to striking the right balance is to ensure that the vision is determinable and is therefore subject to various forms of measurement. An effective vision has to come with a set of indicators that are spelled out within a strategic plan or other widely available documents. When an institution intends to become the best, it must be clear about how it intends to fulfill its ambition, or it will quickly lose credibility. As often happens, if the terms lack definition or local meaning, they will become empty phrases that will be benignly ignored or, worse, will echo in cynical asides around the campus.

Combining Being and Doing the Best in a Strategic Vision

One of the most effective ways to ensure that superlatives have strategic force is to combine reflections about being the best with disciplined explorations of "doing the best." A critical weakness of ambitions that are not specifiable is that they block the processes of precise knowledge, focused reflection, linguistic richness, and integrative judgment that are required to create a sustained and powerful vision. Strategic creativity often has humble beginnings as people with detailed contextual knowledge interact with peers daily to explore organizational problems and opportunities. They start with a sense of what they do best, not of how they can be the best. These issues lead to specific and determinable areas of competence and achievement, the latter into a whole series of complex assumptions that, as we have seen, may be hard to define and measure. Finally, of course, the two forms of "best" should merge, but the order in which the issues are pursued is a critical part of a vision and of leadership.

We touched earlier on the discussion of this issue in Collins's *Good to Great* (2001), and it will be helpful to consider it in greater depth. As we have noted, this study of corporate success has broad implications for other types of organizations, including, unexpectedly perhaps, colleges and universities. Collins discovered that great companies are often built around stunningly simple ideas on which they stayed tightly focused. But it is not just any idea. It "is not a goal to be the best, a strategy to be the best, an intention to be the best. It is an understanding of what you can be the best at" (Collins 2001, 93). In all the cases of moving from good to great, the company made a passionate commitment to being the best in the world in a particular activity or competency. Further, "The good to great companies focused on those activities that ignited their passion. The idea here is not to stimulate passion but to discover what makes you passionate" (Collins 2001, 96).

The concentrated effort to find the areas in which academic organizations have an intense level of commitment and capacity to excel is typically a different process than in business, although there are analogies. A college's greatest claim to talent and distinctive quality may well reside in the values, methods, relationships, resources, and characteristics exhibited in the total educational program and in the campus ethos. These factors cross disciplinary lines and may define the underlying dimensions of a distinctive and powerful approach to learning. To locate its sources, one asks: Where do the people in the organization show substantial and enduring passion for greatness? Where have they built greatness into the middle of the organization without being directed to do so? (Collins 2001).

To disclose these characteristics in the work of strategy is to contribute to a vision as an emergent process of collaborative leadership.

With those distinctive competencies and characteristics as their foundation, the institution can seek to enlarge its level of quality in steps and stages, moving from strength to strength. If the vision is authentic, it will be of decisive importance in helping to drive the momentum of achievement. A vision is fueled by the way these distinctive and generative core competencies are translated strategically from what a place does best into being the best in a carefully defined class of institutions or programs.

Envisioning: An Imaginary Campus Tour

Some strategic plans display an interesting method of developing and testing a strategic vision that uses the narrative form in a distinctive way. Though usually not done systematically or comprehensively, they use a process of envisioning the actual programs, practices, resources, and achievements that would be in place were the vision to be realized or progress made toward attaining it in a given number of years. It involves the effort to imagine coherently what is not yet real in order to bring the future into the present. The strategic imagination works through a disciplined and integrative method of reflection based on various patterns of evidence, for it is not an exercise in creating fantasies and wish lists. It draws on the best quantitative data available, uses collaborative methods, and connects its projections to the institutional narrative and to its current and future strategic position. So, it represents an act of intellectual synthesis.

In an analysis that parallels many of the ideas proposed here, Ramsden suggests: "A vision is a picture of the future that you want to produce…an ideal image… of excellence, a distinctive pattern that makes your department, your course or your research…different" (1998, 139). In a similar vein at a recent seminar on strategy, the leader proposed that we think of strategy as similar to the work of assembling the pieces of a puzzle, and of a vision as the picture on the box that guides the process (Stettinius 2005).

To illustrate one way that envisioning occurs, consider a procedure in which a group of participants is asked to take an imaginary tour through the campus when it has fulfilled the vision established for it (cf. Baylor University 2002, University of Richmond 2003a). The tour will give concreteness and clarity to the meaning of the vision as well as test its plausibility. What will people see as they make their rounds, and how might it be different from what is here today? What are the most significant discrepancies between the way things might be and the way they are now? (Gioia and Thomas 2000). Where are improvement and change most needed and most obvious? What are the most distinctive, compelling, and attractive features of the vision? How is the future described in narrative form?

As we shall show below, the set of concepts and images that emerges from a visioning process can be complex and comprehensive. They will have relevance for virtually every sector of the organization. As a result, the process becomes a useful way for various offices and programs throughout a campus to discern the meaning and possibilities of the vision for its own work. Each area of responsibility will discover special ways that its performance will be altered and enhanced to fit the images cast by the vision. As the analysis goes forward, the central question becomes: Do the concepts and goals of the vision convey authentic meaning and offer criteria that will mobilize commitment to it across the organization?

So, on their imaginary campus tour, people will want, for example, to explore various facets of the academic experience of students. They will ask to see how students and faculty interact in the classroom. What are the forms of teaching and learning inside and outside the classroom that fulfill the vision? What will be the shape of the curriculum in general education and in the majors? What expectations will professors set and students satisfy, as illustrated in course syllabi? What types of assignments and learning experiences will there be? How much writing will be required? What other kinds of individual and group projects will be expected? If we examine tests and papers, what level of rigor and quality of work do we see? How does the total education program fit together, and to what does it lead? What plans do students have after graduation? What contributions do they intend to make to the wider society? When they leave, where do they go, and what are they able to do when they get there?

Imagine that as the tour continues, the visitors follow a similar pattern of questioning as they interact with faculty and staff in a variety of offices and programs. They will be inquiring about and envisioning the professional characteristics and achievements of those whom they encounter, especially the contributions that faculty make to knowledge. The tour will also include an evaluation of the facilities of the campus and its other tangible resources. The group will spend a large amount of time as well collecting and analyzing data concerning the strategic indicators that will tell them the conditions that must be met for the vision to be fulfilled. They will give special attention to the institution's financial position and the assessment of student, faculty, and staff performance.

When all this is done, the group will be able to choose or revise the terms that best express what they have pictured and tested in their minds during your imaginary walk. In a reversal of the usual phrase, here the "talk" gives meaning to the "walk" that is going be required (Weick 1995, 182). Metaphors and symbols will flow from the envisioning process that give color and vibrancy to the vision and capture the institution's identity for the future. If words like "the best," "highest quality," "national leader," "world class," or "superior" can legitimately be used, they will have been tied to specific forms of attainable achievement. They must be able to be imagined and justified with regard to the potential of the institution to dominate the environment that it is likely to encounter. If they are only words, however, they will do more harm than good and produce cynicism, not inspiration. If, on the other hand, the envisioning process demonstrates that the vision resonates with the authentic best possibilities of a place to create educational value, it has created a powerful source of motivation.

The envisioning process is also a way to locate the most important disparities between what we want to become and our current situation. The limitations may come in many forms, but strategically they have to do with the underlying capacities of the organization. Most visions cannot be realized in the span of a normal strategic plan, for they may require several decades, but they are able to focus our attention on the structural issues and causal characteristics that are the primary barriers to the fulfillment of our best possibilities (LeVan 2005). What are the most important gaps that have to be closed? As we consider organizational strengths and weaknesses, this deeper orientation will change the character of our strategic self-assessment.

Whose Vision?

One of the perennial questions about a vision revealed in our earlier analysis of leadership in higher education is whether it is created by leaders and imposed on the organization, or whether the leader serves primarily as the storyteller for the vision that the organization creates for itself. These two ends of the spectrum are better understood as polarities that need each other to be complete, rather than as opposites (Cope 1989; H. Gardner 1995; Ramsden 1998; Sevier 2000).

Since leadership is actively reciprocal, vision is a relational concept. Without opportunities for open exchange and dialogue, absent active and continuing collaboration to learn his or her constituents' needs and aspirations, it seems impossible to imagine how a leader's vision could inspire an organization, especially a professional one like a college or university. The conclusion that as to leader and organization, a collegiate vision is always both/and, never either/or, seems inescapable.

Yet it is also clear that listening is an active process in which the leader is contributing ideas, synthesizing information, integrating recommendations, testing boundaries, and drawing on privileged knowledge and experience from outside the campus. Finally, it falls to the designated leaders of organizations to articulate a clear and compelling sense of direction. To communicate the story and the vision is, then, always far more than neutral discourse that repeats an inchoate set of wants and needs. It is a central act of leadership as both sense making and sense giving.

Narratives of aspiration are not only integrated and changed in the telling; they also have to be sustained and enacted by the leader's commitment. Depending on circumstances, the articulation and implementation of a vision may rise to the level of transforming leadership that involves systematic and pervasive change or decisive moral leadership. The assertion of a bold vision could mean that the president or other high officials have to take a stand in the name of the defining values of the organization itself. At such times, the balance shifts to the side of initiative by the leader in the assertive formulation, communication, and enactment of a vision.

Summary: The Criteria for a Vision

The project of transforming strategy into a process and discipline of leadership clearly turns on its capacity to develop, articulate, and implement a vision. If leadership is to accomplish this task, a variety of criteria have to be satisfied. Since many of them relate to the development of an effective mission as well, it will be helpful to pull these together here in an explicit summary form. To serve the purposes of leadership, a vision statement should be (cf. Kotter 1996; Sevier 2000; Tierney 2002):

- Clear
- Concise
- Focused
- Differentiated
- Aspirational
- Plausible
- Motivational
- Shared
- Authentic
- Worthwhile
- Measurable

MISSION, VISION, AND STRUCTURAL CONFLICT

We have argued that strategic leadership is able to address the structural value conflicts in collegiate governance systems in ways that make a practical difference. Similar to the integrative power of narratives of identity, penetrating statements of mission and vision also provide a framework for transcending the deepest conflicts and worst complications of shared governance.

A vision is not a romantic ideal that a leader has plucked from some hidden world, but an authentic contextual articulation of purpose that has arisen through open debate and dialogue. As to process, it expresses and builds trust. As to substance, it provides values that differentiate, mediate, and reconcile the structural conflict between autonomy and authority, and the intrinsic and instrumental worth and measurement that typify academic decision making. The values of the mission and vision have to become embodied in a specific organization and enacted in its identity. They provide an academic community with professional and moral purposefulness that reconfigures the meaning of both autonomy and authority. It renders authority more conscious of the academic and moral responsibilities that it carries, and autonomy more aware of the organizational requirements it must satisfy. As we shall see in other places, the exercise of strategic leadership is about the resolution of structural conflict at a variety of levels and in different forms throughout the organization.

We can also see that the development of strategic consciousness provides new resources for some of the other perplexing dynamics of organizational decision making, including the decoupled choice system. As we have seen, in such a world of decision making, participants carry around personal and ideological preoccupations that they would like to unload on a decision, whether it is relevant or not. Yet the meaning of the context changes where strategic leadership has been able to define a sense of institutional legacy, mission, and vision. Now there are strategic criteria that assert both subtle and overt rules of relevance to establish the framework for decision making. Instead of carrying lots of excess idiosyncratic baggage, participants can more easily devise strategies and construct agendas to make decisions and solve problems.

In some ways, we have moved ahead of ourselves, for the ways to think about the challenges and the possibilities of the future have been assumed, but not yet defined. We have knowingly explored the questions of mission and vision in isolation in order to penetrate more fully into their meaning for leadership. In a sequential sense they are always considered with reference to the broader social, economic, and cultural contexts in which academic institutions find themselves. We now turn to the task of considering methods to analyze the wider field of strategic forces with which colleges and universities must contend.

CHAPTER

Strategic Position: The External and Internal Contexts

A s we begin to analyze the idea of strategic position, it is important to emphasize that strategy is an iterative process. The same topics may be considered several times in different contexts before taking form in a written document. In terms of chronological order, for example, the assessment of an institution's position in its environment might logically be done before a vision is created. Without defining the institution's external context, how can one project its best possibilities? But it is equally true that the meaning of trends in the external world can only be understood with reference to the organization's identity, mission, and vision. The tasks of external analysis and internal self-definition stand in reciprocal relationship to one another. Thus, there should be continuous connection among the different steps in a strategy process, especially when it is driven by the integrative orientation of strategic leadership. Findings are subject to revision and reformulation as the work proceeds. The image of a spiral rather than a straight line best captures the process.

STRATEGIC LEADERSHIP AS A DISCIPLINE OF CHANGE

Echoing ideas presented in our earlier review of leadership, James MacGregor Burns keeps us riveted on the centrality of change: "Of all the tasks on the work agenda of leadership analysis, first and foremost is an understanding of human change, because its nature is the key to the rest" (2003, 17). We find once again that the leadership perspective takes us below the surface of events to seek their deeper significance. Just as it is with narratives, values, and vision, so is leadership also preoccupied with change. Each of these concepts provides a depth dimension to the strategy process that helps it to see human and social realities that are hidden in the segmented steps of strategic management. In this chapter we shall focus on the external forces of change, and in chapter 12 on intentional change within the institution. When strategic planning functions at its best, it often reaches the level of leadership tacitly by making sense of change systemically and by creating a compelling agenda for action.

Change and the Paradigms of Human Agency

We should recall from our earlier discussion of paradigms that a discipline of strategic leadership requires a conceptual framework that can effectively interpret the meaning of change. We encounter again the fascinating and central question of how academic organizations and the professionals who inhabit them should think about their work in relation to change and external realities. Once more, thinking about the presuppositions of our own thinking becomes a preliminary step in understanding strategic leadership as a discipline of change. Organizations devoted to learning need to become learning organizations.

In its purest form, the teleological assumptions in the paradigm of the academy define the highest good as a self-sufficient world of ideas where change does not really exist. In such a perspective, the university is the place where a collegium of scholars sets unchanging standards of excellence for a scholarly community. Although this model creates a powerful narrative of meaning, it cannot create an understanding of the nature of change and how to respond to it. Change falls outside its systems of significance and intelligibility.

The concepts that change can improve things, that innovation is able to enrich tradition, that initiative is possible, and that discontinuities offer new possibilities all belong in a different order of thought. These perspectives all fit with the master image of responsibility. As we have seen, this paradigm of thought is rooted in the capacity of human agents for intelligent response, adaptation, and initiative in coming to terms with the changing field of forces in which they live (Niebuhr 1963). The motifs of responsiveness and response-ability take us into a world of thought that illuminates the ways that leadership functions strategically in response to the reality of change. Effective leaders seek to anticipate and understand change creatively and congruently, all in dialogue with a community as they together choose a direction for the future.

THE ENVIRONMENTAL SCAN

If strategic leadership is to respond effectively to change, it needs a set of disciplinary tools, not just models of thought. It has to find appropriate ways to grasp the realities of change in the wider world. In the standard practices of strategic planning, this is called an environmental scan. As we have seen in other contexts, strategic leadership must try to turn the insights about social and historical forces into occasions for self-understanding. Ultimately, an understanding of change outside the institution has to be transformed into intentional change within it.

The first step in that process requires a disciplined method to discern the driving forces in the wider world.

Ironically, the strategic plans of many institutions, especially of smaller colleges, often offer little, if any, serious analysis of the realities of their context. When they do, they often contain a long and fragmented list of events, data, trends, and contingencies that may or may not have a significant bearing on the institution itself. In another common approach, strategic plans often describe in general ways the unprecedented pace of technological and social change, but its implications are not translated into an agenda of intentional change. The lack of focused attention on the meaning of change represents a void in the fabric of strategy development.

There are good reasons to be cautious about environmental scans, but not enough to abandon them. Like strategy development itself, everything depends on how it is done. To be sure, they often misfired in earlier generations of strategic planning, frequently because they tried to predict the future. Fifteen years ago, for example, planners inside and outside of the academy knew for a fact that information technology would make most brick-and-mortar universities obsolete by the early twenty-first century. Both in higher education and the corporate world, the enthusiasm for futuristic thinking dims when it tries to predict specific events and trends and their precise impact on an organization. Whatever else it may be, the future is inherently uncertain.

PEEST

The proper diffidence about prediction should not, however, discourage a disciplined approach to reflection about change. The aim should be to develop a multidisciplinary capacity to think systematically about the meaning and direction of trends that have already appeared, and that are inescapably shaping the institution's future. Technology, for instance, may not replace fixed-site universities, but it is transforming the practices and capacities of education within them. The capacity to assess systematically the future consequences—the futurity—of inexorable driving forces such as technology becomes an essential dimension of the work of strategy, especially as a method of leadership.

To analyze the forms of change, many institutions use a strategic approach that has come to be called the PEST method, which is an acronym for the basic categories of political, economic, social, and technological trends. Depending on the industry, organizations may add other trend lines. Natural resource and manufacturing companies would be shortsighted not to add environmental trends to their list of domains to watch closely. Educational institutions should obviously include educational trends within the set of realities to which they must respond. Thus, we have PEEST as an acronym for an environmental scan for higher education. Already apparent is the need for flexibility in devising the factors to analyze continuously. If the PEEST categories strike the members of a planning team as too limited or artificial, they can and should define a set of classifications or issues that are more illuminating for their work. The groupings are simply a device used to focus on the characteristics of change and to think systematically about them (cf. Bryson 1995; Rowley, Lujan, and Dolence 1997; Sevier 2000).

The systematic collection of information about external influences becomes a precondition of effective strategy formation. In large institutions, planning and research staffs are available to spearhead the effort, while in smaller colleges the task can be divided among several offices. In all cases, the work is substantially assisted by sources of analytical and quantitative information that are readily available. National educational associations, regional consortia, and state and local governments are repositories for data, as are periodic special projects on higher education's future. Needless to say, publications devoted to higher education offer timely and easily available trend analyses. The World Wide Web gives access to dozens of other possibilities for accessing information, both about higher education and other spheres of activity, including a wealth of comparative information from IPEDS, as noted in chapter 5 (cf. Morrison and Wilson 1997 for an excellent list of sources).

A PEEST Illustration

To make the issues more concrete, we shall use an abbreviated PEEST analysis to display some of the trends and challenges that institutions of higher education are facing. Even though it is intended only to be illustrative, our exploration will allow us to draw several general conclusions about the prerequisites of environmental scans within a process of strategic leadership (cf. Alfred et al. 2006; Newman, Couturier, and Scully 2004; Yankelovich 2005).

In the early years of the twenty-first century it has become clear that higher education is being shaped by:

Political Forces:

- **Accountability and assessment:** steadily increasing regulatory controls and demands for accountability by state and federal governments, including the measurement of student performance and debates about educational policy driven by sharp ideological divides

- **Strained federal resources:** a likely restraint or reduction in programs of federal student assistance and support of basic research that accompanies massive federal deficits looming far into the future and exploding entitlement and defense costs and uncertain tax policies

Economic Forces:

- **Declining state resources:** erratic and uneven financial resources for higher education, accented by uncertain economic growth, volatile equity markets, and gyrating support from state governments, in a general pattern of long-term decline in public revenues as a proportion of total university income, accompanied by a strong pull toward privatization

- **Global economic competition:** the globalization of technology and the economy in an interconnected world with the constant outsourcing of U.S. jobs, creating pockets of unemployment and stagnant middle incomes

Educational Trends:

- **Expanding and uneven educational access and quality:** the steady expansion of participation in higher education by people of all ages to unprecedented levels, accompanied by sharply uneven access and quality, with a heavy emphasis on professional and vocational programs and the loss of centrality for liberal education

- **Affordability:** the continuing escalation of the price of higher education at rates well above inflation and increases in family income, creating a permanent and deepening structural problem of affordability

- **Engaged learning:** a growing focus on engaged, active, and participatory forms of student learning with inconsistency in application

- **Market-driven and global competition in higher education:** an ever-increasing competitiveness in education, propelled by market-driven realities, including new (often proprietary) providers of education; distance learning; the globalization of higher education and research, especially in science and technology; differential pricing through tuition discounting; and various forms of resource-driven entrepreneurial activity and competitive improvements to facilities and programs

- **Rapid expansion of knowledge:** a continuing explosion of new knowledge, with the power to shape the economic future and well-being of human life, both in individual and collective terms

Social Trends:

- **Internationalization:** the continuing and profound impact of global cultural and political interaction in both positive and virulent forms, with a profound impact on curricular content and programs (languages, area studies, cultural and religious studies)

- **Diversity and demography:** continuing growth in social and educational diversity, increasingly driven by immigration, and in rising overall high school age cohorts until 2010, when declines will begin in some regions

- **Public criticism:** widespread public doubt, anxiety, and ideological debates about the cost and the quality of higher education

Technological Change:

- **Technological transformation:** the deep, wide, and continuing global, educational, and administrative impact of information technologies, including the rapid growth in distance learning

Using the Environmental Scan

What becomes of the potential mountain of information that is gathered on these critical educational and other trends? The PEEST categories should provide a framework for integrative and systemic thinking about the institution's context, and for the eventual preparation of a summary analysis of its position. The effort should move systematically by means of statistical and content analysis from specific data points, trend lines, and events to the patterns and driving forces that they reveal. The trends spelled out here represent a powerful set of pressures and opportunities, some of which are approaching end points where change becomes systemic. The problems related to the affordability of higher education are of this kind. At the same time that concern is focused on external realities, there should also be an effort to find connections, themes, and structural relationships in the trends that are most significant for a particular institution. Achieving this level of integrative analysis requires an institution to have full command of its story and identity, its mission and vision, and its management information systems and strategic indicators.

As it makes these connections between the worlds outside and inside the academy, the institution is able to construct its own set of contextual issues and priorities; in effect, it builds a watch list of critical variables and relationships that will determine its future. Those insights about the forces of change with the highest leverage will become critically significant as it goes on to define its strategic position through an analysis of its strengths and weaknesses and its opportunities and threats.

Brief examples will show how the PEEST process should develop a particular center of institutional gravity. Within the sphere of social and political trends, for example, it may be the demography of regional high school graduates, changing federal financial aid policies, and family income patterns that will matter most to institution A, a small regional private university. It follows these trends in depth and develops systematic quantitative analyses because it knows that its tuition increases cannot exceed wage and salary growth in its recruitment area. For nearby institution B, a state university with a large variety of professional programs, it will be patterns and trends of adult educational participation that should receive the most attention. They are heavily influenced by the tuition assistance policies of local businesses and the increasing competition from proprietary institutions and distance-learning providers. They will need to follow employment patterns and policies closely. Across the state, a large research university, institution C, is preoccupied by trends in federal and private funding of scientific research and instrumentation, which are the keys for its overhead income, and its recruitment of graduate students, who also serve as laboratory instructors. It sharpens its abilities to follow and influence trends in Washington, D.C.

The results of the same PEEST process should look very different in these institutions, as each tailors it own analysis. It becomes clear that broad categories like "social" or "economic" are basically markers for the exploration, differentiation, and connection of the most relevant trends. As much as anything, an environmental scan is important because it intensifies and deepens the process of self-knowledge that is at the heart of effective strategic leadership. The institution's identity is sharpened as it sees itself over against trends in the wider world and at other institutions. Participants in the process also learn to question their own arrogance and defensiveness as they come to see that the future guarantees nothing, even to the secure and to the virtuous. By promoting thinking in new ways about change, the work of strategy creates new sensitivities and patterns of cognition to grasp emerging threats and opportunities that differentiate a responsible learning organization.

Strategic leadership has to do with ways to reconceptualize the presuppositions of collegiate decision making itself through the model of responsibility. Sustaining academic integrity precisely in a world of market-driven competition is an increasingly demanding challenge for today's colleges and universities. Both as to purpose, which is understanding change, and as to method, which is informed collaboration, an environmental scan is an important component of strategic leadership. Its aim is to show what truly matters in the forces that affect the organization and to reveal possibilities that will energize people to come to terms with change.

In sum, institutions of higher learning need to learn to worry coherently and creatively about the field of forces that impinge on them. In his study of six extraordinary university presidents (Hesburgh, Friday, Kerr, Gray, W. Bowen, and Slaughter), Arthur Padilla (2005) finds precisely this capacity for systemic thinking to be one of the distinctive characteristics of their leadership. He calls it "an 'aerial' or global understanding of the relationships among different parts of the enterprise and the larger environment" (2005, 255).

Collaborative Strategic Learning

Several other compelling results flow from the analysis of an institution's context through the perspective of collaborative strategic leadership. As persons serving on an SPC or one of its subcommittees are immersed in the same data and engage in a genuine dialogue about trends and realities, something important often occurs in the dynamics of the group. Unless it is spoiled by adversarial conflict, a sense of shared reality, trust, and solidarity takes hold among participants. As people receive the same information and share thoughtful interpretations, they come to see themselves in a common situation. Barriers between people are lowered, and the great divide between faculty and administrators recedes. An environmental scan becomes a pivotal occasion for collaboration, for learning, and for thinking coherently about problems that hitherto were disconnected.

Competitor and Constituency Analysis

The world of higher education is defined not only by change but also by key relationships and competition, which need to be assessed strategically. As we have seen, strategic governance is not limited to the tension between the administration and the faculty but involves relationships with constituencies and stakeholders that have a variety of different expectations (Alfred et al. 2006; Rowley, Lujan, and Dolence 1997).

A process of strategic leadership offers colleges and universities a chance to do something that they often do not do well, which is to listen. What they hear may be distortions or resentments based on emotion or limited information, or complaints that serve political or self-interested agendas, yet the voices of dissent and criticism need to heard. They should be drawn into the institution's self-understanding and become the occasion for hard thinking about its strategic position. The widespread perception that universities arrogantly resist change and are unresponsive to the public's needs casts a dangerous pall over all institutions, whether or not they are guilty as charged. Institutions can use the strategy process to register critiques from their constituencies that they must address. By considering the issues strategically, they can move them to a higher plane of significance and make them an appropriate part of their agendas.

Every college or university is more or less conscious of its competitors, although they are typically so numerous and so diverse that intense bilateral rivalry is more the exception than the rule. As we have suggested previously, an essential dimension of strategic self-understanding comes from the comparative analysis of benchmarks, strategic indicators, programs, and capabilities. Organizations know themselves best when they can see themselves through a reflexive comparative lens. It is impossible to understand one's own strategic identity without competitor analysis since strategy has to do precisely with one's position *relative* to others. Alfred et al. (2006) spell out many of the factors needed to assess competitive position, including (1) cost, (2) convenience, (3) form of program delivery, (4) quality, (5) innovation, (6) systems and technology, (7) networks with other institutions, (8) administration and governance, (9) culture, (10) reputation, (11) resources, and (12) distinctiveness.

Competitor analysis leads in many directions. It may help to reveal and to define the need for a long-term commitment to increase donor support or show that salaries must become or remain competitive with a group of peers. In some cases, the competitive analysis is pointed and specific and leads to the construction of new facilities or to the introduction of a new program of scholarships. If an institution comes to believe that its competitive position is being challenged, it often will try to move heaven and earth to keep its place.

SWOT ANALYSIS: STRENGTHS AND WEAKNESSES

Based on experiences in strategic planning seminars on both sides of the Atlantic, I would conclude that if anything is always associated with strategic planning, it is the SWOT analysis. The analysis of an institution's strengths, weaknesses, opportunities, and threats (SWOT) is itself a form of integrative thinking that describes an institution's position in the world. If it is done well, it achieves an insightful synthesis of the internal and external realties that define an organization's possibilities. Scanning the environment with a focus on what matters most to a given institution prefigures some of the tasks of an effective SWOT analysis. The scan describes what is happening in the outside world, and the SWOT analysis makes sense of it at home.

A SWOT analysis does several important things. It picks out those features of both the context and of the institution that represent threats and opportunities, strengths and weaknesses. As it does so, it turns outward to focus on threats and opportunities, and inward to examine its strengths and weaknesses. But in both cases, the analysis is relational and contextual. One college's threat is another's opportunity. Similarly, the strengths and weaknesses of an institution have greater or less salience depending on external trends.

A SWOT workshop early in a strategy program can be especially useful. It provides an opportunity for participants to begin to share insights based on the institution's story and vision and its strategic data. Based on the findings of the environmental scan, the development of lists of strengths, weaknesses, opportunities, and threats can be a productive exercise as a first step in the process (cf. Bryson 1995).

Let us look first at ways of analyzing strengths and weaknesses, and subsequently threats and opportunities. Colleges begin the task by reviewing a list of institutional elements like the one included in our framework of the strategy process in chapter 4. As we review the typical components, we find that tangible resources are of critical importance, starting with the organization's financial resources and its space and place both with regard to the nature of the campus and its facilities and its geographic location, either as resources or deficiencies, or often as both. Other tangible resources such as technology, equipment, and collections also differentiate an institution's capacities. Human resources are at the core of an academic organization's ability to create value, including the capacities of faculty and staff. Relative levels of scope, quality, and achievement have to be assessed concerning educational programs, including the curriculum, teaching and learning, research, and student life. Systems and processes—especially those concerning admissions, enrollment, image, constituency relationships, and fund-raising— are critical success factors, as are the mechanisms of governance and decision making. Organizational culture includes strengths and weaknesses regarding campus relationships, values, community, and identity. As a point of departure, it is logical to create and debate lists of strengths and weaknesses around these elements (Alfred et al. 2006; Sevier 2000).

But one must be cautious. Strengths and weaknesses come in many forms, some of which are relatively trivial or have no particular strategic or competitive significance. Many problems may simply be short-term operational issues or may represent conflicts over governance or between personalities. A modest operating deficit for one year may not a strategic issue, while the inability to solve the problem within a specified time period decidedly is. The tendency for negativism and complaints to overwhelm an analysis is real, so the effort should be made to move the discussion away from the symptoms of the problem to its causes. The aim should be to find the distinctively strategic and structural forms of vulnerability and opportunity, of capacity and incapacity. What forms of strength and weakness go to the distinguishing and defining characteristics of the organization? What propels or impedes its ability to compete effectively for resources and talent to fulfill its mission? Where are the real points of leverage? Using contextual analysis and relational thinking, the focus should be on the strategic fit between an organization and its environment.

A good SWOT process produces a substantial amount of organizational learning. In particular, those leading the process have to be sensitive to whether people are able to understand the connections between issues, and to see that strengths and weaknesses and are part of an interdependent system of relationships.

The learning is not didactic but involves new levels of awareness and enlarged capacities for systemic thinking. In a word, leaders of the process are often teachers. As Peter Senge puts it, "Leaders are continually helping people see the big picture: how different parts of the organization interact, how different situations parallel one another because of common underlying structures, how local actions have longer-term and broader impacts than local actors often realize" (1990, 353).

CORE COMPETENCIES

Over the past two decades, a variety of novel methods of strategic analysis have shown their value in business and are now beginning to appear in colleges and universities. They cannot be drawn into higher education without careful reconceptualization, much as needs to occur with the process of strategic planning itself. One of the responsibilities of strategic leadership is to ensure that the work of strategy is enriched by insights and methods that will improve its effectiveness.

We intend to explore two analytical methods that can be used to shape strategic conversations on campus. One has to do with the analysis of an organization's core competencies as a way to assess its strengths and weaknesses, and the other with the use of scenarios to study the impact of future trends. We shall begin with a look at core competencies and related issues, such as a strategic reading of organizational assets.

As we pursue an inquiry into strengths and weaknesses, we begin to note that some of the most significant characteristics are not specific programs or assets, but broad capacities or abilities that generate a range of strengths and achievements. A high rate of acceptance into graduate study, for instance, may point beyond itself to a capacity for excellent faculty advising, to rigorous and imaginative teaching, or to a set of distinctive pedagogies. Behind a set of specific strengths, we may discover what students of business organizations have come to call core competencies, a concept that we have already found useful in exploring mission and vision (Hamel 1994). Known by many names, these concepts shift our focus to underlying forms of activity, away from surface characteristics. The concept of core competencies takes us to the set of skills and abilities that are the source of the more visible and identifiable strengths of the organization.

In the business world it is not a successful product that constitutes a core competency, but a distinctive level of skill, ability, and knowledge that produces market leadership in a whole range of products. Canon, the Japanese manufacturer of copiers and cameras, for instance, developed a dominant ability in lens technologies in the 1970s. This broad capability can be qualified as a core competency since it serves as the generative source for a variety of specific product innovations. Many of the innovations are not even used by Canon but are components in the products of other companies (Hamel 1994).

Besides being a generative activity or skill, a core competency is also distinctive. It is hard for others to duplicate, so it represents a powerful competitive advantage. Much of the management task itself resides in nurturing the development of core competencies (Hamel 1994).

Academic Core Competencies

The idea of core competencies offers a powerful way for institutions of higher education to understand themselves and make strategic decisions (Dill 1997). When seen as competencies, for example, an institution's academic program shows itself to be a repertoire of capabilities by which it defines itself in a world of challenge and change. To be sure, specific courses and programs of study consist of important intellectual assets—subjects, topics, and disciplinary methods that have been created by academic experts and approved by their peers. Yet at the same time, a program reveals and depends upon a wide variety of distinctive skills and abilities possessed by the institution's faculty and its students. These may be distinguishing capabilities or competitive advantages, or they could reach the level of being a core competency. Consider how the following list of demonstrable and generative abilities in teaching, learning, and research exemplify the idea of core competencies in the work of different programs, departments, and institutions:

- Creating consistent innovations in teaching
- Developing new academic programs
- Establishing rigorous academic expectations
- Producing effective experiential and active learning opportunities
- Involving students in research
- Producing exceptional levels of original faculty research
- Attracting and retaining outstanding scholars
- Stimulating high levels of student intellectual maturity
- Building thematic connections among courses and programs
- Creating a rich array of interdisciplinary programs
- Using technology creatively and extensively in fostering student learning
- Building exemplary programs in diversity
- Constructing powerful programs of international education

- Employing comprehensive and effective ways to assess student learning
- Preparing students for lives of leadership and service
- Decisively raising moral consciousness
- Involving students in the critical and integrative study of original texts
- Contributing to personal religious development

The list could be expanded at length, and many educators could suggest the names of institutions that have become known in the literature for possessing one or more of these competencies. They are often part of a legacy of identity for what a place does best. Strategically, the development and articulation of a broad academic portfolio of competencies and capabilities creates educational worth and potentially constitutes the competitive advantage of a college or university.

The competitive advantages may play out, of course, in an enormous variety of directions, depending on the mission of the institution. Institutions may display several core competencies, not all of them limited to the academic domain. The concept of core competency is not a finished doctrine, but an exploratory lens for discerning activities and skills that cut across an organization's programs (Cope 1994). Core competencies point back to the identity of the organization and beckon forward through a vision to renew and innovate in those spheres in which it has developed particular strengths.

Administrative Core Competencies

The analysis of core competencies applies as well to administrative responsibilities. The process begins again with an effort to single out defining characteristics, assets, and key operational results. The self-evaluation can then be brought to a new level of strategic insight as it is translated into a consideration of core competencies. What are the critical processes and activities—the distinctive skills and abilities that stand behind exceptional administrative performance? Of many possible examples, consider the following.

Financial Capabilities

Strong or weak financial capabilities, for example, are a function of many things, including accurate budget projections, good operating controls, effective data systems, and skillful planning and management. Many institutions have financial management competencies that achieve levels of effectiveness and efficiency that set them apart from the competition. They are able to build and fuel a financial system that stays in equilibrium, and they can both support innovation and generate long-term financial flexibility, even in difficult environments.

Gift and Grant Capacity

The ability to generate gifts and grants has become a defining strategic issue for all institutions, whether public or private. Successful institutions, regardless of the wealth of their constituencies, are those that know how to capture a high proportion of their potential support. Effective fund-raising is always systemic because it depends on everything from good organization to a powerful story. The ability to generate resources has become a foundational core competency at many institutions, and where it has not, it may represent a lost opportunity or a telling strategic deficiency.

Strategic Leadership and Campus Decision Making

The flaws and weaknesses that are often noted in campus decision-making systems and cultures, and that have been described at length in this work, are not a matter of fate but of capacities that can be changed and improved. No matter how brilliant the idea or promising the innovation, it will go nowhere without a method of decision making and leadership that can implement it. Institutions with ponderous or dysfunctional governance systems mired in distrust are not only wasting time and energy, but they are also damaging themselves by their inability to respond to change. Effective systems of strategic governance, leadership, and management have become a critical capacity, a key success factor, in the contemporary world of higher education. Institutions that can develop core competencies in strategic decision making have a powerful competitive advantage.

These examples of core competencies from both the academic and administrative spheres could be multiplied in many directions, including the vital area of student life and co-curricular programs. One of the important methods that connects the illustrations is the strategic differentiation of strengths and weaknesses in terms of levels and forms of fundamental capacity. There is a natural strategic order to the logic of self-assessment that judges a program or service to be (1) deficient, (2) adequate, (3) a distinguishing capability, or (4) a core competency. The process of analyzing strengths and weaknesses can be given more focus and pertinence by these kinds of distinctions. A strategic weakness is tellingly dangerous when it prevents an organization from mobilizing its capacities to respond to its threats and opportunities.

Although the differentiated assessment of levels of strength and weaknesses is a necessary step in strategic planning, it is not a sufficient one for the work of strategic leadership. Seeing strengths and weaknesses in terms of capacities and competencies brings them within the context of human agency and choice, opening them more clearly to the influence of leadership. The shift in perspective empowers people to take on problems that otherwise seem impenetrable. The chance to develop a set of generative competencies is deeply motivating for it enables people to take initiatives that include them in a larger process of leadership and responsibility. As the work of strategy moves from description to action, it implicates motivation, which is achieved through interactive leadership.

STRATEGIC ASSETS

The analysis of strengths and weaknesses performed in a leadership context also sets the tone for the assessment of the fixed characteristics and given assets of an institution that may seem impermeable to change. An uncertain mission, poor location, and lack of resources typically represent serious weaknesses for the members of a campus community. If strategic self-analysis makes the weaknesses seem insurmountable, or if assets and characteristics are only portrayed negatively, then the results are likely to be counterproductive and dispiriting. As a facet of leadership, the aim of the analysis should be to create a sense of urgency and possibility by mapping assets rather than just listing weaknesses. To do so the first step is to create a clear sense of the positive assets that the organization possesses, including the talent and commitment of its people and the possibilities that flow from its identity, mission, and circumstances.

Suzanne Morse (2004) describes this orientation to strategic thinking in *Smart Communities*, her study of successful community development programs in a variety of cities. Typically the process of seeking improvements in hard-pressed cities has started with making a list of the deficiencies and problems obvious to any observer, from empty storefronts to high crime rates. Although the analysis of the negatives cannot be ignored, it is not the place to begin or to focus the inquiry. To dwell on the negative is to create an attitude of dependence and defeatism. If the process begins with a mapping of assets—with an analysis of the relationships, organizations, people, programs, and resources that are available to foster improvement—a sense of possibility and empowerment can take hold. "The fundamental payoff of this approach comes when people see that they and their neighbors are capable of taking charge of their lives and the future of their community" (Morse 2004, 90).

Although the particulars are different, there are parallels between strategic thinking in colleges and universities and communities. If institutions of higher learning become preoccupied with what they are not, they often enter a downward spiral of self-doubt and self-judgment that drains off energy and initiative. They tend to compare themselves with an unarticulated model of prestige that displays their deficiencies and blocks an appreciation of what they are and might be. If, however, the process of self-analysis is oriented by strategic leadership, it uses the logic of self-affirmation and possibility. It begins by defining its assets and distinctive characteristics, and by seeking the potential that may be hidden in its identity and aspirations. The success stories of the "new American colleges" charted by Berberet (2007) and described in the preceding chapter provide evidence for this claim.

Virginia Commonwealth University

In the early 1990s Virginia Commonwealth University (VCU) embraced a vision of leadership as an urban research university. Characteristics that might easily have been defined as negatives, such as a dispersed urban campus, were reconceived as strategic opportunities. The university resolved a lingering contentious dispute with a neighborhood bordering the campus that feared absorption. VCU decided to grow on the other side of its urban location, adding new economic life and opportunity to an otherwise unpromising commercial zone. As VCU affirmed its distinctive urban mission, it also committed itself to the economic development of the city and the region. The university addressed the immense financial challenges of providing health care to low-income patients in its hospitals. It developed an innovative new school of engineering and launched an ambitious biotechnology research park adjacent to its downtown medical center. By leveraging the traditional research strengths of its medical programs, it brought over 1,500 new jobs and hundreds of millions of dollars of capital investment to the city in less than a decade. In spite of an unpredictable cycle of both substantial budget cuts and increases by the commonwealth, the university has been able to grow to become the largest university in the state. It has substantially enlarged funded research and private contributions and has received several multimillion-dollar gifts. VCU has gained strength and prominence by affirming the logic of its urban opportunities, emphasizing innovation, and framing issues in the sphere of possibility. President Eugene Trani and his colleagues have consistently used strategic planning and strategic leadership to enable VCU to be what it is and might become, rather than pursuing a wistful search for what it is not (Leslie and Fretwell 1996; Virginia Commonwealth University 1997).

In many of the other examples in chapter 7, we saw a similar process at work. In mapping assets, the goal is to understand and unfold the promise that comes with particularity, to unleash the significance of being who one is. Focusing on assets does not deny the negative or hide it from view but places it in an actionable context. The findings that show weakness and vulnerability are accepted and confronted, but not considered in isolation. They are interpreted within a larger pattern of meaning and responsibility, which are components of strategic leadership as a discipline of possibility.

SWOT ANALYSIS: OPPORTUNITIES AND THREATS

The analysis of strengths and weaknesses prepares the way for a translation of the environmental scan into a specific set of challenges and opportunities for an institution. As we have suggested, the first step, which is to develop a systematic, structural, and thematic understanding of the meaning of the driving forces of change, should be completed within the scan itself. The next step is to analyze the bearing of these factors on the institution's strengths and weaknesses, understood as its core competencies, assets, capacities, vulnerabilities, and deficiencies. The insights about the most significant threats and opportunities will be determined through a process of relational thinking that systematically connects the most important external trends and internal characteristics. The interpretive process is highly collaborative and integrates the insights and judgments of a variety of participants in the strategic conversation. It is driven by quantitative information (comparative benchmarks, strategic indictors, and the environmental scan) and qualitative perspectives (identity, mission and vision, strengths, and weaknesses) that lend themselves to the integrative task of interpreting and defining the institution's basic strategic position. For threats, the primary concern is to find structural situations in the environmental scan, like the affordability of tuition, that touch on basic organizational vulnerabilities. Conversely, opportunities, such as the creative use of technology, match an institution's capabilities with a defining feature of the context. From a strategic perspective, the aim is to locate those threats that disable or frustrate the institution's ability so that it can respond effectively to change, as well as those opportunities that enable it to dominate its environment and the competition.

Matrix Analysis

Some students of strategy suggest that this task of sorting out opportunities and threats (and strengths and weaknesses) can best be done by the use of a cross-impact matrix that asks participants to rate the influence of factors in the environmental scan on the institution's key performance indicators, which are essentially what we have called strategic indicators. Rowley, Lujan, and Dolence (1997) explain a procedure to create a matrix with a horizontal axis that records major factors in the environmental scan, and a vertical one that lists key performance indicators. The task for participants in the process is to give a numerical weighting to the influence of environmental factors (governmental policies, high inflation, population increases, etc.) on the key performance indicators. The different weightings offered by individuals are then averaged and analyzed in terms of standard deviations, and conclusions are drawn about the institution's most significant threats and opportunities. The process, adapted from Rowley, Lujan, and Dolence (1997), is represented in table 8.1.

The attempt to do integrative thinking about threats and opportunities through cross-referencing trends and organizational characteristics is sound, but the quantitative calculus is problematic. To be successful it has to be understood as but one step in a process that finally depends on rational analysis, dialogue, and judgment. It may well be useful as a way to start a strategic dialogue about threats and opportunities but should not be the primary or exclusive way to conduct the inquiry.

The reasons are obvious. It is artificial to display external forces in a table that presents them as isolated events or trends, when in actuality they are always systemically related to one another. It is equally artificial to try to dissect their impact on a list of separate strategic indicators that are themselves related to one another

Table 8.1

Strategic Indicators	Political Trends	Educational Trends	Economic Trends	Social Trends	Technological Trends
#1 Create as many indicators as needed.	Put a numerical weighting in each block.				
#2					
#3					
#4					
#5					

in a system that is controlled by a large number of variables besides the single external factor that may be under analysis. How, for example, does one translate a new governor's pro-education campaign platform (as a political trend) into an influence on indicators such as the number of applications, the state subsidy, or retention rates? The governor's ideas may never be enacted, and the influence of other variables on each strategic indicator makes a numerical measure a misleading indicator, providing more apparent precision than is warranted.

If one uses cross-matrix analysis in a comprehensive way for the ten steps of the strategy process, as the Rowley, Lujan, and Dolence suggest, it becomes an extremely elaborate and complex process. It would involve measuring dozens of trends from the PEEST analysis plus countless more calculations to sort out opportunities and threats and strengths and weaknesses, as well as to assess policies, procedures, strategies, and goals. The problem is not to do the calculations, but to be confident of what they mean. What is described as a strategic engine appears to become a forbidding contraption with no off switch. Surprisingly and significantly, there is no determinative place in the engine for a vision of the future (Rowley, Lujan, and Dolence 1997).

TOWS Matrix

A helpful use of a matrix is to juxtapose the conclusions about an organization's strengths and weaknesses against the threats and opportunities that have been defined in a planning process. The diagram is simple, but it helps to focus the work of strategy on the issues that most deserve to be pursued and that will yield the best results. It marks a useful way to begin to turn the strategy process toward the selection of the strategic initiatives and projects that rank as priorities. Each of the four quadrants in the matrix below suggests an appropriate way to respond to the various interconnections between opportunities and threats and strengths and weaknesses: to develop opportunities where there are strengths, to confront threats with strengths, to consider opportunities to overcome weaknesses, and to avoid threats where there are weaknesses. What

Table 8.2

Threats	Confront	Avoid
Opportunities	Develop	Consider
	Strengths	**Weaknesses**

some call a TOWS matrix follows this form (see table 8.2, adapted from the East Lancashire Training Council, n.d.)

SCENARIOS

Environmental scans and SWOT analyses are clearly one of the important steps in a strategy process. Without trying to predict the future, they are able to monitor and anticipate the way that various trends already in evidence are likely to affect the organization. Yet even when there is no pretense to predict the future, the anticipation of the influence of major trends is subject to error and distortion since forces and events bring constant surprises. In order to deal with these contingencies, many business organizations have turned to the analysis of alternative scenarios to describe several plausible patterns for the unfolding of future events. First developed by Hermann Kahn of the Hudson Institute, scenarios became a celebrated feature of Shell Oil's strategy process and its preparedness for the 1973 oil price shock (Van der Heijden 1996). The use of scenarios is beginning to appear in higher education (Morrison and Wilson 1997).

As the term suggests through its use in plays and films, a scenario is a basic plot-line out of which a full story or script can be developed. A literary scenario often follows any one of an enormous set of recurrent patterns of dramatic interaction, such as triumph over adversity, the solitary hero, love versus duty, loyalty and betrayal, beauty and the beast, and rags to riches. Out of these themes a scenario is developed that serves to outline the plot.

As they have come to function in organizational planning, scenarios have kept something of this dramatic flavor. Their creators try to find evocative story lines that can be easily remembered. Scenarios writers often use images or metaphors borrowed from the animal world or mythology to capture a motif. So, avoiding or ignoring problems is the ostrich scenario, while Icarus (the mythical figure who flew too close to the sun), is the overly ambitious scenario in which the participants initially soar, only to fall to destruction (Schwartz 1991; Van der Heijden 1996).

Scenarios begin in much the same way as a standard PEEST and SWOT analysis, with a careful analysis of driving forces in the environment and their likely impact on the organization. Yet important innovations come into play. Scenarios recognize the truth that the future always consists of factors and trends that are largely predetermined, as well as developments that are uncertain and unpredictable. The world, for example, is sure to run out of oil, but no one knows precisely when.

Although the prediction of future events is impossible, much of the uncertainty of the future can nonetheless be made more intelligible and become subject to more effective managerial decision making. To accomplish this, several different scenarios can be created to capture the most plausible eventualities.

The creation of a scenario is a demanding task. It begins with an awareness of important events and then seeks to understand them as part of broader trends, some of which are largely inescapable and others which are uncertain. Once a series of trends has been recognized and analyzed, then the task is to look at the structural patterns and the causal forces and relationships that are producing the trends. A scenario is produced out of these analyses. As Van der Heijden puts it, "The scenario is a story, a narrative that links historical and present events with hypothetical events taking place in the future" (1996, 213).

It is possible to trace, for example, the interlocking events, trends, and economic and cultural realities involved in the extraordinary development and global influence of the Internet, as Friedman (2005) has done in *The World Is Flat*. Those analyses can then be combined with others to create scenarios on such topics as the future of international scientific research or international student flows among countries or economic development through information technology.

Although often misunderstood, the purpose of the process is not to develop the best or most predictive scenario. Rather, the goal is to reduce uncertainty to manageable proportions by developing several scenarios, each of which is a plausible possibility for the future. The task is demanding because each scenario must be internally coherent and based on good supporting information. One cannot try to make things fit artificially simply to make a point. The causal relationships in the scenario have to mimic the real world of interacting events, trends, forces, and powers (Van der Heijden 1996). If they are able to do this, they also serve the critical purpose of challenging the existing assumptions and models of reality of the organization's decision makers. We again find the theme that organizations can learn best when they clear away outworn mind-sets.

Once several scenarios have been created, how are they to be used? They function as a testing ground for strategy at a variety of different levels (Van der Heijden 1996). The focus of scenario analysis can be to test a strategic vision, a broad strategic initiative, a single project, or a major decision. Whatever the level, its purpose is to assess whether the option in question is adequate to meet the contextual challenges of each of the scenarios. If not, it will have to be modified to function effectively under all the plausible conditions it may face. Obviously, one or more of the scenarios may define conditions that are more favorable for a given strategic option than the others. Yet the test of the strategy against an adverse set of future circumstances prepares the organization for success under a wide variety of contingencies. Based on its analysis, the organization may decide that its proposal meets all the tests, or it may choose to reconfigure aspects of its strategy in order to come to terms with various threatening or opportune circumstances; or it could delay acting on the strategic option until a later time or abandon it.

Scenarios at John Adams University

A brief example from higher education may help to give concreteness to the idea of scenarios. Consider John Adams University, a small public institution in the West that is developing a strategic plan and is ready to define a series of new initiatives. It wants to test the coherence of its ambitious strategic vision to become a state and national leader in funded applied research and in the assessment of student learning. In particular, it has decided to create a truly comprehensive and expensive program of institutional and academic assessment to enhance its quality. To test these and other strategies, the SPC develops three scenarios based on a PEEST analysis that reflects changing trends both in the state and nationwide.

Many aspects of the future environment are known and will be constants in each of the scenarios, including a consistently high and increasing demand for educational services in the state, supported by steady population growth. Changes in the economic fortunes of the state and region are automatically translated into growing or declining state subsidies, so the nature of the state relationship and different political philosophies are the primary differentiating characteristics in each of the scenarios. Over the past decade the state legislature has provided erratic levels of support for its public institutions, dictated strictly by the state's revenues. Tuition rates at Adams were cut for one four-year period and then increased dramatically. There have been some strong signs that the state wants to foster institutional autonomy, but others indicate that bureaucratic regulation is a fixture of government. Based on a careful analysis of these and other trends and political tendencies, the university develops three scenarios for plausible futures: Business as Usual, Creative Self-Reliance, and the Competitive Marketplace.

Business as Usual

In this scenario, it is clear that the intricate patterns of governmental, bureaucratic, and university interactions and expectations will not change substantively or structurally. As far as the eye can see, there will be erratic funding based on the state's changing economic situation, as cycles of political and bureaucratic control alternate with some movement toward more autonomous forms of governance, but not in fundamental, coherent, or predictable forms. Tuition will follow gyrating patterns of stability or increase based on the state's revenues, and capital funding will be reactive rather than proactive and a function of the political timing of bond issues.

Creative Self-Reliance

In the second model, the picture is different. This scenario sketches a coherent plan driven by political leadership to make constructive self-reliance a model of governance and decision making. State funding increases modestly for the public universities, but in ways that are targeted to build capacity and to encourage initiative. Research facilities are funded, for example, but operational support for them declines after a start-up period. Institutions are enabled to set tuition themselves and to keep the funds they save in annual operations but are expected to generate resources for repair and maintenance of their physical plants. Financial aid funds for low-income students are increased by the state, though it is expected that the university will share the costs through fund-raising. Incentives for performance in designated areas are periodically defined and funded by the state by one-time incentive awards, such as matching gifts to endow professorships.

The Competitive Marketplace

The third scenario shares many features of the second. The decisive difference is that the state's political leadership now believes deeply in privatization. The scenario also reflects a latent resentment toward higher education that has taken hold in the media, the legislature, and the governor's office. Substantial new levels of autonomy, as well as significantly reduced funding, are provided for public institutions. In effect, the relationship between the state and its institutions is conceived as contractual rather than as statutory. While the state does not disavow its legal control and responsibility, it believes that all agencies, including institutions of higher education, have to function on a market-driven, competitive basis. Financing for all facilities is now on a strictly one-to-one matching basis, with student fees or private fund-raising an essential part of the funding equation. As intense competition for dollars and students takes hold, some institutions fare well and raise their tuitions significantly, while other suffer since they cannot increase revenues in their markets. A gradual decline takes place in the number of student spaces available in the four-year system. as funds for the expansion of facilities and programs are not available. Noting the quality of the state's community colleges, the availability of low-cost education from a number of new providers, and the easy accessibility of Web-based education, the state's leadership is not disturbed by the trend.

Scenario Analysis

Having developed these scenarios, Adams University now has a set of templates against which to assess various aspects of its strategies and goals. Its aspiration to be the state's leader in applied research is compatible, even desirable, in each of the scenarios. The analysis also reveals that Adams must make it a priority to expand its staff and its capacity to secure grants from the government, foundations and corporations, and donations from individuals. Enlarged financial self-reliance is an important expectation in each of the scenarios.

Other strategies can also be tested and modified. The project to develop a core competency in program assessment also proves to be an essential goal in each case. Because of the near certainty that success will depend on capacities to perform well in competitive markets for students, resources, and recognition, the ability to demonstrate achievement will become increasingly important. Thus, the assessment project moves up the ladder of priorities for funding. Each of the scenarios also makes it clear that admissions, marketing, and fund-raising will require enlarged resources, although they were not originally projected as major needs.

As it examines its capacities in information technology, the university decides, counter to its early expectations, that it does not have the capacity to be a substantial independent provider of distance degrees. The market-driven scenario leads it to conclude that it will join an alliance of schools that provide online degrees in certain professional fields.

Scenario Conclusions

The scenario process is stimulating and imaginative, but it is also demanding. Unlike small colleges, multibillion-dollar corporations and large universities have the resources to invest in a continuing capacity for scenario building. Yet even the smallest institutions can ask several staff and faculty members to develop enough background to lead a scenario workshop as part of its environmental scan, perhaps with the help of a facilitator experienced in the art.

The development of scenarios is not, of course, an end in itself, especially in the context of strategic leadership. Scenario thinking offers yet another systematic language with which to understand change and the organization's relationship to it. It offers a mechanism by which to embed strategic thinking within the life of the organization, and to challenge and enlarge the thought patterns of the campus community. Seeing the interrelationship of forces in a scenario sensitizes the ability to anticipate what is up ahead, and to grasp new challenges and opportunities that are just appearing. It renders change less daunting, less strange, and less unwelcome. To be fully effective, strategic leadership has to touch the values and thought patterns of many, if not most, of the decision makers in an academic organization, including a good cross-section of the faculty. As they shape habits of perception, reflection, and judgment, systematic procedures like PEEST, SWOT, and scenario analysis help to domesticate change. They make it clear that even academic institutions are situated contextual enterprises that live in constant interaction with society and time itself. We come again upon our theme of the cognitive dimensions of leadership and the importance of the paradigm of responsibility.

STRATEGIC POSITION

These disciplines for understanding change not only contribute to thinking in terms of the image of responsibility; they play an explicit role in the step-wise process of strategy formation. They shape an institution's understanding of its strategic position, of the specific powers, assets, and competencies that it possesses that help it to make its way in a competitive world. Without a clear-headed self-estimate that takes form at least tentatively early in the process, the content of strategy can become vague, diffuse, and an exercise in wishful thinking. A crisp statement of institutional position in several paragraphs provides focus to the process. It draws out the implications of the SWOT analysis and the environmental scan and enables a purposeful and coherent selection of specific strategic issues for intensive analysis and action. Adams University says of itself, for example,

> The university is poised to capitalize on its distinctive strengths in applied research and the assessment of student learning to meet the educational and economic needs and opportunities of a growing population in its state and region. It has the focus, resourcefulness, and decision-making systems it needs to respond to changing circumstances. Through partnerships with state government, the private sector, and individual donors, it can attract the resources required to reach its goals. Adams can plausibly set high ambitions for its future.

In choosing the issues to address in its strategies, the analysis of an institution's position sets a series of demanding conditions. It places the focus on matters that are genuinely strategic, not primarily operational. An analysis of position also will be able to put the spotlight on strategic possibilities that offer the best returns for the effort and resources invested. To choose its priorities meaningfully, an institution has to be able at a minimum to accomplish what it sets out to do (Bryson 1995). The clearer sense of itself that it gains through the definition of its position provides deepened knowledge of the capabilities that are required. The goal of strategic leadership is ultimately to find ways to dominate the environment and to have the abilities and the resources to meet the demands of change resiliently and responsibly. One of the tasks of leadership is to anticipate what is required to build a sustainable level of effectiveness to fulfill a vision of the future.

We have proposed that the motif of institutional position is one component of the fourfold infrastructure of strategic self-definition. When a college or a university articulates its narrative of identity, states its mission, creates a vision of its possibilities, and develops a statement of its strategic position, it has put in place a comprehensive foundation for strategic leadership. On this basis it can move forward with confidence to craft the specific strategies that it needs to address the challenges and opportunities of its future. We turn to those subjects—first the form of strategies and then elements of their content—in the next two chapters.

CHAPTER 9

Strategies: Initiatives, Imperatives, Goals, and Actions

Throughout this inquiry, I have tried to show how a method of strategic leadership functions within the decision-making world of higher education. The time has come to examine the logic of the approach in designing specific strategies and courses of action. The aim of this chapter is to indicate how strategic leadership operates as a discipline of decision making by making strategies understandable, persuasive, and actionable.

INTEGRATING LEADERSHIP AND THE STRATEGY PROCESS

Even as our point of view shifts to focus on some of the details of strategic planning, we shall not lose sight of the differentiating aspects of leadership in its applied form. We will expect the various levels of strategy to bear the authentic stamp of the organization's narratives of identity and aspiration. In terms of leadership, they must be able to orient choice and motivate action, even if the proposed strategies stir up some measure of conflict and require difficult decisions. Coping with conflict and change is always on the agenda of leadership. To be effective in doing so, strategies have to be grounded in the institution's story, mission, and vision as sources of inspiration and legitimacy and must be able to anticipate the challenges to their enactment. At whatever point one taps into the strategy process, its different aspects should reflect that they are part of an integrated effort. The vision can be read in the goals, which in turn give the vision a purchase on reality. Since a vision reflects both limits and possibilities, it portrays goals as indicators of deeper commitments and perspectives. In the work of strategic leadership, the vision and goals are transparent to one another though the sense-making and sense-giving power of the narrative that frames them.

As strategies of integrative leadership, the strategies cannot merely be suspended in midair for all to admire and promptly forget. The ultimate goal of strategy is to capture the best thinking of an academic community and to enlist its members in a serious pursuit of shared aspirations. Agreement and enthusiasm are not required, but a critical mass of the organization must find itself influenced and even moved by the strategy. The community and the smaller communities within it have to own the most important strategic directions and share a commitment to enact them.

Anticipating a subsequent chapter on the implementation of strategy, I want to emphasize that leadership as an applied discipline has to be integrally oriented toward action. The conditions for successful implementation must be woven into the strategies and goals themselves. The very act of choosing strategic priorities requires an integrative understanding of the total circumstances of the institution. To launch a strategic initiative is already to have considered the actual or potential conflict with judgments about the significance of other worthy possibilities, not all of which can be made priorities. As a discipline of action, leadership anticipates the responsibilities and tensions of enactment. Since it is rooted in narrative, it draws on this resource to resolve the drama of choice and conflict in the strategies it chooses.

The Reciprocity of Leadership and Management

These thoughts and those that follow reveal another aspect of the relationship between strategic management and strategic leadership. Like all disciplines, including those in applied fields, strategic management gravitates toward methods that are systematic and rational. Its aim is to find a logic of decision making that can be used similarly in all situations. Its methods of design, description, measurement, evaluation, and control tempt it to think of itself as a science of management. In its drive toward a deductive pattern of reasoning, however, it begins to lose intuitive touch with the ever-shifting complexity of the real world, or it tends to become mechanistic and pointlessly elaborate, as we have found in some of the proposed models for strategic planning in higher education.

Strategic leadership does not eliminate the systems and methods of strategic planning and management but reorients their meaning. It places them in the context of human agency rather than rational deduction, of narrative rather than description, thereby creating a discipline of engagement whose intention is ultimately to motivate commitments and actions to fulfill common purposes. Strategic leadership depends on logic, rational decision making, and measurement to provide evidence and establish good reasons for action, but the case it builds is addressed simultaneously to humans as subjects and as responsible agents of choice. As a discipline, it honors the norms of truth and seeks out what is right, but it translates its findings into patterns of enacted sense making and responsibility, not just into decisions or propositions to which one might give just verbal assent. The decisions that flow from strategic leadership follow a logical sequence, but they must as well be adequate to change and unpredictability, to conflict and challenge. They will be able to motivate others only if they relate to the story and values through which individuals and organizations understand themselves and fulfill their purposes.

As we have seen and will see again, although management and leadership are different phenomena, they are intimately related. Management sets the conditions and provides the procedures without which strategic leadership could not function. Yet through the context provided by the larger horizons of leadership, management is able to find greater coherence and purposefulness for its own processes. In the real world, the promptings of leadership usually migrate into management to protect it from becoming deductive and mechanistic. Beyond that implicit relationship, management needs leadership to deal with tasks that are beyond it, including the capacity to motivate people to reach demanding goals.

The Choice of Strategies

From a purely theoretical point of view, there is no reason for a strategic plan not to cover every office and program in a college or university. To develop full-blown strategies for each of a dozen or more major spheres of activity (see "Framework for an Integrative Strategy Process" in chapter 4) and then do the same for five to ten major subcategories in each area is logical but not possible. The results would be a largely unusable catalog of staggering size and complexity that could never be implemented.

Ideally, the selection and development of strategic priorities is a highly disciplined, not expedient, process. This is true both in terms of the rigor and coherence of strategic thinking and the more practical considerations of the form of the final planning document. Colleges and universities have to follow the law of parsimony in developing their strategic initiatives. Time and attention are the scarcest commodities on a campus, and there is no special "research and development" or "project engineering" department for the academic program, and, at best, skeletal ones for the administration. Strategic initiatives often die a quick and ignoble death from neglect because too much has been loaded onto an operational system that is already fully charged. Those with the responsibility to implement the strategies can only correlate, integrate, and control a limited number of priorities. Faculty members in particular are appointed to be teachers and scholars, not strategists.

In describing the characteristics of the eight organizations (including one university) that were recent Baldridge Award winners in the category of effective planning, John Jasinski notes that they were able to "identify a manageable number of strategic objectives (perhaps four to six), tied to inputs that systematically address the challenges that they face" (2004, 29). To be sure, unusual circumstances and institutional variability in size and complexity make any hard-and-fast rules about the number of strategic initiatives ill advised. Yet it is far better to succeed on a small set of essential and manageable initiatives than to flounder over an imaginative but impossible agenda. Thus, it is hard to imagine how most colleges and universities could design and execute more than eight to ten major institution-wide strategic initiatives at one time, assuming that each would contain two or three strategic projects and programs.

To help winnow down the list of potential strategic issues, it should be remembered that important problems that surface in strategy deliberations can be handled through annual operating plans. Further, if the strategy process is continuous, then the annual planning cycle can modify strategies and revise goals to address changing circumstances. If the cycle between intensive forms of planning and reporting is relatively brief—not more than the typical five years—then the campus has a sense that a new round of planning will begin in the foreseeable future. Projects deferred in the past may prove to be top priorities in the next planning cycle. Setting strategy in the context of leadership makes it not only more integrated, but more flexible as well. When leadership is the goal, strategies both individually and collectively require a focus that is logically related to the institution's self-definition. As suggested in the preceding chapter, institutions have to define their strategies around those critical success factors that will provide them with the greatest leverage in reaching the destinations that they have charted for themselves.

LEVELS OF STRATEGY

The effort to develop a disciplined and persuasive set of strategies can be strengthened through the creation of several levels of definition, starting with broad themes, issues, and goals, and moving to specific plans and proposed actions. A content analysis shows that in almost all cases, strategic plans are built explicitly or implicitly around three or four levels of argumentation and explication, although the language used to describe them is very diverse. From the point of view of both the methods of management and leadership, what matters most is the effort to construct strategies through a coherent pattern and sequence of analysis and argumentation. The persuasiveness of a strategy depends on presenting evidence and ideas systematically to show their relationships with each other and the institution's story, purposes, and goals. The force of reason and of information are joined to the resonance of the story and the vision (H. Gardner 2004). Through such an approach, questions are answered before they are asked, tensions are resolved through the dramatic resolution suggested in the narrative, and the logic of the strategies builds on one another to make a persuasive case.

Lest one think that these ideas apply only in the world of higher education, let us note that the planning model of the large industrial materials corporation 3M is based on narrative strategy. 3M's strategic decision making relies on the central business story and principles that differentiate its success, which becomes much more persuasive when presented in narrative form, rather than in a set of bullet points. The narrative form allows people to see themselves in the goals and actions of the plan (Shaw, Brown, and Bromiley 2002).

It is helpful to develop strategy at the four levels of (1) strategic initiatives, (2) strategies, (3) goals, and (4) actions. The terminology used in the literature and in the practice of strategic planning is widely variable and determined by context, though there is almost always a set of terms that parallel the usages proposed here (cf. Bryson 1995; Cope 1985; Hunt, Oosting, Stevens, Loudon, and Migliore 1997; Rowley, Lujan, and Dolence 1997; Ruben 2004b; Sevier 2000). Based on context and usage, it becomes clear that one plan's "strategic initiatives" are another's "strategies," "directions," "themes," "issues," or "goals." What some documents designate simply "strategies," we are differentiating here as "strategic initiatives," and strategic projects and programs as "strategies." In some plans, strategies are designated as "goals" or even "objectives." We, and many others, reserve the word "goal" for a specific and measurable target of opportunity, but the word frequently used for this is "objective." We call the fourth and most specific level "actions," which is the predominant usage, though it is also common to refer to this stage of strategy as "tactics." And so it goes in the terminology of strategy, making it impossible to establish definitive terms of art or usage. The least one can expect, however, is a definition and justification for the terms chosen, as well as a sense of the levels and forms of strategic thinking as a pattern of argumentation.

Table 9.1

STRATEGIC INITIATIVE	A theme that describes one of the major issues, priorities, or aspirations in the strategic plan, consisting of one or more strategies, each of which is defined by goals
Situation Analysis	A rationale that gives the evidence and reasons for the significance of the strategic initiative in terms of the institution's identity, mission, vision, and position
STRATEGIES	A strategic initiative usually has several strategic projects or programs within it. They each define a discrete activity with one or more goals that address one aspect of the larger theme. Each strategy has a rationale and a definable pattern of accountability with measurable goals, designated responsibilities, deadlines, and actions.
GOALS	An aim to achieve results that do not currently exist
Measurement	Goals are determinable and should be subject to various forms of measurement.
Accountability	The achievement of a goal should be assigned explicitly to groups or individuals who are responsible to attain it.
Timeline	The achievement of goals should have milestones and deadlines.
ACTIONS	The specific actions that are required to achieve the goal

An analytical chart (table 9.1) will help to clarify terms and display the relationship of terms, and each will be discussed in the text.

STRATEGIC INITIATIVES AND IMPERATIVES

Strategic initiatives are central strategic themes or issues. They consist of one or several strategies that define projects and programs that are of high priority, both in solving problems and in seizing opportunities. Strategic plans often involve themes like enhancing student engagement in learning, expanding funded research, or internationalizing the curriculum, as strategic initiatives or directions. Each strategic initiative provides a clear rationale or situation analysis that explains the significance of the theme. In effect, each strategic initiative translates identity, mission, vision, and position into a set of several identifiable strategies, which in turn should include measurable goals and specific actions. The realization of the institution's strategic vision is closely tied to the achievement of the goals. Taken together, the strategic initiatives form a coherent set of priorities and designs for the future that have been selected through the various steps and stages of the strategy process.

Why use the word "initiative"? Indeed, many other terms are possible, including, as we shall see, the word "imperative." The use of the word "initiative" accomplishes several things. First, it places a strong emphasis on action since it suggests the self-motivated and intentional exercise of will, effort, and energy. Further, the phrase "strategic initiative" suggests several forms of closely related strategic activities to address an important strategic issue.

A number of institutions have found the expression "strategic imperative" to be especially effective in defining the major priorities in a strategic plan (cf. Baylor University 2002; Bridgewater College 2002; Rhodes College 2003). At one level, it is interchangeable with strategic initiative since it refers to the same type of broad strategic theme and issue. The advantage of the word "imperative" is that it communicates a sense of urgency. It gets and holds people's attention because the language is clear, evocative, and uncompromising. It defines issues that must be addressed if the institution is to fulfill its vision.

This perspective accords well with the motivational intent of strategic leadership, so the term has clear advantages. At the same time, there is danger in over-dramatizing every strategic problem or opportunity. Emotional energy can be spent quickly if everything is always and equally urgent. When used prudently to ignite a sense of authentic concern, the word "imperative" clearly has a place in the lexicon of strategic leadership.

Generally it is best not to define a strategic initiative or imperative by generic areas such as "academic affairs," "the curriculum," "student life," or "finances," unless the term calls to mind a set of activities and priorities that people can easily identify in specific terms. Strategic initiatives are thematic issues that crystallize priorities through careful explanations and arguments as the institution's story, values, and vision are passed through the analysis of its position.

Strategic Initiatives at Brown University

Brown University's "Plan for Academic Enrichment" (2004) discusses ten themes, called "areas of strategic focus," that can serve to illustrate our understanding of strategic initiatives.

- Enhancing undergraduate education
- Excellence in graduate education
- Faculty excellence in teaching and research
- Leadership in biology, medicine, and public health
- Fostering multidisciplinary initiatives
- Enhancing excellence through diversity
- Building a shared sense of community
- Diversifying and expanding the university's sources of revenue
- Collaborating with the local community on Iissues of mutual interest and benefit
- Enhancing the quality of our facilities, infrastructure, and administrative support

In Brown's lexicon, each of these initiatives is translated into a set of "specific objectives" (we would call these strategies or goals), which is followed by a set of illustrative "Proposals" that represent, to us, a mixture of goals and actions. The different levels in the presentation succeed on the whole in communicating several differentiated stages of definition, assisting Brown to articulate a clear and ambitious direction for the future. Yet, because so many of the "proposals" are actually goals ("ensure competitive staff salaries and benefits," "enhance and expand research facilities,") that are not accompanied by measurable indicators, the plan loses some of its focus, sense of actionable sequence, and persuasiveness.

It is clear, however, that Brown's ten areas of strategic focus are intended to play the critical role of translating the university's story, mission, and vision into a set of priorities that define specific strategies, plans, and needs. Brown's vision is to maintain and to strengthen its preeminent position among American universities in fulfillment of its mission as a university-college, and its strategic initiatives play the pivotal role in giving definition to that ambition (Brown University 2004).

Levels of Strategy at Monnet University

To examine more of the dynamics of strategic thinking in a leadership context, it will be helpful to look at examples of the way that it can orient decision making at all four levels of strategic definition, starting with a situation analysis of a given issue. Then, at appropriate places later in the text, we will examine other illustrations of ways to craft strategic goals and actions. We will use Monnet University, a hypothetical institution that reflects real-world characteristics and has chosen to focus on international education as one of its strategic priorities. (This example is drawn from my personal involvement in international education in several institutions and in study abroad, and influenced in a general way by two excellent reports (Jenkins 2002; National Association of State Universities and Land-Grant Colleges 2004).

Position Statement

Monnet University is a small private university in a coastal city in the Northwest of the United States that enrolls 3,500 undergraduate and 500 graduate students. It sees itself as carrying a legacy of regional leadership and educational innovation based on a strong sense of collegial decision making. With excellent resources and a strong admissions profile, it has developed high aspirations for its future. During the early stages of a new planning cycle, it has tentatively decided that one of its six strategic initiatives will be international education. Reflecting views that are widely shared on campus, it has included the development of student global awareness and competency as an explicit aspect of it educational mission.

Strategic Initiative

As the plan begins to take shape, the SPC decides that it will take a distinctly strategic approach to defining its ambitions in international education. Its SWOT analysis has developed evidence to show that the quality and scope of its work in international education make it a distinguishing capability of the institution and a competitive advantage. After inviting response to the idea with several faculty audiences and the administration, the SPC concludes that it will propose that Monnet should develop international education as one of its defining core competencies, and that it should seek to gain national recognition for the quality and scope of its programs and capabilities.

Situation Analysis

Based on the work of its task force on international education, the SPC provides a brief rationale for the strategic initiative and the goal that it recommends. It places its thinking squarely in the context of the university's identity, mission, and vision and demonstrates the appropriateness of the commitment to develop students who will be able to think coherently and act responsibly in a global context. The situation analysis characterizes the strengths of the existing international programs and notes that the faculty and staff no longer think of international education as the responsibility of only two or three departments. The university's success is also traced to the ways that both academic and administrative programs have developed formal as well as informal procedures and practices to create a system and a culture that integrates international students and faculty members into campus life. The SPC emphasizes that Monnet can create a core competency precisely because it has shown a distinctive ability to deploy its resources and mobilize its abilities to integrate an international orientation into all its educational programs. The SPC's report is itself an effort to present a systematic and integrative argument that is supported by the organizational story, factual evidence, demonstrable university capacities and commitments, and documented challenges and opportunities.

Strategies: Programs and Projects

The SPC's report presents eight strategies for the development of international education into a core competency: (1) a continuing program of faculty development that provides the opportunity to study foreign languages and cultures and to participate in annual travel seminars sponsored by Monnet and its consortium; (2) the establishment of a much-enlarged interdisciplinary international studies major with several new area concentrations and international themes, replacing the single-track concentration currently in place; (3) the appointment of a new dean of global studies; (4) the expanded study of five additional foreign languages both abroad and through the use of Web sites, audiovisual study materials, and tutors on campus; (5) the enlargement of the undergraduate enrollment of international students, including both exchange students and degree candidates, to 15 percent of the student body; (6) an increase in study abroad participation by Monnet students to 80 percent of the student body in programs of eight weeks or longer; (7) a plan to add both continuing faculty members and visiting faculty members who have international backgrounds or have been trained in other countries, so that every large program or department has at least one such an appointment; and (8) a plan to integrate an international focus into campus events, lectures, and arts programs through the establishment of a new Institute of Global Studies that will also have the authority to appoint visiting international faculty and artists.

Goals and Actions

Through carefully defined goals, measures, deadlines, accountabilities, and proposed actions (several of which will be illustrated below) for each of these strategies, the strategic initiative in international education develops a comprehensive set of dimensions.

The Monnet case describes an ambitious strategic initiative that touches many facets of the university's academic and administrative life, and that has important implications for the way it will use its resources. Several characteristics of strategic thinking and leadership are in evidence. The proposed improvements to the program are built on the passion and commitment of many members of the university community. They take root in an authentic set of beliefs and values about how the university can excel, based on a narrative of accomplishments in which people take legitimate pride. The conditions are in place to build motivation for the initiative based on a strong strategic foundation. The leadership task of inspiring new levels of attainment is enabled by integrative and systemic patterns of thought and argumentation, which are supported by the different types of evidence that are presented in the narrative of the strategic initiative. The argumentation becomes even more pointed and persuasive when translated into goals, actions, and accountabilities.

STRATEGIC GOALS

As we consider the place of strategic goals within strategies, we have to reckon with the fact that many campus strategic plans are light on measurable goals. Goals are often expressed in general terms unaccompanied by any form of measurement, milestones, or deadlines. Sometimes a set of more determinable goals can be found in accompanying reports or in documents that do not circulate widely, but they are not usually commanding features of collegiate plans.

The resistance to define strategies by measurable goals is understandable in many contexts but remains a significant strategic weakness. It also defies the advice of those who study and write about the best practices of strategic planning in higher education (Coleman 2004; Hunt, Oosting, Stevens, Loudon, and Migliore 1997; Rowley, Lujan, and Dolence 1997; Ruben 2004b; Sevier 2000). The flaw surely reflects some of the characteristics of collegiate culture and governance that we have examined from several angles, including the lack of top-down authority, the uncertainty of resources, political infighting over priorities, and the inability or the unwillingness to take responsibility for the organization's future.

Whatever the explanation, much of the influence of the strategy process, especially as a tool of leadership, is lost if systematic vagueness characterizes its goals, understood here as specifiable objectives. An effective strategy process should challenge this conventional practice by differentiating and clarifying the issues. Correctly defined, strategic goals motivate people to achieve them, especially if they incorporate central aspects of the vision of the institution and are understood to be testable hypotheses, not rigid formulae. They can function as powerful tools of continuous leadership and management, of motivation and accountability, and of learning and self-discovery.

Characteristics of Goals

Whatever else they do, goals announce an intention to achieve desirable results or create positive conditions that do not currently exist. What we set as a goal cannot be reached by the normal course of events, or the continuation of regular operational decisions, but requires a special set of initiatives, choices, actions, and efforts. Goals are by nature aspirational and uncertain. Included in the very idea of a goal is an element of risk that we might not achieve the desired results.

As most commentators suggest, goals should represent a challenge, but one that is attainable (Sevier 2000). To propose too lofty an ambition is to create frustration that leads to cynicism about the process or the institution. To create goals that do not require people to stretch realistically is to fall short of the institution's best possibilities. Once again, goals embody the institution's story and the vision and share in the tension between aspiration and reality, between dreams and their fulfillment. They embody both leadership and management in everyday decisions.

The Measurement of Goals

Setting a goal carries with it a need to know whether or not progress is being made or success has been achieved in reaching it. The measurement of what we intend to achieve is a given condition of its being meaningful as a goal. Absent some form of determination, the mind boggles over the very meaning of the term. Perhaps the measurement is difficult or complex or depends on a series of indirect indicators, but without it, the word "goal" does not seem to be the right one to describe that to which we aspire. Our movement toward the future through goal-directed behavior has its own forms of intelligibility, among which is that goals are determinable.

To suggest that strategic goals must be measurable does not mean that they are all quantifiable, or if quantifiable, that results are equivalent to objective scientific facts. If, for example, a college intends to develop a program to heighten its students' commitment to democratic citizenship, it cannot measure the influence of its efforts by the strictest canons of scientific cause and effect. Rather, it will do well to establish a series of indicators, such as involvement in volunteer service or participation in the political process, that serve as proxies for its goals. Although interviews and questionnaires are always limited by their subjective nature, a systematic use of student self-assessments can provide reliable information about experiences related to civic values and responsibilities. As we shall see in a subsequent chapter, the ability to implement strategic goals depends heavily on their being subject to assessment.

Nor does the measurement of goals suggest that they must be mechanistic and inflexible. In the context of strategic leadership, they reflect the larger possibilities of the organization and connect to the drama of its story. Goals represent ways of testing the validity of the strategy they are intended to enact. If problems are found in reaching goals, there is much to be learned from the failure and the frustration of the effort. The problems may lie in tactics that can be changed or adjusted, or the difficulties may be deeper and reveal weaknesses in the strategy itself. Perhaps the goal was poorly crafted, and its intent is being fulfilled in other ways. Whatever the problem, the measurement of goals produces invaluable forms of learning for the ongoing work of strategy.

Effective Goal Setting

Even when goals are easily and relevantly quantifiable, many institutions do not seize the opportunity to develop effective measures. One often encounters vague goals in planning documents, such as this one from a small southern college: "Increase the proportion of alumni participation in the annual fund." After careful study and definition of the strategic intent of the goal and the operational issues it involves have been conducted, it makes eminent sense to define a specific level of alumni participation as a goal. In doing so, the organization benefits in a number of ways. It is forced to examine the strengths and weaknesses of its fund-raising operations and to explore alumni attitudes as a critical part of its narrative of identity. When a goal has been properly crafted, an organization can confidently put itself on public record with what it intends to accomplish. A goal that captures the institution's authentic possibilities provides a powerful form of motivation that operates continuously to shape people's imaginations and daily choices. It builds a sense of individual and collective leadership and accountability, which are critical components of the total strategic leadership process.

The creation of effective goals to serve the ends of leadership is a demanding task. Even quantifiable goals can be subject to manipulation, so they require careful and thoughtful definition. A steel factory, for example, may successfully meet its goal to reduce scrap, only to find that its percentage of on-time deliveries declines as workers take longer to complete each order. Or the college that defines 50 percent as a goal for alumni giving may find itself flooded by $10 contributions. Without careful consideration of the goal, staff time can be drawn away from attending to gifts from larger donors, so as participation rates climb, total giving could drop.

These eventualities suggest that effective goal setting requires disciplined analysis. The place to begin is always with the strategic intent of the goal as defined in the rationale for the strategic initiative or project of which it is a part. As a consequence, it may be helpful to use a series of quantifiable measures to avoid distortion of the goal. So, for example, the goal to raise alumni giving to 50 percent should be one of a series of interrelated goals that might include the overall totals of cash gifts and contributions from major donors, and the size of the median gift from individuals. People working in the trenches need to understand the strategic intent of the goals they are responsible for fulfilling. When they do, and as measurements match intent, goals are far less likely to be distorted and more likely to become a source of motivation.

Accountability for Goals

Another crucial part of any strategy is the establishment of accountability and deadlines for the achievement of goals. These elements are often omitted in collegiate strategy reports and documents. With the omission, there is a loss of the focus, motivation, and expectation that can come from a public definition of responsibility. Once a person or a team has accepted responsibility for a goal, a new dynamic takes hold. In a healthy organizational culture, people feel intensely responsible to one another and depend on each other to reach common objectives. Having responsibility for a goal releases energy and commitment, born of both the satisfaction that comes from achievement and the fulfillment of sharing in a common enterprise. On the side of negative motivation, the desire to avoid looking bad to one's colleagues and to stakeholders is not unimportant. The willingness and capacity to take initiative and responsibility is one of the defining elements at the core of a reciprocal and dispersed process of leadership.

Strategic Accountability at Villanova University

Villanova University has shown its commitment to achieving its twelve strategic goals (the equivalent of what we have named strategic initiatives) by naming goal attainment teams to monitor progress in reaching each of them. The teams include the faculty and staff members who are in the most logical position to assess and influence the goals. One member of the team is also on the university's primary planning body, which is comprised of academic deans and senior administrators. The charge to the teams is "to concentrate on a specific goal in order to monitor progress, facilitate and suggest strategies for actualizing goals, and in other ways to enhance goal-driven strategic planning" (Kelley and Trainer 2004, 99).

Goals and Deadlines

Nor can accountability function effectively without time-defined goals. Deadlines have a marvelous ability to focus the mind. Especially in academic communities, where strict deadlines for curricular projects are not customary, they are essential ingredients in strategic thinking and planning. They build a sense of urgency for both individuals and groups, especially committees. For groups in particular, they create a sense of shared reality and motivation. Deadlines and time lines also help to create a sense of systemic connection between and among strategic initiatives and diverse goals. Projects lead logically from one to another, from one initiative to the next. The connections between goals, the achievement of which is facilitated by differential deadlines and timetables, become a crucial dimension in the creation of strategic momentum.

Strategic Academic Goals

Students of strategic planning might logically suggest that measurable goals, explicit accountabilities, and timetables make sense in the administrative, but not the academic, sphere. Although there are major differences between the two decision-making systems, explicit goals are relevant and important in both arenas. The effectiveness of goals that relate to academic programs and to teaching and learning depend on a variety of aspects of the strategy process that we have emphasized. An academic strategic initiative needs to be described carefully in terms of the external or internal factors that are prompting a proposed change. The rationale for change sets the conditions that a new or revised program must meet in order to satisfy broader strategic aspirations. The connection to other strategic issues and opportunities should be made explicit. As we saw in the example of Monnet University, if international studies is to become an extensive new major, the goals of the undertaking need to be explicitly tied to the environmental scan, the capacities and interests of students and faculty, the availability of learning resources, and the ways other academic and university programs will contribute to it and be strengthened by it.

As we have suggested above and in our earlier description of the role of the SPC, recommendations for academic programs that emerge from the strategy process will eventually have to be shaped, considered, and approved by the appropriate faculty committees and decision-making bodies in order to be implemented. In this case, its consideration will have the benefit of the analysis to which it has been subjected in the planning process. The recommendation comes to the academic decision-making body accompanied by a clear strategic rationale, with many of the essential issues already addressed. By returning to the example of Monnet University, we can expand on the case in terms of the way the creation of an enlarged interdisciplinary major in international studies would be appropriately fashioned.

After the governing board endorses the strategic plan, the president asks the provost to send the recommendation to the Monnet University curriculum committee, along with the report of the SPC task force on international education. The provost calls the committee's attention to the strategic initiative on international education, and in particular to the rationale and the goal related to the proposed new multi-track interdisciplinary major. Since the curriculum committee has been involved in deliberations about the strategic plan and is considering other interdisciplinary programs based on it, it is well versed in the general issues. The strategic plan's goal concerning the proposed major reads as follows: "The curriculum committee should develop the requirements for an enlarged and reformulated interdisciplinary program major in international studies that will include six new concentrations. In collaboration with the interdisciplinary international studies faculty group and the dean of global studies, it should consider the rationale and characteristics described in the enclosed report. The proposal is expected to be ready for final action by the end of the current academic year, at which time the curriculum committee and the dean of global studies will present the recommendations to the faculty."

In some colleges and universities, the statement of a goal in this way would be novel since it involves a formal authoritative recommendation on a curricular question initially coming to, rather than from, a faculty committee. Moreover, it establishes explicit accountabilities and deadlines for a faculty committee and for named academic officers. Although these steps may not appear customary, in point of fact, administrative and faculty leaders often use parallel but less formal methods of leadership, consensus building, problem solving, and political influence to move issues onto the agendas of academic decision-making bodies.

As a method of strategic leadership, the approach is appropriate and responsible. It sets an agenda through a legitimate strategy process that is part of the total governance system. It defines goals to be achieved within a given time frame and holds specified groups and individuals responsible to do so. As a consequence, it builds a sense of focus and urgency. Yet it does so in ways that respect shared governance and the professional judgment of the members of the curriculum committee. Professional responsibility is a powerful resource that can be elicited and given coherence by strategic leadership, or it can work in fits and starts as part of a fragmented decision-making process. Alternatively, as often happens it can be alienated by real or perceived administrative arbitrariness or bureaucratic controls. Goals that define academic issues in time-wise strategic terms with designated accountability can create a sense of purposefulness and responsibility that may otherwise be difficult to achieve.

Change in the academic sphere is the test case for the effectiveness of strategic leadership, and the issues come into sharpest focus in initiatives that propose new or revised programs of study or methods of teaching and learning. As has become clear in this example, strategic decision making and leadership in the academic sphere must reflect possibilities that are rooted in the actual or potential interests and capabilities of the faculty. As Burton Clark suggests, the "viability [of academic institutions] does not depend on the capacity of top-down commands to integrate parts into an organizational whole," as it does in hierarchical organizations (1987, 268). Strategic leadership recognizes that academic change almost invariably moves from the bottom up. The responsibility of leadership, whether official or unofficial, is to define educational issues, to motivate, to challenge, to support, and to integrate emergent academic possibilities into the institution's strategic priorities.

ACTIONS

The fourth dimension of strategy is the development of a series of proposed tactics or actions, often called action steps. Once again the language used in strategic plans to differentiate "actions" from "goals" or "objectives" is not very precise. One often finds that strategic plans do not differentiate effectively between the terms,; long lists of purported goals or objectives often look more like specific actions. To sort out the usage, it seems appropriate to call an action a specific decision, choice, or specifiable activity undertaken to support the achievement of a broader goal. In most cases an action also tends to fall within the authority and available resources of an individual or group. There is less risk, constraint, or uncertainty in achieving it than the more inclusive goal that it supports and enacts. Besides defining a broader scope of accomplishment than actions, goals are more transparently strategic, while actions are more operational. Clearly, there is also a stronger volitional and broader motivational aspect to a goal than an action step.

Using the example of alumni-giving rates, we can see some of the concrete differences between goals and actions. The goal of raising alumni participation depends on actions such as gathering more e-mail and residential addresses, finding current phone numbers, installing up-to-date software, using the alumni Web page creatively, organizing the staff, and creating better annual fund publications. In many ways, the proposed actions test the validity of a goal and reveal the true dimensions of its possibilities. Where suggested actions may encounter resistance or require new resources, we quickly find ourselves dealing with the strategic meaning of the broader goal. Alumni participation is related to the strategic effort to build more resources for the long term, but also to other actions to enhance the total alumni relations effort. It may require new initiatives to build alumni involvement in career networks, student recruitment, social events, and continuing education and travel programs. Strategically, higher rates of alumni giving not only provide more resources but may respond to expectations of potential major donors such as foundations and enhance the institution's profile with the media and in various rankings.

Testing Proposed Strategic Goals and Actions at Monnet

If we return to Monnet, we notice some other important aspects of actions and goals that relate to the central question of resources and priorities. As we have seen, as Monnet develops its goals on the enrollment of international students, it sets a target of 15 percent, comprised of two-thirds degree candidates and one-third single-semester or year-long exchange students. Since Monnet does not offer graduate programs in science, technology, or business, which generally attract the largest proportion of international students, its goal—essentially to double the international enrollment in five years—is a demanding one. The dean of admissions, the dean of global studies, and the provost are responsible for achieving the goal.

During the development of the actions that will be required to reach the goal, it becomes clear that the project will be expensive. The resource projections include $1.4 million for financial aid increases over four years. A new position and additional travel expenses in admissions plus two new staff members and program expenses in global studies will add $250,000 to the budget. As the costs of these actions steps are defined, they are assessed within the strategic plan's financial model and ideas are explored for their funding. It is projected that the current operating budget can only absorb $750,000 of the costs over five years. The ability to support another $500,000 through annual and endowment gifts is a stretch possibility, but a worthy target, since the project will be attractive to many donors. It will be made a focus of the proposed capital campaign. The remaining needs cannot be met, so a number of the actions relating to staffing, financial aid strategies, and the geographic mix of international students are redesigned to fit the projected resources of $1.25 million that will be available incrementally over five years. The goal remains in place.

Clearly, the differentiation of goals from actions is an important and useful exercise in the total planning process, and a task that merits more careful thought than it often receives. As suggested, it provides a way for the plausibility of goals to be tested, especially concerning the resources that they will require. The effectiveness of strategic planning as a discipline depends in good measure on the precision, the coherence, and the integration of the various methods, insights, and concepts that it uses.

Presenting Actions in Reports

We should also keep in mind several cautions concerning the use of lists of action steps in strategic plans. Sometimes one finds reports that are filled with a potpourri of tactics and proposed actions, including everything from repainting the faculty lounge to adding new part-time staff. The source of these loosely related proposed actions is usually the reports of subcommittees or task forces and suggestions that people have offered at some point during the group's deliberations. Committee chairs are often reluctant to drop them for the sake of political goodwill, even though they may represent the special interests of those who proposed them. The SPC should carefully winnow down proposed lists of actions in any reports that it intends to circulate widely, scrutinizing and systematizing but not eliminating them. In doing so, its aim should be to find tactics and actions that test, illustrate, and give concreteness to the main themes and content of the strategic vision and of the plan's major initiatives. The reports that include detailed action steps can be circulated among those who will be responsible for implementing the strategy, for they are an important source of ideas at the operational level, and they are a useful control mechanism.

If strategic initiatives and imperatives, strategies, goals, and actions are each developed carefully and artfully, they provide reinforcement to one another. They build a case for action through the construction of a disciplined and affecting argument. Each of the facets of the strategy speaks to the mind's need and the person's desire for direction, purpose, coherence, and definition. A good strategy contains an inner logic of sense making and sense giving that draws its audience of participants and interested parties into a coherent and intelligible pattern of analysis, reflection, judgment, and choice. It communicates credibility and invites commitment, and it does so through the ways its strategies, goals, and actions convey a compelling narrative of challenge and opportunity.

CHAPTER 10

Strategic Leadership in Context: From Academic Programs to Financial Models

Thus far I have described and illustrated several of the key components of the strategy process. Ultimately each institution has to bring these methods to bear on specific areas of organizational responsibility. The actual content of strategic initiatives, goals, and actions is determined by the planning that occurs within the different spheres of each institution's diverse activities, from academic to financial affairs. As a result, there is no way to import detailed strategic content from external sources. The story, vision, contextual position, and deliberative processes of each college and university are embedded in a unique identity, so strategic content has to be grown at home.

While giving full weight to uniqueness, it is still possible to highlight the general features of strategic leadership as different organizational operations and programs come to terms with the changing world around them. In doing so, we shall examine briefly and selectively the way strategic leadership differentially shapes the consideration of:

- Academic programs
- Student learning
- General education
- Admissions
- Student life
- Facilities planning
- Financial resources
- Fund-raising

In analyzing these areas, the goal is to answer basic contextual questions that may be on the minds of those leading or participating in a strategy process. What difference does a strategic orientation make in approaching issues in various contexts? What are some of the most telling strategic challenges and opportunities facing institutions in today's world? Within what frameworks of thought should issues be situated and analyzed? To anticipate some of our findings, we shall regard the tracings of strategic leadership as an applied and integrative discipline in the ways that it is contextual and analytical, conceptual and data driven, integrative and systemic, value centered and action oriented, and motivational and collaborative.

STRATEGIC THINKING AND ACADEMIC QUALITY

For many of the reasons that we have analyzed, the introduction of an authentic strategic perspective is an especially demanding task in the sphere of academic specialties. Consider the ways in which we ordinarily think about the quality of academic departments. Let us do so by examining the profile of two history programs inspired by actual models, one in a major university and the other in a very small college. The comprehensive undergraduate history program at a large regional research university with a departmental faculty of fifty-four offers five majors, eight program concentrations, and 110 courses. Its faculty is well published and many of its members are widely recognized, two of its specialties are in the top twenty-five in graduate program rankings, and it attracts talented doctoral students, though it is much less selective in some fields than it would like. Most of the lower-division courses are large lecture classes supported by teaching assistants, the courses for majors enroll thirty to forty students, and honors students take a senior seminar. The number and quality of its undergraduate majors have declined moderately in the last decade, though most students perceive history to be a popular program that makes moderate demands.

Consider next the history department at a small liberal arts college that has a solid reputation in its region. With a faculty of five, it offers a single major with concentrations in European or American history. Its largest class enrolls twenty-five students, its entire faculty is full time, and it places a major emphasis on the use of original texts and documents in all its classes. Its majors have always been among the most talented students at the college, and it has a reputation for being a demanding department.

The realities of institutional mission, culture, size, and resources have shaped two radically different history departments, even though there are some formal parallels between them in courses and requirements. As we compare the two programs strictly with the professional eye of a historian, we have to judge the small college's program to be marginal in quality and viability. It is very weak in scope, in depth, and in the professional reputations of its faculty. In terms of disciplinary measures, one cannot begin to compare the comprehensive range, depth, and prominence—that is, the quality—of the university program with the impoverished version that exists in the college.

Yet as we turn our attention to the culture of student learning in the small college's department, other characteristics come to the surface. We learn that many of the leading graduates of the college studied history, and that a dispropor- tionate number of them, including several eminent historians, went on to earn doctorates in the field. Whenever these graduates tell their stories, they consis- tently note that their professors required them to learn history by doing it—by studying original texts and documents, writing countless interpretive papers, and participating constantly in discussions and presentations in small classes. Their teachers held them to rigorous standards but also encouraged them. Faculty mem- bers often became mentors to students and interacted with them frequently both in and out of class. The faculty's narrative of academic quality concentrates on the character and depth of student learning. They hold themselves to these values and make professional decisions in terms of this understanding of quality.

These cases allow us to raise an impertinent question. Which of the two under- graduate history programs is of higher quality? Which one creates more educa- tional value for students? The answer depends, of course, on the values that a person privileges in his or her understanding of academic quality. In the college, educational worth is measured by student learning as intellectual engagement and transformation, while in the university, quality is defined around the creation of knowledge. For most of us, the question brings up a series of conflicts in academic purposes that can never be entirely resolved, but that can be reconciled through effective leadership.

Although it seems deceptively basic, the strategic articulation of principles of educational worth is a difficult task for most disciplines. This is so because it is often carried out, as we have seen, in a context defined by the internal criteria of an academic specialty alone or is imposed by an external management system. When disciplinary logic encounters managerial logic, the tensions are inescap- able. Although the transition to a broader pattern of reflection is initially chal- lenging, when a program's educational rationale is explicitly connected to the more inclusive aims of liberal education and student learning, to special institu- tional characteristics and capabilities, and to changing methods of the discipline and the needs in society at large, the process becomes more strategically vital and fruitful (Association of American Colleges and Universities 2004). As these steps occur, the model shifts from emphasizing the requirements of management to focusing on the responsibilities of collaborative strategic leadership.

STRATEGIC LEADERSHIP AND POWERFUL LEARNING

The purpose of strategic leadership is to look inside and outside an institution simultaneously and to align the two perspectives. As it searches for the structural trends in contemporary higher education, it finds some markers that should rivet its attention. One of these is the intensifying focus on student learning. Long- simmering changes in the methods of teaching and learning have taken form as a self-conscious movement. There is a growing preoccupation with the nature of learning itself, with what and how students learn in ways that are motivating, enduring, and powerful (Association of American Colleges and Universities 2002; Bok 2006; Gaff, Ratcliff, et al. 1997; Kuh, Kinzie, Schuh, Whitt, et al. 2005; Levine 2006).

Engagement in Learning

Common in many expressions of the learning movement is a focus on student engagement—on forms of teaching and learning that make a successful claim on the interest, energy, and motivation of the student. The emphasis is on ways the student becomes personally engaged in a process of learning. The implied contrast is with learning that is passive, in which the student receives knowledge and information from a teacher. In engaged learning, students are agents more than observers, makers of meaning rather than recipients of information (Morrill 2002).

Learning as the Development of Human Powers

One of the critical presuppositions of this intensified focus on learning is that liberal education has to do with the development of deep and enduring intellectual and personal abilities. One commonly finds that institutions express their rationale for liberal education in terms of the development of complex cognitive abilities such as critical, analytical, and integrative thinking; effective communication; global and multicultural awareness; and technological and quantitative literacy (Bok 2006). Included as well are intellectual dispositions and values such as curiosity, mental resilience, and imagination as well as commitments to the values of an open society.

From the perspective of strategic leadership, more important than these lists is the unspoken presupposition that liberal education has to do with the development of fundamental human powers, the enhancement of the intellectual and moral capacities through which the human project itself unfolds. In tracing the evolution of liberal education at the University of Chicago, Donald Levine (2006) finds and formulates the inner logic in its concern to develop the multifaceted powers of mind. As Thomas Green suggests, "Coming into possession of the powers that we have as human beings . . . is the defining presence of educational worth" (1982, 182). So, engaged learning is also powerful learning because it intends to make a compelling difference in the ways that humans as agents create meaning and act in the world.

Why does any of this matter for the strategy process? It does not if strategic planning is simply a discipline of the market. To contribute to academic leadership, strategy has to be integral; it must connect with the deepest purposes of the organization as it has been shaped in response to the context in which it lives. For a college or university to understand its differentiating characteristics, it has to know what it believes in, what it intends its education to be, and how it can create for its time and place the practices and conditions on which powerful student learning depends. It has to ask itself continually what it means to be an educated person, and in the plurality of answers to that question, it must reflect on the center of educational gravity in its own methods and programs. It especially has to do this in a time when liberal education is neglected and misunderstood. Is liberal learning about information or knowledge, methods or content, the powers of the mind or the habits of the heart, or what? How does it relate to the unrelenting demand of society for a well-trained workforce and of students for careers? (Bok 2006). In pursuing this inquiry, the institution has to consider where, if anywhere, it has developed generative core competencies that distinguish it from others and that deeply mark its programs and its environment for learning. A review and self-assessment of the following list of some of the components of powerful learning will help institutions see what characteristics of learning truly set them apart and understand strategically where they excel or should or could excel (cf. Association of American Colleges and Universities 2002).

The Characteristics of Powerful Learning

Powerful learning is:

- **Transformative:** It intends to develop human intellectual powers, moral capacities, and personal abilities at fundamental levels and in enduring forms.

- **Intentional:** It help students become aware of the interconnected aims and results of liberal and professional education and learn how they can design their studies to connect in purposeful ways with their own goals.

- **Engaged:** It involves students in learning actively through collaboration, discussion, writing, speaking, performing, doing research, leading projects and presentations, and forming relationships with teachers who have high expectations.

- **Global:** It involves students in the study of other languages, cultures, and societies, optimally through living and studying in another country.

- **Broad:** It requires students to master content, methods of reasoning, and ways of solving problems in a variety of fields and disciplines.

- **Coherent:** It designs and presents programs of study with a clear rationale and goals that connect themes, courses, and learning experiences in meaningful and explicit patterns, both in general education and in the major.

- **Useful:** It demonstrates how cognitive powers and knowledge are deeply practical in preparing students for employment and civic responsibilities.

- **Inclusive:** It features programs that address the diversity of human experience and cultures as enriching educational resources.

- **Integrative:** It encourages an understanding of the relationship of fields and disciplines in the study of intellectual, moral, and social issues and offers programs based on interdisciplinary and integrative methods.

- **Enriched:** It draws upon a wide variety of resources, including facilities, technologies, scientific instrumentation, books and periodicals, cultural events, and local organizations.

- **Technological:** It uses information technology to draw on the new universe of Web-based knowledge to develop computer literacy and to make learning and communication continual, global, interactive, and motivating.

- **Experiential:** It uses a variety of ways to involve students in learning through experience in service projects, internships, and field research, closely coordinating theory and practice.

- **Responsible:** It prepares students to understand and to act on their responsibilities in a democratic society and fosters their commitment to its basic values.

- **Substantive:** It explores the structure, methods, languages, and content of various disciplines and bodies of knowledge and uses landmark original texts and materials in doing so.

- **Rigorous:** It sets exacting standards and has high expectations concerning both the quality and the quantity of student educational achievements.

- **Assessed:** It uses a multiple set of methods to evaluate the effectiveness of learning and feeds these results into the teaching and learning process to improve future performance.

- **Encompassing:** It occurs in many campus contexts and relationships both in and out of the classroom and is strengthened by an ethos that carries, communicates, and reinforces a clear and strong set of consistent messages about the institution's identity and educational purposes and practices.

Strategic Thinking and Powerful Learning

The effort to evaluate which forms of learning are most in evidence at an institution is a rewarding strategic task, and the preceding list of characteristics offers a place to start. Groups of faculty and staff in a strategy process can analyze and map their own institutions and programs by asking several questions about each characteristic: Which most resonate with our narrative of educational identity and quality? Where are we now, and where would we like to be in the future? Where are we deficient, where adequate? Which of these forms of learning are distinguishing characteristics? Are there any that are or could become core competencies? What strategies and goals would move us forward? The process of analysis should stir the interest of many faculty and staff members, for it offers a systematic template for defining issues about which they care deeply.

In the process of discussing and evaluating its culture and characteristics, an institution begins to gain a clear sense of its own identity and its vision as a community of learning. Its self-evaluation should be realistic and recognize that generally no more than several of its characteristics can become core competencies. The discussion should also be guided by all the forms of available evidence, such as a content analysis of its academic programs and practices, its results on the National Survey of Student Engagement, and other forms of assessment and strategic evaluation.

One of important affirmations in this book is that the character and quality of student learning are a central strategic issue. The study by George Kuh and his associates (2005), *Student Success in College*, shows the intimate connection between student learning and this wider view of strategy, even though the authors do not use that term in describing their findings. As we have already seen, the study describes the characteristics of twenty campuses whose graduation rates and engaged learning practices exceed what would be expected in terms of their institutional and student profiles. The colleges present features that bear directly on aspects of strategic leadership because, among other things, they demonstrate: a "living" mission and "lived" educational philosophy, an unshakeable focus on student learning, an improvement-oriented ethos, and a sense of shared responsibility for educational quality and student success. Moreover, they each embody a strong culture and highly resonant identity that marks out paths for student success and an environment that enriches student learning. The leadership of these institutions is also focused on student learning both in terms of the actions of those in positions of authority and as distributed in processes and relationships throughout the organization. In our terms, the narratives, values, and visions of these colleges and universities are expressed in their organizational cultures, programs, and collaborative practices, all of which are sustained through a distributed process of strategic leadership.

Perhaps it is no clearer than in the sphere of student learning that official leaders are often followers in strategic leadership. Teachers and students take the lead in shaping the practices of engaged learning, which those in academic leadership positions may then help to clarify, systematize, and support. In the sphere of teaching and learning, the idea that strategy emerges from practice is entirely apt and accurate. When the University of Richmond issued its strategy report entitled *Engagement in Learning* in the mid-1990s, it chose a theme that arose from the educational practices that were emerging in and outside its classrooms. The strategic consciousness of those practices arose in dialogue with faculty members and students who shared with the planning committee their uses of collaborative learning, interactive classes, experiential learning, study abroad, service learning, and student research. The report carried a title and explored themes that would soon emerge prominently in the wider conversation in higher education.

General Education

One of the places where the strategic analysis of student learning should concentrate is general education (cf. Gaff, Ratcliff, et al. 1997). Because it occurs at the intersection of a series of defining organizational commitments, it is a quintessential strategic issue. To begin, general education typically represents a major investment of institutional resources. Its special courses and requirements draw heavily on faculty time and energy and require a large number of faculty positions. In most institutions, more than half of a student's first two years of study are devoted to general education, so its influence on a student's early educational experience is often decisive. Typically a student makes some form of intellectual connection with the campus during these years or may never do so. Thus, the relationship to retention and enrollment is crucial. Most importantly, many institutions explicitly define the meaning of liberal education around the purposes of their general education programs.

In terms of the motif of powerful learning, it is often in general education that institutions make explicit their distinguishing characteristics, core competencies, educational values, and credos. In the course of the work on the Association of American Colleges and Universities' *Greater Expectations* (2002), it became clear that institutions were increasingly tying their general education programs to their special characteristics and competencies. A college or a university's distinctive academic profile in teaching, curriculum, and research was translated into ways to engage students in coherent, intentional, and integrative forms of general education.

As we consider strategic leadership in the context of student learning and general education, we see the depths to which it must reach. It must draw on the institution's most powerful conceptual resources in order to address comprehensive educational questions. In working on general education, faculty members and academic administrators have to be encouraged and enabled to be educators, not just field-specific experts. It may appear odd that institutions committed to higher learning need to focus on the conceptual foundations of programs of study, but that is a requirement of strategic leadership. A well-founded, distinctive, and rich program of powerful learning in general education and throughout the undergraduate curriculum and co-curriculum brings into focus an institution's specific educational capacities, reflecting its story, values, and identity. It creates a sense of common enterprise and seeks to involve students and faculty in the experience of a true educational community. If this intense focus on learning is to be sustained, faculty as educators need to reach periodically for the best current literature on student learning, study model programs, and continue to think deeply and coherently about educational design and execution, all in terms of a differentiated concept of quality (cf. Bok 2006; Levine 2006). Such is the nature of strategic thinking in the academic sphere. As a form of leadership, it moves through conflicts and disagreements to find the shared values and concepts to which people are willing to make commitments.

ADMISSIONS: BRANDS OR STORIES?

As we have seen, many practitioners of strategy locate the core of the process in the way an organization differentially positions its products and services in a competitive marketplace. In consumer products companies, the analytical and quantitative methods of marketing have become the queen of the business sciences and drive much of the corporation's strategy. Some of these same trends have migrated to the campus. In sharp contrast, we have located the strategy process at a deeper level by rooting it in collegiate narratives of identity and aspiration. In today's world the contrasts between these two starting points often show up most vividly in the work of admissions offices.

The strategic plans of most colleges and universities include a strategic initiative or, more aptly, an imperative concerning admissions and enrollment. Since many private institutions are only several bad years in admissions away from extinction, and virtually every institution depends heavily on tuition, marketing usually has a prominent role in collegiate strategic planning reports. As a consequence, its language and methods are increasingly in use on campuses, no matter how distasteful most faculty members find the terminology of markets, brands, and customers. Based on visits to many campuses David Kirp (2003) reports that the language of marketing is here to stay, whether we like it or not, both for good and for ill.

Our question is similar to one that he poses: When it comes to the use of strategic marketing, is it possible to reconcile the values of the academic commons with the marketplace, or will colleges and universities sell their birthrights? In considering admissions in a strategic context, we have the test case of an issue that we have examined in several guises, and that, as we have seen, has been the focus of many studies, including those by Kirp (2003); Bok (2003); Newman, Couturier, and Scully (2004); and Zemsky, Wegner, and Massy (2005). In general terms, it concerns the limits of commercialism and market competition in higher education. In this specific case, the question is focused on the appropriate use of the terminology and methods of marketing in admissions.

Strategic Leadership and Marketing

We can begin to address this question by examining several basic characteristics of integral strategic thinking that differentiate it from a discipline of marketing. In particular, deep strategy requires integrative and systemic forms of thought and action. What may be invisible at an operational level comes into full view in strategy. It reveals the connectedness between and among academic and administrative activities and programs.

Consider what is required to reach virtually any goal in admissions, whether to increase applications or yield or to attract more students with certain talents, backgrounds, or levels of family income. The admissions program is simply the leading edge of a complex and connected strategic system. No matter where one touches it in such a structure, that point connects to all of the structure's major components. A strategic system requires faculty and administrative leaders throughout the organization to understand its interconnections.

When seen in this light, effective admissions work begins with the integration of several different forms of knowledge, from narratives to data. The institution's story and vision, its distinctive educational characteristics and core competencies, should be woven into virtually every facet of the verbal and visual messages that an admissions office communicates. These are drawn from a complex set of beliefs and information about the institution that are both discovered and validated in a process of deep strategy. Strategic thinking brings a discipline to this process of integration and makes the creation of the message a differentiated, authentic, and focused process.

Branding

A proponent of branding and integrated marketing claims that "At root, a brand is the promise of an experience. Understanding and communicating the validity of that experience to target audiences are parts of the branding process" (Moore 2004, 57). From this it is clear that branding and marketing depend on a complex strategic task that precedes it, which is "understanding... the validity of the experience." The validity of soda pop, a coffee shop, or an automobile is one thing, but the validity of an educational experience is quite another. The word "experience" does not mean the same thing in describing products and education. Products are experienced through functional use and consumption, while education involves an intangible process of intellectual and personal transformation. Products are infinitely modifiable to meet the desires of the customer, while education sets standards that learners can only satisfy through changes in their capacities and knowledge, based in good measure on their own will and motivation. Especially since branding has its origins in selling consumer products through repetitive and sometimes deceptive mass advertising, if we omit the essential step of discovering and articulating an institution's authentic identity, its purposes could be reduced to whatever the inventiveness of marketing chooses to make of them. One of the responsibilities of strategic leadership is to ensure that education is not reduced to commerce.

These considerations offer a clear perspective on the use of the methods and language of marketing in higher education. The terminology that we use matters, and not just to spare the sensitivities of the faculty. Language conveys a system of thought and values. An authentic university generates and conveys knowledge as a public good and is constructed around a different set of values and purposes from those used by businesses that sell products and services. The issue is whether the methods of thinking and decision making used in business can fit that world of thought. Some business practices do fit, including the methods of marketing and the tools and concepts of strategy, as we have been at pains to show. To do so, the language and the relevant processes of management can and should be translated into the idioms, values, and methods that illuminate educational issues and university decision making. If that happens successfully, then the methods of integrated strategic marketing can bring new insights and disciplined processes to the work of admissions and other departments. Yet some terminology, like the use of the word "customer" for student and "brand" for identity, image, and reputation, resists translation and cannot be made into central strategic concepts without distorting the meaning of education.

THE STUDENT EXPERIENCE

Whereas admissions is often at the center of institutional planning documents, student life is rarely at the core of institutional strategy. Ever since the doctrine of in loco parentis was swept away in the late 1960s, a vacuum has existed in the articulation of the educational purposes of student life. To be sure, many student affairs officers have an intellectual perspective that animates their work. Most campuses try to build linkages between residential and academic life, often through ingenious practices and programs. Nor is campus life lacking in countless opportunities for student learning and personal development in everything from volunteer service to artistic programs to athletics. Yet typically there is no coherent or compelling conceptual vision of how all these activities contribute to student educational growth. More often than not, it seems that "edutainment" is at the strategic center of things, with consumer satisfaction the goal.

Rarely, in particular, do faculty members show much interest in or understanding of the ways that campus or residential life might be an important part of the institution's educational mission. More typically, the prevailing sentiment is annoyance at the coarseness of student social life and the way it distracts from the pursuits of learning.

Then there is the dark side of student life, which is itself a strategic issue, as troubling realities from the wider culture invade the campus and shape its character. Levels of alcohol and substance abuse are high and inexorably give rise to instances of violence, vandalism, and sexual exploitation. Virtually every contemporary campus has developed special programs and interventions to address binge drinking and its effects on students.

Strategy and Campus Life

Over against this challenging picture are strategic opportunities for distinctive educational achievement through the campus experience. Probably more than in any other national educational culture in the world, American institutions have made the campus experience an important part of what it means to go to college. The investment of resources in staff, programs, athletics, facilities, and campus events is massive. Yet in most institutions, the *educational* purpose of it all is neither conscious nor articulated.

At a strategic moment that makes late adolescence a challenging time in personal growth and sees technological forms of distance education rising dramatically in popularity, the educational meaning of student life on campus is a neglected conceptual and strategic theme. It requires a new articulation by the institution's academic leaders, especially the ideas and voices of the faculty. Ironically, before long, the campus experience may become one of the primary differentiating competencies of colleges and universities. What does it contribute that cannot be found at a computer terminal?

Intellectual Leadership and Student Life

If this strategic challenge and opportunity are to be seized, higher education needs to use the available theoretical, conceptual, and empirical resources to understand and enact its student life programs. The insights and the findings are there, as for example, in the voluminous research and publications by Alexander Astin (1977, 1993), or more recently in the work of George Kuh and his associates (1991, 2005). The developmental theories of writers such as Arthur Chickering (1969), Douglas Heath (1968), and William Perry (1970) have enlightened both past and present generations of theorists and practitioners. Pascarella and Terinzini (1991, 2005) have analyzed many studies over the years of the impact of the college experience on students. Working within the same Harvard context as William Perry before him, Richard Light offers these conclusions from his decade-long work in the Harvard Assessment Seminars: "I assumed that most important and memorable academic learning goes on inside the classroom, while outside activities provide a useful but modest supplement. The evidence shows that the opposite is true. . . . When we asked students to think of a specific, critical incident or moment that had changed them profoundly, four-fifths of them chose a situation or event outside of the classroom" (2001, 123).

These scholars and many others provide conceptual frameworks and touchstones that give rich educational meaning to the encompassing forms of students' intellectual and personal development. In doing so, they reveal some of the cultural infrastructure and patterns of campus life that accelerate and facilitate a student's successful engagement in higher learning. Terms that one often finds in mission statements or hears on campus, like "personal growth," "intellectual maturity," "responsibility," "commitment," "autonomy," "democratic citizenship," "leadership," and "community," are made intelligible and actionable as they are connected to coherent models of human development that interpret education as the unfolding of fundamental human powers and possibilities. They provide the integrative perspectives that are needed to make powerful learning an institution-wide commitment and strategic priority.

Once again, the strategy process becomes a form of leadership. It does so as it urges connection among the parts of a system, and as it reaches for the conceptual resources that can do justice to the richness and variety of education as a form of human empowerment within an intentional community. As Ernest Boyer put it when issuing the influential report *Campus Life: In Search of Community*, "We believe the six principles [of campus life] highlighted in this report—purposefulness, openness, justice, discipline, caring, and celebration—can form the foundation on which a vital community of learning can be built. Now, more than ever, colleges and universities should be guided by a larger vision" (1990a).

STRATEGY AND FACILITIES

Under most accreditation standards, institutions are required to have a campus master plan. A plan that defines the location of future buildings and the use of campus space would seem to be a classic exercise in long-range planning, not strategic thinking. After all, the major variables are spaces and physical masses that are under the control of the designers and the design. They can be reduced to precise drawings and blueprints, whatever the driving forces of the surrounding world may be.

Strategic Space

Yet at the level of strategic reflection, it is clear that campus and building plans are part of a system of beliefs and distinctive educational purposes. The plans of today's colleges and universities display a sharp consciousness of how the goals of an engaged educational community should determine the places, shapes, and forms where learning takes place. Campus spaces are configured to facilitate collaborative learning in small groups, to create places where people can interact, to connect to technology, to allow for the placement of laboratories so that faculty and students can do research together. Physical space increasingly has become transparent to the educational goals that it serves.

A Sense of Place

Strategic plans and similar studies of campus life also reveal that the campus is *lived* space, so it is often lodged in memory and in personal experience as a major theme in the institution's story. A sense of place is commonly a defining element in the shared values of a community, and many students, staff, and graduates develop intimate connections to the campus, its landmarks, and special natural and architectural features. Places carry meanings that contribute to the larger purposes of education.

Salem College and a Sense of Place

Salem College in Winston-Salem, North Carolina, is located in the restored Moravian village of Old Salem, whose roots reach back to the mid-1700s, when German-speaking Moravian settlers arrived in Salem from Pennsylvania to create an intentional community of faith and labor. The sense of historic identity of the village is interwoven with the college and the neighboring academy, which grew from a school for girls that the Moravians started before the American Revolution. College and village also share a common architectural signature defined by simple geometric forms, pitched tile roofs, arched windows, brick structures in Flemish bond, rhythmic green spaces, and pathways of worn brick. The campus leads off the large village square into intimate quadrangles created by buildings that largely conform to the style of the eighteenth-century town beyond. Historic artifacts are everywhere, from antique furniture to embroidered samplers created by young women over 150 years ago. A sense of intimacy and community, of historic fabric and authenticity, defines the place. These very values shape the human transactions and relationships of those who dwell there as students, deepening bonds between them as responsible members of a historic community of women, and marking their experience for life.

Countless campuses have similar stories that give the campus a voice in its narrative of identity. So master plans and decisions about major renovations also are crucial parts of educational strategies for the future. A building has an impact on its human community and the natural environment, which is itself a vital issue in contemporary decisions about facilities. Its physical fabric and infrastructure are critical considerations for efficiency, effectiveness, and sustainability but also for the meanings that it carries. Campus designs and buildings ground the identity and the heritage of a community. In all these ways campus space and architecture are parts of an integral strategy that moves the organization toward the vision it has defined for itself.

STRATEGY AND FINANCIAL RESOURCES

Those who study collegiate strategic planning reports and documents soon come to a surprising realization. Many plans do not include either a financial model to test the cost of the initiatives being proposed or a method to fund them within a designated period of time. This is more than a little odd, since strategic planning has precisely to do with creating goals and allocating resources to translate them into reality. Without a sense of financial capacity, many of the goals in a strategic plan become what its critics complain that they are anyway, either wish lists or a safe place to store the excess baggage of campus opinion and desire. Without financial feasibility, a strategy compromises its credibility and loses an effective mechanism of decision making and leadership.

Many institutions are diffident to define their financial capacities and priorities because there can be political risks in doing so. To signal that some units or programs may have a higher priority than others is dangerous. In adversarial contexts, the setting of priorities may unleash a torrent of conflict. Yet these challenges should not prevent us from exploring the possibilities of an optimal process, even if its application may have to be tailored to a variety of circumstances.

Financial Models

A fundamental requirement for effective strategic planning is the use of an analytical financial model. The model can be quite simple but should capture the key points of leverage that determine the institution's financial position. Effective decision making requires that these leverage points be deeply understood and carefully charted, including the key ratios that indicate financial position. Our suggested dashboard of strategic indicators in chapter 5 shows data that should be included in a model or in an accompanying analysis of financial position. Key ratios and indicators such as debt to assets, debt payments to revenues, net tuition after discounts, and unrestricted net income have to be understood both operationally and strategically. Most accounting firms can provide a set of analytical and comparative ratios for colleges and universities, and bond agencies create powerful sets of metrics in issuing ratings. Strategic thinkers and leaders focus on these comparative trends and ratios and attend particularly to both marginal income and expense and to the danger zones in their financial metrics (cf. Townsley 2007). Every institution's financial engine drives results precisely through the interaction of its most important variables in revenue and expense, assets and liabilities. Strategic leaders are often skilled in relating the dynamics of the engine to the critical success factors in the educational program (Collins 2001, 2005). Although most of the revenue and expense streams have differing rates of increase and decrease, they can be translated into an analytical and quantitative model that is able to test the financial consequences of various strategic decisions and economic trends.

Each of the major task forces and groups developing strategies should use the model to test the financial results of its proposals and should highlight these as part of its report. The SPC will select options for further consideration and implementation with a clear sense of the resources that they will require, and the steps they will take under adverse circumstances, such as high inflation or serious recession. Without a clear window into the inner workings of its own financial world, it cannot meet these responsibilities.

Transparency and Financial Information

A financial model can project plausible scenarios for the future, but the institution's basic financial position has to be communicated clearly as well. As we noted in our discussion of SPCs, governing boards and presidents do well to disclose all the basic financial information that is relevant to the work of strategy. Although it can be difficult if the institution is in a weak position, or an especially strong one, it is far better in the long run that these issues be shared rather than hidden. The tendency of some faculty members to deflect hard financial choices to administrators, and for administrators to keep problematic financial facts from the faculty, is part of the same unhealthy syndrome. A credible process requires both shared information and shared responsibility. An ability to deal honestly with limits and possibilities as defined by context is one of the characteristics of effective leadership. MacTaggart (2007a) makes this point repeatedly in discussing institutions that began their academic turnarounds by becoming transparent about their often-precarious financial positions.

Strategic Priorities

In an environment in which resources for higher education have become perpetually strained and erratic, each institution will also have to reconfigure continuously the relationships between its resources and its goals. As a matter of course, institutions will use their strategy processes to redefine many of the assumptions about what programs they offer, to whom, and how. The criteria for priorities in the operating budget will have to become more transparently and consistently strategic. For some time now, collegiate institutions have used criteria, often tacitly, that weigh programs in terms of variables such as (1) quality, (2) centrality, (3) demand, and (4) cost (Dill 1997, Ferren and Stanton 2004). The more systematic use of criteria of this kind should become an explicit part of strategic plans and their implementation. They have to become the constant canons of decision making that keep an institution in strategic balance both within itself and with the environmental forces that affect it. In developing a useful series of detailed procedures to achieve ongoing strategic balance, Robert Dickeson notes that "Balance can be defined as 'bringing into proper proportion,' and such is the nature of the ultimate task of institutional leadership" (1999, 121). The effort to think and act responsively and responsibly in all aspects of decision making, from the cost-effective design of each course and program to the best combination of all programs, has to become a new center of strategic gravity.

Selective Excellence at Yale University

An example will help to illustrate these points. Although institutions often have used phrases like "selective excellence" to describe their efforts to target their resources, their decisions have not always produced either excellence or clarity. Does selective excellence mean that we will be good at some things and mediocre at others, or just what? In describing Yale's University's future several years in advance of its three hundredth anniversary, President Richard Levin offered an illuminating strategic interpretation of the phrase. Yale, he said, would strive for excellence in everything it does while concentrating on its demonstrated strengths. In some fields, like the humanities and the arts, Yale could aspire to comprehensive excellence across most specialties. In other fields, however, such as the physical sciences and engineering, it would have to choose several specialties and concentrate its resources on a few distinguished faculty groups. "The range of human knowledge is so vast and so rich in variation that not even a great university can aspire to comprehensive coverage of every subject worthy of study" (Levin 1996, 10).

The special features of strategic thinking are placed in sharp relief in financial decisions. The analytical, integrative, and systemic characteristics of strategy as a discipline have to confront the continual tendency to think of budgets in strictly operational or political terms. Lacking a strategic perspective, financial decisions are driven by a grab bag of urgencies. With effective strategic thinking comes the ability to integrate purposes and meanings with facts and numbers. Either annual budgets are integrated into strategic priorities and plans, or the institution loses its purposefulness. Since leadership is all about purpose, it has to make its guiding presence known in responsible and coherent financial decisions.

Financial Equilibrium

A strategic orientation offers not only a framework for thinking about financial issues, but it insists on content as well. One of the goals of an effective strategy is the achievement of long-term financial stability for the organization. For most colleges and universities, this means achieving financial equilibrium, the characteristics of which can most easily be illustrated for independent colleges and universities but that increasingly have direct parallels at state-sponsored institutions as well. Being in equilibrium involves (1) maintaining a balanced operating budget; (2) keeping the rates of increase in expenditures and in revenues in line with one another while accounting for discounts in financial aid; (3) making annual provisions for the depreciation of the physical plant and equipment that should eventually reach 2 percent of replacement value; (4) creating annual budgetary flexibility by building in contingencies for enrollment variations and other factors, and using any proceeds to create funds for new initiatives and reserves up to designated levels; and (5) safeguarding the purchasing power of the endowment while providing for a steadily enlarging stream of endowment income.

Financial equilibrium sets a rigorous standard that many institutions can only aspire to as a model. Nonetheless, the concept illustrates the structural depths that strategy must reach in order to be an effective method of leadership. To achieve equilibrium, all the options and tools of policy and decision making are on the table within a long-term horizon of aspiration. Every choice and issue, from increasing tuition to the effectiveness of the financial leadership of the president and board, are part of the strategic equation of financial equilibrium.

The task is to build a financial engine that can meet the test of sustainability by operating in perpetuity at the highest levels of effectiveness and efficiency. The engine will always need more fuel, but it has to be built so that it can operate under adverse conditions, switch to resilient strategies when fuel supplies run low, and continuously replenish some of its own resources from within. From a strategic perspective, the goal is constant: to create a financially self-renewing organization that is able to dominate its environment by exercising choice about its future.

Affordability: Hitting the Wall

As our environmental scan has suggested, the challenge of creating financial equilibrium has intensified for almost all institutions over the past decade because of structural shifts in the affordability of higher education. Strategic thinking and the goal of financial sustainability are strict taskmasters in the current environment. Years of tuition increases beyond rates of inflation have lifted college prices well beyond the growth in average family incomes. The average price for room, board, and tuition at major private universities in 2007 was only a few thousand dollars less than the median family income before taxes. Many public universities face parallel challenges as they cope with declining state subsidies from an incoherent trend toward privatization that results in escalating tuition charges.

Colleges have responded by discounting their charges based on need and merit aid, creating a vicious fiscal cycle in which higher charges produce lower marginal new revenues as more and more families become eligible for discounts. As a result, countless colleges have begun to "hit the wall" financially because the price of tuition has reached a structural limit in families' financial capacities. If the trends continue, it is just a matter of time before students from all but the top 5 percent in family income will receive ever-enlarging discounts, progressively diminishing net tuition income and slowing starving many institutions.

Many institutions with the right locations, programs, and innovative capacity have responded strategically and creatively to the new limits by finding new revenue streams that build on existing administrative and faculty overhead. They create professionally oriented graduate programs, open centers for adult education around the region, and expand offerings and enrollment in low-cost fields with a practical turn, often using distance learning to expand their reach. In many cases, these programs produce income on which the academic core of the institution has come to depend, even as the core itself shrinks in size. The situation is not unlike the patterns in large research universities, where undergraduate tuition, research overhead, and programs with high net revenues fund the research and teaching in the arts and the humanities (cf. Zemsky, Wegner, and Massy 2005).

In some cases, however, the new financial engine will not be sustainable, since it is subject to intense competition from other institutions and low-cost educational providers, and rapid shifts in demographic and economic trends. Strategic leadership forces these issues into the open and tests financial models for their staying power and durability. The "brutal truths" and structural vulnerabilities have to be confronted before the best options can be chosen. It will take changes in structural elements, not just budget reallocations, to address these issues. Options such as the three-year degree, collaborations between community colleges and four-year institutions, alternating work and study programs, new educational services for a growing retirement population, and more educational alliances with organizations in workforce education and management development are examples that change the financial model in more structural terms. In addition, the ever-present need for new capital to initiate and sustain programs and scholarship budgets has to be filled through large doses of philanthropy, which brings us to our next topic.

FUND-RAISING

No matter how successfully a campus implements a system of strategic priorities to manage its expenditures, it will constantly need to enlarge its resources. Inflationary pressures in salaries and benefits can only increase over time, and cost increases for facilities and financial aid are inexorable, especially in the highly competitive world we live in today.

As new strategic needs and goals are developed and approved, they will always require funding. When these priorities are formulated according to the disciplined processes of strategic planning, they connect directly to the institution's capacities to generate large sums of capital and operating funds from sponsors and donors. This capacity is a defining element in the institution's strategic position and aspirations, and both public and independent colleges and universities increasingly need to make it a core competency.

Gift Capacity

One of the most critical strategic indicators of an institution's ability to meet its goals is its capacity to generate gift and grant income. Consider, for instance, the amount of gift and grant revenues for all purposes (excluding contract research) per student that an institution receives per year over a ten-year period compared with a group of similar institutions. If the institution cannot generate comparable cash gifts per student, over time it will eventually lose its competitive position unless it can generate resources from other sources, such as tuition, the management of physical assets, or endowment returns (or state subsidies for public institutions.)

Assume that institution A, with 3,000 students and a moderate level of gift capacity, receives $5,000 per year per student for ten years, or $15,000,000 annually to total $150 million for the decade. Compare those figures with those of institution B, which also enrolls 3,000 students but has a superior gift capability of $15,000 per student annually. These projections are based on actual gifts received by twelve colleges and universities from 1998 to 2001 (University of Richmond 2003). Over the course of the decade, institution B receives $45 million annually and $450 million in total. Unless balanced by other sources, institution B has a $300 million resource advantage over institution A, and the differences will only increase over time. Gift and grant income obviously influences decisively the most fundamental form of strategic and competitive capacity, which is the ability to generate resources.

Telling the Story

Strategy sets the fundraising agenda in a variety of ways. It helps to sort out projects that are candidates for support from different sources, such as government, corporations, foundations, alumni, and major donors. In doing so, it also differentiates the organization's capacities in staff and expertise to be successful in these different domains. Most importantly, the strategy offers a systematic rationale for the programs that the institution intends to support. The strategy document should pass into the hands of the development staff and be regarded as a storehouse of ideas that help to frame and even to compose a large number of proposals for support.

Often the completion of an intensive strategy process can and should be timed to coincide with the planning of a capital campaign or similar long-term development program. As this occurs, a well-crafted planning document offers the central arguments and defines the major elements of a case statement. Donors want to hear cogent reasons why the projects they are asked to support really matter in setting the course for the future. A good strategic plan shows precisely how the project will make a difference both in itself and in the synergies that it will create to fulfill the institution's larger vision.

Charitable giving depends on many things, including good ideas, reliable information, personal relationships, and a well-organized staff, as well as a motivated group of volunteers. But it is also driven by the values that people claim and the causes in which they believe. The pride and loyalty of friends, trustees, and former students are strategic assets that have to be galvanized into personal financial support and a commitment to secure contributions from others. When an organization integrates its story and vision into a persuasive strategic argument, it creates a powerful source of motivation. An elegant strategy can inspire generosity, both by persuading the mind and lifting the spirit. It represents a form of personal address to all those who participate in the organization's narrative of identity and believe in the values on which it rests. It calls on them to take responsibility for the well-being of an organization that has been entwined in their lives and that serves vital human needs. Knowing and telling the story are among the central tasks of strategic leadership in the advancement work of colleges and universities.

Strategy as Conceptual and Integrative Leadership

I have argued that there is more to a strategy process than meets the eye. Even when it may not be conscious of its own depths and possibilities, strategic thinking embraces immediate concerns but reaches beyond them. As it deals with specific issues and decisions, strategy also carries presuppositions, forges connections, and builds a foundation for action that has wide significance as a form of leadership. We have traced these dimensions of leadership in the establishment of a contextual mind-set for considering academic decisions and as integrated forms of reflection that fuse the quantitative and qualitative dimensions of issues. At critical points we also have found that strategy becomes leadership as it offers unifying conceptual perspectives that provide resources for the development of educational programs and practices.

Strategy as leadership also creates a disposition to connect decision making to action, because it reveals the systemic relationships among various projects and programs. The cycles of connection tie various academic and administrative strategies and actions to one another, showing patterns of interdependence that operational thinking alone does not perceive. Through the goals that define strategic initiatives, a sense of possibility is given form, and motivation is made concrete. As information is made transparent and hard choices appear in every priority, strategy becomes credible. For all those reasons, it is appropriate to designate strategy an applied discipline of reciprocal leadership. If it is to fulfill this demanding possibility, it must be able not only to make decisions, but to execute them. So now we turn to the agenda for the implementation of strategy.

CHAPTER

Implementation: From Strategic Leadership to Strategic Management

The popular literature on leadership sends the message that management is mundane and blind to change, while leadership is noble and visionary. Practitioners, however, know that the relationship between the two is much more complex. In describing strategic leadership, I have tried to fill the managerial frames of strategy with new images of leadership. Yet I have sought as well to show that a leadership vision must create a clear picture of the tasks of enactment. In sum, leadership without execution creates an empty vision, while management without leadership is nearsighted.

In order for strategic leadership and management to work reciprocally, the first task is to analyze the resources, practices, structures, and culture of an organization to find vehicles for the implementation of strategy. The key to strategic effectiveness is a new intentionality that continuously seeks ways to incorporate a strategic orientation into the workings of the institution. Practically every facet of college and university operations presents itself as a possibility for reconceptualization and reformulation. In discussing a diverse series of successful steps to move the plan off the shelf and into action at the University of Wisconsin at Madison, Kathleen A. Paris notes: "For the plan to be taken seriously, faculty, staff, and students must see it as infused throughout the organization. It must be part of routine academic life" (2004, 124). Her thoughts parallel other recent motifs in the literature on strategy that emphasize the importance of linking institutional research with initiatives to improve quality, plans with budgets, goals with teams responsible for attaining them, and strategies with control systems. An emphasis on the translation of strategic thinking and planning into action has come to characterize contemporary strategy programs (Dooris, Kelley, and Trainer 2004).

In the sections that follow, we provide analyses that illustrate the way that several critical contexts, activities, and relationships can become resources for the implementation of strategic leadership. There are countless opportunities on each campus besides these, but they are significant ones that often appear in the literature on the execution of strategy (Alfred et al. 2006; Bryson 1995; Keller 1997; Rowley, Lujan, and Dolence 1997; Sevier 2000). We shall focus on:

- Communication about strategy
- Strategy and organizational culture: Norms, stories, rituals, and ceremonies
- Authority: Leadership, management, and control systems
- Strategy and accreditation
- Strategic assessment
- Strategic program reviews
- The governing board and the implementation of strategy
- Strategic integration and momentum

COMMUNICATION ABOUT STRATEGY

Most theories of leadership give a central place to the importance of communication in order to engage and motivate constituents. Ultimately, strategic leadership becomes influential in the intentions and actions of individuals and groups through effective communication. Narrative leadership is successful because it reaches people at the level of their personal and cultural identities and thus is tied to their values and actions. Communication is the critical link in forging these connections.

Goals for Communication in Strategic Leadership

As we consider the role of communication, several familiar themes will reappear. It will become apparent that to serve a process of strategic leadership, communication must meet a series of tests. Both during and at the conclusion of a strategy process, communication will show itself to be characterized by:

- **Reciprocity:** Most of the values and strategies developed in the process come from the campus community itself and are given back to it, perhaps in new forms, in the final vision and goals of the plan.
- **Participation:** There are ample opportunities for people to be heard and for genuine give-and-take in the development of the strategy.
- **Urgency:** Effective communication gains attention, shows that strategy matters, and summons effort and commitment to succeed in the face of obstacles.
- **Learning:** In an effective strategy process, everyone learns about the institution and how it really works, as well as about the challenges it faces in the environment.

- **Narrative:** The strategy uses the story and the narrative voice to embody the institution's identity, capture its spirit, resolve conflicts, and create a sense of connection between the past and the future.

- **Validation:** Invitations to experts on and off campus to speak and write about the plan can both clarify and verify its claims.

- **Motivation:** Leadership is always about motivation and inspiration, and communication is one of the primary vehicles through which it is achieved.

- **Repetition:** The periodic and consistent communication of the key messages of the strategy in a variety of contexts is a necessity.

Not surprisingly, various guidebooks and studies of strategic planning consistently emphasize the centrality of effective communication (Alfred et al. 2006; Keller 1997; Sevier 2000). Echoing that theme, one of higher education's most influential voices in matters strategic, George Keller, frequently affirms the need for effective and repeated communication in developing strategy: "The communication must be effective and continued, from the inception of planning through the several years of its implementation" (1997, 165). He advises us to communicate and then to do so again, and again. This communication has several goals, including the creation of a sense of urgency to respond to tough external pressures, and to seize the attention of busy academics who are preoccupied with the many other claims on them. As March puts it, decisions "depend on the ecology of attention: who attends to what and when" (quoted in Keller 1997, 165). If strategic issues are to engage an academic community, they must be communicated skillfully and persistently and, at times, movingly.

Forms of Communication

Both before and during an intensive cycle of strategic planning, there should be a variety of forms of communication. Institutions should use the vehicles that best fit their cultures to build awareness about strategic planning, from Web sites to newsletters, from large public meetings to smaller gatherings, from informal conversations to major speeches, and from the agendas of regular meetings to special presentations. There should be good opportunities in these contexts, and many others, to present and elicit ideas and reactions to the strategy project, both as to its methods and content. The efforts to inform and to establish a sense of importance for the process should themselves be considered strategic objectives.

As the strategy process gets underway, the SPC will have gathered a set of articles and documents for its own use. Information about the collection can be made widely available, and some articles and reports should be provided on a Web site. At various moments in the process, people across campus will be invited to offer opinions on surveys and questionnaires, or to attend meetings, roundtables, or workshops to offer ideas or to respond to a task force or council draft. As the process moves forward, a draft document of the SPC's final report should be circulated for comment or should be made the subject of formal or less formal discussions or open meetings. To increase participation at these events, personal invitations should be sent from the chairperson of the SPC, the president, or the relevant dean or director. As a result of these interactions, a good cross-section of the campus will feel informed and involved in the main issues under consideration. The reciprocity of a process of leadership will have been achieved.

Larger campuses will have a harder time than smaller ones in building an effective communication system, but modern information technologies make the goal a realistic one. In large institutions, each academic unit or subdivision becomes an important spoke in the wheel of communication. Success will depend on the ways that deans of schools and colleges are drawn into the strategy process and then communicate on its progress and results. The chairperson and the staff of the SPC should monitor and encourage that process, calling on the authority of the president or chief academic officer as needed.

The Strategy Report

The leaders of every strategy process have an important decision to make about the nature of the reports or documents that will issue from the project. Often one hears that it is the process itself, far more than the resulting document, that matters. People claim that reports have a short shelf life, and no one has time to read them. For these reasons, and others, some writers suggest that a final strategy document should be no more than twenty to twenty-five pages (Rowley, Lujan, and Dolence 1997).

There is no easy rule of thumb for the appropriate length or nature of a final strategy document. The character and length of the document is a consequence of the goals that each institution sets for the process and the uses that it intends for the report. It ordinarily should appear in several different forms and lengths to accomplish its purposes. Although the report is not an end in itself, it can be an influential means to achieve a variety of critical goals.

Consistent with our emphasis on the tasks of leadership, it is important for the report to be a primary source for teaching and learning about the strategic future of the institution. As such, a strong case can be made for making the final report a longer and more elegant document of fifty to seventy-five pages of text, plus charts and data. Carefully crafted language can serve a variety of purposes, many relating to the themes of leadership. The most important issues should be treated in clear and exacting prose, although some sections can use bullet points and summaries. In presenting strategic initiatives relating to the use of resources, or involving conflict and change, there should be a premium on well-reasoned and documented argumentation rather than extreme brevity. Much of the document's persuasiveness is achieved by drawing on the institution's story in building its case, and using the narrative form to reach the audience as participants or stakeholders in the process.

The capacity of a report to inform and inspire those who have not been close to the planning process is often at stake, so the document carries an important burden. The report teaches. What do we mean when we seek national status? What is the balance between legacy and change? What does it suggest to be the best in our class? What is the specific content of diversity? What is the resource picture for the future? Why were these and not other construction or renovation projects chosen? Why are we being asked to establish priorities and to cut expenses yet again? The final report becomes one means to create a sense of urgency and significance, which is essential to drive the plan to realization.

Tactics to Communicate the Strategy

A final report does not, of course, stand alone as the product of a strategy process. It functions as the source for a large variety of other communications and for a set of emphases and actions that, in effect, comprise the tactics to communicate the strategy. It is much easier to accomplish these steps if the final report has a suggestive name that describes its major themes, rather than the generic "Strategic Plan, 2005–2010." Centre College entitled one of its plans "Education as Empowerment," a theme that captured some of the goals of a transformative liberal education.

The steps in a communications plan can include:

- The preparation of attractive summary reports to be circulated to special audiences, like advisory groups and the press, and to be included in alumni publications, perhaps as a pullout section

- The development of articles to be used in faculty, staff, and alumni publications, often as a series

- The development of stories and features based on the analysis of proposed programs and facilities, to be used by the admissions and development offices

- The creation of Web sites that provide the plan, progress reports on its implementation, and coverage that may have appeared in press releases, stories, and articles

At the basis of the communications effort, is the systematic distribution of the full report to the campus itself. In the hands of many key decision makers, it becomes a coherent set of directions and goals for their own priorities and plans, as we shall see. If it is clear that budget decisions will be made in terms of the priorities of the strategy, it will get everyone's attention. A good final report also prompts admissions directors, development vice presidents, and communications directors to underline key ideas and narratives in the report. It offers them a coherent story to tell about the institution's direction for the future. The ideas and even the language of the plan come to shape the way these key divisions communicate with a wide variety of the constituencies of the university. As a result, the organization's identity and its messages become much clearer and more coherent.

Brown University Web Site

Brown University has created a superb Web site to communicate its "Plan for Academic Enrichment." In addition to the plan, it includes several backup reports on the campus master plan, financial resources, and other strategic issues. Some features of the site are distinctive and effective. Among these are links that take the viewer to recent developments in each of the university's ten strategic initiatives. The excellent graphics and photographs, press releases and stories, announcements of grants (including $100 million from one donor for financial aid), and descriptions of new academic programs give the reader a vibrant sense of the content and progress of the plan.

STRATEGY AND ORGANIZATIONAL CULTURE: NORMS, STORIES, RITUALS, AND CEREMONIES

A central theme of our analysis is that collegiate organizations function as cultures as well as formal organizations. Campus communities live by norms and beliefs, customs and rituals, and stories and traditions that suggest what people should know and do in order to fit into the organization. As we have seen, the power of organizational culture has a strong influence on the effectiveness of leadership both as an engaging process of influence and as a formal position. The implementation of strategy depends on knowing the folkways, pathways, and leverage points to get things done within the culture. Strategic leadership is always looking for ways to read the meaning of these lived realities in order to embed strategy with the grain of the organization's understanding of itself and its ways of doing business. In doing so, it brings a systematic and focused approach to the cultural tasks of leadership.

The culture of a community also has a more visible way of enacting itself through the formal and informal rituals and ceremonies by which it celebrates its history and identity. Traditions and rituals are plentiful on many campuses, less so on others. But virtually every institution has ceremonial moments when it opens and closes the academic year, celebrates a founder's day, provides students and faculty with awards, and welcomes new members of the community. At the University of Kansas, entering students participate in a powerful initiation into campus lore and culture as they celebrate Traditions Night and learn songs and chants and hear stories about the Jayhawk, a mythical bird that represents the struggles of the early Kansas settlers (Kuh, Kinzie, Schuh, Whitt, et al. 2005; cf. Toma, Dubrow, and Hartley 2005). All such occasions become ways for aspects of the institution's narrative to be presented and celebrated. Rituals and traditions connect faculty, staff, and students with a lived expression of the community's heritage and purposes, reinforcing and deepening the formal definitions of identity and vision found in a planning document. Strategic leadership draws respectfully on these resources to relate its goals to the interwoven cultural dimensions of the community.

AUTHORITY: LEADERSHIP, MANAGEMENT, AND CONTROL SYSTEMS

More than communication and cultural resonance are necessary to implement a strategic plan. Required as well is a sense of the legitimacy of the total process and an effective use of authority to accomplish designated goals (cf. Bornstein 2003). Unless hindered by adversarial hostility, faculty and staff will be inclined to accept and own a strategic agenda that has been developed collaboratively and legitimately. With appropriate forms of consultation and interaction, opportunities to contribute and be heard, and responsiveness to any signals of discontent about the process, the strategy agenda gains legitimate authority in the academic sphere. If the leaders of the strategy process have exposed the academic issues in the report to open faculty debate and consideration, it will be seen as conforming to the expectations of shared governance.

If legitimacy is essential in the academic sphere, both ownership and authority are vital in the administrative arena. Strategic leadership captures the best ideas and professional aspirations of the staff as well as the faculty. Many of the primary champions of the process and the products of strategic planning will have to come from the highest ranks of the organization, and others will be found at all its levels (Keller 1997). The designation of named academic and administrative positions and offices in the context of goals and accountabilities will establish public expectations for the enactment of the strategies.

Yet the daily work of the implementation of goals also depends upon the authority of those who hold leadership positions. Although reciprocal leadership is not defined by authority, the full and consistent institutionalization of strategy depends on it. In the words of Jean Monnet, one of the architects of the European Economic Community, "Nothing is possible without individuals; nothing is lasting without institutions" (quoted in H. Gardner 1995, 15).

The Role of the President and Other Executives

The authority and commitment of the president and other senior officers are necessary conditions for the successful implementation of strategic initiatives and goals. Whatever role the president may play in leading the strategy process itself, there is no doubt about the central responsibility of the president in implementing the results. In analyzing eight case studies of successful strategy programs at widely diverse institutions, Douglas Steeples notes: "Successful strategic planning requires...presidential leadership of the highest order" (1988, 103).

For strategic leadership to take hold, far more is required than formal presidential assent. Other senior officers and members of the faculty will know from the start whether the president values the strategy process and has the skills and inclination to use it as a form of interactive leadership. They will take their cues from the president's actions and expectations, giving greater or less weight to the goals of the strategy as they read the president's intentions. If the president is truly committed to strategic leadership and strategic management, the strategy process will be continuous and its goals will be in evidence in the way that conversations take place, speeches are given, priorities are set, resources are allocated, and decisions are made. It will be equally clear if the president only pays it lip service and prefers to handle issues politically or through a strict chain of managerial control.

Commitment by the highest officer in each unit that undertakes the process is also critical for successful implementation. The top officer can use the tools of authority to embed the strategy in the everyday decisions of the organization. Individuals in authority can command attention, control resources, reward and punish, control systems of communication, and hold people to account even in the world of autonomous knowledge professionals. These capacities are the mechanisms of authority exercised by position. They provide a framework within which the work of leadership as reciprocity can be given form and continuity.

To be sure, the tasks of implementation become far more difficult or impossible if the members of the organization are not invested in the ideas and strategies of the plan. Especially in the academic sphere, but throughout the organization, there will be minimal compliance, grudging acceptance, or all the intricate tactics of resistance, avoidance, and delay where commitment is lacking. Authority *over* others has to be transformed into *authority with* and *for* others in the development and implementation of a strategic plan.

Control Systems to Monitor Results

The commitment to strategic management will also become evident in the way the president and other officers use and create control systems to monitor the implementation of the strategy. Strategic goals take primacy over operational objectives, which are gradually reorganized to implement the strategy. One basic but effective way for the top administration, including the academic deans, to achieve one aspect of this task is to construct the annual planning and operational cycle explicitly around the goals of the strategy. As a result, each senior officer's and division head's annual report and budget plan would give central emphasis to the status of each strategic goal. Commentary on problems and successes in reaching the goals would be expected, along with reports on steps to overcome obstacles. If circumstances merit revisions in goals, the annual report is one of the places to propose them. Since many of the vice presidents and their staff will carry explicit responsibility for implementing goals, the report connects to existing public expectations. The annual review can also be made a part of the individual's own performance evaluation and be one of the factors determining compensation. In a strategic context, the annual report is not just paperwork, but a tool of leadership that can link operations with strategy.

There is also merit in making an annual report to the campus on the institution's progress in meeting the plan's goals. The report can be presented orally in the annual opening faculty meeting, in other campus presentations, in written summaries, in analyses and materials posted on Web sites, and, as we shall see, in reports to the governing board. If there have been changes in the goals, these adjustments and the reasons for them can be explained as well. Whether simple or complex, the reporting process itself communicates the message that strategy matters, as do those whose ideas have shaped it.

Some presidents and administrators choose to make the monitoring of strategic goals a continuous and structured administrative process. A midyear retreat to review the progress of the strategy, including intensive review sessions with each of the vice presidents, and in turn with their direct reports, is one way to exercise controls. Another option, more bureaucratic, requires top officers or their subordinates to report in writing on progress in meeting goals on a quarterly basis, typically on matrices that cross-reference issues and goals with deadlines and costs. Being strategic in scope, the goals may be difficult to measure quarterly, but the method produces an acute sense of responsibility and ensures that the control system is strategically oriented (cf. various articles on control systems in two collections on strategic planning, e.g., Dooris, Kelley, and Trainer 2004; Steeples 1988).

Strategic Goals and a Steering Core

There are other ways to link the strategic goals of the whole institution with the goals of academic and administrative units. In large and complex universities, the strategic initiatives themselves will have to be defined thematically and broadly to encompass the responsibilities and interests of the various academic and administrative subunits. If that is done effectively, then each college, school, or administrative area can be expected to carry out its own strategy work in ways that reflect the larger educational and strategic commitments of the whole institution. The strategy process is able to make clear that the viability and success of each element of the university ultimately depends on the reputation and strengths of the others. Turbulence in the wider world may be so daunting that it requires responses that no one unit can make alone.

We may have reached the logical organizational point of diminishing returns in radically decentralized patterns of institutional decision making. Duplication in academic programs becomes rampant, inefficiencies in administration and staffing multiply, common dangers go unattended, commercialism takes hold in some programs, and donors complain of being constantly solicited by multiple units of the same organization. Burton Clark writes: "One university after another finds that a strengthened, steering core is needed, one central body or several interlocked central groups of administrators and academic staff who can legitimately and effectively assist the interests of the university as a whole" (1997, xiv).

An example of educational leadership at the core of a large, complex, and celebrated research university can be found in the efforts of the University of Wisconsin at Madison to focus its energies on improving undergraduate education.

Based on the recommendations of its 1989 North Central Association self-study for reaccredidation, the university provost decided to do something bold—to actually implement a plan developed for accreditation. Among other priorities, the effort involved investing resources in undergraduate education, making it a thematic strategic focus that was relevant across virtually the entire institution. It produced new initiatives in advising, an effort to transform residences into learning communities with close ties to faculty, and enlarged opportunities in both classroom and community learning (Paris 2004).

Strategy and Human Resources

Another critical contribution of strategic leadership is its influence on a college or university's human resource program, including its system of faculty appointment and tenure. A sharpened sense of identity and vision translates into clearer profiles of the people needed to enact the strategy and helps to define and refine criteria and expectations for performance, including that of the president. The tasks of recruiting, retaining, evaluating, and developing people become more intentional. Programs of faculty and staff orientation and of management and leadership development become more differentiated and purposeful. The inner workings of the strategy system itself can become a worthwhile subject of study and a focus of leadership development. Many of its methods can be taught and learned and embedded in decision-making processes throughout the organization. Without the right people with the right skills to give it life, strategy will become dormant and ineffective.

STRATEGY AND ACCREDITATION

In the academic sphere, many strategic goals will be directed to specific committees or departments for follow-up and eventual action. Others will have a more general impact across many academic programs. As examples, one frequently finds that strategic plans include initiatives to implement international and multicultural studies, to expand interdisciplinary work, to encourage the uses of technology in teaching, to develop new pedagogies, to revise the general education program, to make advising a more effective process, and to create effective methods for the assessment of learning. These strategies cannot be reduced to the work of one or two faculty committees. Broad academic initiatives like these need to be related to the ongoing work of academic programs and departments. The connections are usually difficult to make, and academic administrators are often frustrated in trying to create them. The specialized focus of the department and the pressures of everyday responsibilities work against the time and energy required for new ventures. If the push for change comes from the top in the wrong form, resistance and resentment immediately rise to the surface.

In dealing with challenges of this kind, strategic leadership always looks for existing methods and processes to help accomplish its work. Cross-cutting academic initiatives can, for example, be tied to program review, to self-study for reaffirmation of accreditation, and to the ongoing work of assessment. These suggestions will grate on many ears, since each of these processes are scorned by a hefty percentage of the faculty, and not without good reason. Much of accreditation has consisted of busy work necessary to comply with regulations, program reviews have been scripted and perfunctory, and assessment has never engaged the imagination or interest of the faculty. Nonetheless, there are opportunities for strategic change in each activity.

More recently the accrediting processes of both specialized and regional associations have allowed or required institutions to become more expansive in their self-studies and to focus on the quality of student learning. Jon Wergin (2003) documents the recent emergence of the strong emphasis on student learning in the seven regional accrediting bodies. In a parallel way, Ann Dodd (2004) analyzes the increasing focus in accreditation on the self-assessment of educational quality, curriculum development, and leadership. The emphasis is on encouraging institutions to relate their ongoing strategy processes to the tasks of a self-study. The approach makes eminent sense for several reasons. One is that it gives priority in accreditation reviews to issues that have strategic significance across the institution; another is that it focuses energy on a substantive set of responsibilities that must be fulfilled by the entire campus.

The 2002 guidelines of the Commission on Colleges of the Southern Association of Schools and Colleges emphasize precisely these points. Each institution undergoing review is expected to develop a quality enhancement plan and to demonstrate that it is part of a continuous process of planning and evaluation. "Engaging the wider academic community, the quality enhancement plan is based upon a comprehensive and thorough analysis of the effectiveness of the learning environment for supporting student achievement and accomplishing the mission of the institution...with special attention to student learning" (Commission on Colleges 2002, 5).

To fulfill these requirements, institutions obviously need to have an ongoing strategy program. Existing or contemplated strategic initiatives provide the content and the context necessary for charting the development of a quality enhancement plan. That plan may, as suggested, be one or more of the topics already on the institution's strategic agenda. If a topic is chosen that cuts across the curriculum and teaching and learning, it will have to be considered at the departmental level and translated into plans and actions that become part of the institution's formal responsibilities. The goals of each department are perforce connected to the larger educational and strategic objectives of the institution, which are ultimately approved by the governing board. The obligations of accreditation can be transformed into an opportunity for integrative decision making.

STRATEGIC ASSESSMENT

We have already seen that strategic indicators are an important part of institutional self-definition. Those same indicators often provide the basis for measuring and monitoring an institution's achievement of its strategic goals, especially if they are easily subject to quantification, such as goals relating to admissions, enrollment, finances, and fund-raising. The implementation of goals is strengthened by effective forms of quality assessment that open lines of inquiry into the institution's performance.

Performance measured by strategic indicators offers a wealth of critical information. It prompts important inquiries about the meaning of the data and the achievement of strategic goals that specify the vision. Where have the goals been achieved or exceeded? Where have they fallen short? For what reasons? What actions are underway to reach the goals? What do we do to improve our performance? Are there unanticipated results? What do the data tell us about where we stand with the competition? Are the data a reliable indicator of the institution's achievements? What follow-up studies are required to probe important findings and glean new insights? Do the goals or the measures need to be revised?

In a similar way, each major administrative service and program should assess its own performance periodically through surveys and interviews and relate its evaluations to its own and the institution's strategic objectives. The ability to make continuous progress in reaching ever-higher levels of service and achievement depends on knowing how well the organization is performing its work in all spheres, which is one dimension of what it means to be a learning organization. Quality is of a piece. The effort to enhance quality across the campus contributes to a spirit of pride and achievement that builds on itself and creates momentum. Recent studies, including ones on projects at the University of Iowa and Rutgers, focus on the importance of a strategic orientation to measurement and goal setting (Coleman 2004; Lawrence and Cermak 2004).

The Assessment of Student Learning

Typically the assessment of academic and student learning goals will depend on evaluations that do not lend themselves easily to quantifiable results, or to trends that can be simply reduced to numbers. The desire to reduce students' intellectual development to a simple set of comparative metrics or the results of high-stake tests is a misconception that blocks coherent thought about the kinds of assessments that are possible. To look for simple answers, one would have to displace the larger and most important goals of liberal education—a passion for learning, critical judgment, moral purposefulness, civic responsibility, and a resilient imagination—because they are not directly quantifiable.

Student learning is best assessed with a variety of methods, many of which are useful, if not purely scientific. They can provide proxies and indicators of achievement that have meaning in the context of the inquiry and as a way to probe the issues in an institutional framework (cf. Bok 2006; Burke 2005; Ewell 2006). Institutions, for example, do and should gather data through interviews and questionnaires about student and alumni interpretations of their campus and academic experiences. A wealth of data is available in the results of teaching evaluations, in the patterns of students' course selections and grades, in retention data, and in many other sources that are part of the everyday life of most institutions. Useful information is often collected about alumni achievements in the workplace and graduate school. The data can be mined for significance through various analytical and quantitative techniques (Kuh 2005). With the right disposition and processes, all this information can be used to build a culture of evidence about student learning.

Institutions may also choose to participate in important projects such as the National Survey of Student Engagement, which, as we have seen, seeks to determine the level of active student involvement in learning. It collects and analyzes data from thousands of students at hundreds of institutions and offers a variety of quantitative analyses and institutional comparisons of the various dimensions of student engagement in learning. Carefully interpreted, findings from these kinds of inquiries can assess broad strategic initiatives and goals with regard to important aspects of the quality of student learning, as opposed to subject matter recall (Kuh, Kinzie, Schuh, Whitt, et al. 2005).

A variety of newer methods of assessment are especially appropriate in a strategic context as well. The growing practice of using student learning portfolios, often created electronically to function as an elaborate transcript of student experiences, achievements, and abilities, is promising for several reasons. They can be the basis for student, peer, and faculty assessment of a student's intellectual skills and competencies, as demonstrated through a wide range of experiences and accomplishments in and out of the classroom, or they can contribute decisively to student self-awareness and purposefulness in setting and achieving educational goals that reflect the institution's special strengths.

In terms of strategic issues, the gold standard for assessment is the ability to determine the value that a particular educational program adds to the student's intellectual development. Students come to college with such different levels of motivation, talent, and preparation that absolute measures of student achievement provide only a partial indication of the educational power of a given program or institution. Were we able to measure the degree of a student's progress, however, educators would have ways to improve their teaching and programs in response to assessments of learning. They might also find critical evidence in support of their claims about their distinctive achievements and ways of creating educational value. The ability that strategic assessment offers to create, reinforce, and promote authentic comparative advantages and core competencies should motivate the work of value-added assessment. The findings should reflect and authenticate the institutional narrative and become embedded in the ongoing work of strategy.

The National Survey of Student Engagement , as we have seen, offers a promising line of inquiry about the culture and the form of student learning. Another variable in the learning equation has to do with the cognitive skills students develop and points toward the assessment of differences in intellectual growth. Working in cooperation with the Council for Financial Aid to Education, the

Rand Corporation has developed a test to measure acquired intellectual capacities in communication and in critical, analytical, and integrative thinking, echoing the focus on cognitive skills we discussed in the preceding chapter. Called the College Learning Assessment, it gives students a real-life problem to analyze and resolve by drawing on different types of information and using various forms of reasoning. Instead of responding to multiple-choice questions, students write their analyses and proposed solution to the problem in a complex prose argument. The test can be administered at the early and more advanced stages of a student's career, so the patterns of value-added intellectual growth among students can be charted and compared. The results can also be correlated with other measures of student capability, such as test scores and college grades. The College Learning Assessment intends to measure cognitive capacities that most colleges and universities describe as one of the aims of liberal education (Erwin 2005; Ewell 2006; Rand Corporation / Council for Aid to Education 2004). Using predominantly multiple-choice questions, both the Educational Testing Service's Measure of Academic Proficiency and Progress and ACT's Collegiate Assessment of Academic Proficiency also offer tests that aim to measure academic skills, though the emphasis is not as clearly focused on real-life situations.

Embedded Assessment

If strategic leadership is to be successful, it matters whether or not specific academic and administrative goals are achieved. Yet the most significant accomplishment of strategic leadership is to embed a system of productive self-evaluation and strategic decision making into the institution, one that continuously translates into efforts to raise the bar of academic and organizational achievement (cf. Banta 2002; Bok 2006; Ewell 2006). Strategic assessment then becomes a distinctive activity of a learning organization by determining whether educational goals are being met, and by using the results of the process to move to the next level of achievement. Data on student learning must migrate from the institutional research office into the self-assessment of academic programs and individual faculty members. Although this is no small task, it can be gradually achieved by establishing a strategic context for disaggregating, considering, and using the data. The data can come to include the results of small-scale studies and experiments teachers themselves can perform to compare results on different types of assignments and classroom strategies. In *Our Students' Best Work*, the Association of American Colleges and Universities (2004) provides ten recommendations for creating campus cultures of accountability and assessment, emphasizing liberal education as a standard of excellence, the need for articulation of goals for learning in each department, the development of milestones of student achievement, and continuous assessment that includes external reviews and public transparency of student achievements.

Done effectively, assessment contributes to a culture of evidence that characterizes the work of strategic leadership. These issues ultimately go to the strategic question of providing evidence for educational quality. Whatever else it does, a college or university first needs to have meaningful information about whether or not it is fulfilling its mission to foster students' intellectual growth and achievement. Then it needs to have mechanisms to give visibility to its findings and communicate them to programs, departments, and individuals. Finally, it must have strategic linkages to act on what it has learned about itself. As difficult and unpopular as assessment is among many faculty members, institutions do not have the option to avoid the issue, especially from the perspective of strategic leadership. Unless it knows what it intends its intellectual signature to be and can assess the impact that it is has on students, it will not be able to create a focus for its aspirations to attain higher levels of educational quality. It may fall into the common strategic trap of wistfully claiming that all it needs are better students, rather than becoming passionate about ways it can make a greater difference in the education of the students it has.

STRATEGIC PROGRAM REVIEWS

We can illustrate some of the challenges and opportunities of institutionalizing a new strategic orientation to assessment by considering changes that have been made in the practice of academic program reviews. Especially in larger institutions, one of the primary forms of assessment involves the periodic review of each academic department and program, often with regard to its separate graduate and undergraduate offerings. Most program reviews, not unlike accreditation, consist of a departmental self-study and a campus visit by a panel of two or three faculty members from another institution. When used to greatest advantage, there is a clear process for the review, active participation by the university's academic leadership, and timely communication of the results back to the department (Mets 1997).

Not unexpectedly, the process and the results of program review are of uneven quality and usefulness. Most faculty members participate in the process with sentiments ranging from grudging acceptance to repugnance (Mets 1997; Wergin 2002). Yet if good information about the faculty, the students, and the program has been collected, and insightful consultants have been retained, the recommendations can be beneficial to the department's self-understanding and its plans for the future.

From the point of view of strategic self-assessment, the process represents an important opportunity at several levels, many of which have not always been characteristic of the practices of program reviews. First, it provides the occasion to connect the strategic vision of the institutional or unit-wide plan with the self-understanding and planning of each department. Additionally, it offers an ongoing process that can be oriented toward strategic thinking, goal setting, and continuing self-assessment, especially with regard to the quality of student learning, a topic that is not traditionally the focus of the process. The link to strategy is not an illusion. In a helpful study of program reviews across 130 campuses, Wergin asked the provost of a research university with a model program how he would introduce it into another institution. He replied: "First I'd take a measure of the institution and its vision for the future.... I would try to find ways of articulating a higher degree of aspiration; if there weren't a strong appetite for this, then program review would be doomed to failure" (quoted in Wergin 2002, 245–46).

Although some processes show these characteristics, there should be no illusion that these proposed strategic shifts in the perspective and purpose of program review will be easy to accomplish (Mets 1997). The culture of academic autonomy that makes leadership so difficult is in fullest flower at the departmental level. It is not surprising that proposals for academic change that do not originate in the department, such as reform in general education, are often perceived as a threat to departmental autonomy.

Program Reviews and Student Learning

One should not expect or even desire to change program reviews radically, for they are properly a creature of the judgments of professionals in their fields. Yet one can seek to alter the process to make it fit more naturally into a process of strategic thinking and self-evaluation. This could mean that each program would be asked to focus on the quality of student learning (in addition to research, faculty productivity, and program content) with specific attention to the larger strategic goals of the university. Protocols and methods would be built into the process to achieve this orientation, giving space to the department to develop or modify assessment methods that it would find beneficial to improve its own work with students.

An important part of the self-study would be focused on questions that the program faculty would shape themselves and would find meaningful. Zemsky, Wegner, and Massy (2005) write of a fascinating project in academic quality assurance at the University of Missouri that can guide some of these questions and has inspired the following list: *What are the goals of learning in the department?* What do we want our students to learn and to be able to do? How do our goals reflect the distinctive mission and vision of the department and the institution? *What should be the design of the curriculum?* Is there a coherent logic for the relationship of courses in the program? How do the courses relate to the goals of learning? *What are the department's primary methods of teaching and learning?* How do our students learn? Are teaching and learning active or passive, individually or group oriented? How is technology used? What types of assignments, learning experiences, and levels of expectation predominate? *How do we know if students are reaching the department's and the university's goals for learning?* How do we assess learning? Who is responsible for the evaluation—the faculty member, the department, the school, or the university? What validates a student's choice of this program as a major? *How do we use the results of our evaluations to improve the quality of student learning?* Are the results actually being used effectively? What are our priorities in light of what we know about teaching, learning, and our program? What should change?

In an approach such as this, the department would go on to create a self-study that would provide external reviewers with samples of student work, such as papers, projects, and exams. Assessment data about student accomplishments and the results of exit interviews and alumni surveys would be provided. The visiting team would read much of this material in advance and spend considerable time on campus, interacting with students, perhaps hearing and seeing the results of student research. The effort to create a culture of evidence for student learning as a basis for program reviews would make the process more strategically effective and rewarding.

If the questions alone were to become a central concern of all program reviews, they would more clearly become strategic activities. The questions about other broad strategic goals of the university concerning graduate programs or research might be structured in similar ways. Whatever the focus, they would become vital links in the effort to connect the program's goals with the strategic objectives of the larger institution and would build the strategic self-assessment into the ongoing work of the department. In systematically using the program review process to respond more nimbly to change and the university's vision, departments would find themselves participating in the process and discipline of strategic leadership.

THE GOVERNING BOARD AND THE IMPLEMENTATION OF STRATEGY

One indispensable but neglected resource for the task of implementation of a strategic plan is the governing board, whose role in strategic governance we explored in chapter 7 and can now supplement. At this stage of our study, it has become clear that the board's acceptance of a strategic outlook is a critical dimension of its own work, and one that involves many-sided opportunities and responsibilities. Its participation in a total process of strategic leadership takes it well beyond simply insisting that the institution develop a strategic plan as one activity alongside many others. Rather, the governing board serves as the ultimate guarantor that strategic leadership is empowered by strategic governance and translated into strategic management (cf. Association of Governing Boards of Universities and Colleges 1996, 2006; Chait, Ryan, and Taylor 2005; Morrill 2002). In a strategic context, its responsibility to monitor, evaluate, and ensure accountability for the fulfillment of the institution's purposes takes on a new pertinence.

Having examined the importance and the content of strategic visions, initiatives, and goals, we can more easily appreciate the centrality of the board's role in the implementation of the plan. The governing board and each of its committees now have a rich set of issues to address through the content of the strategy and its measurable goals. The goals form a natural agenda for each board and committee meeting, giving trustees a coherent set of topics to keep under continuous review.

Monitoring Performance

In responding to strategic initiatives and goals, the board's first responsibility is to raise pertinent questions. As it does so, it exercises far more influence over the university than it might otherwise expect. The strategic questions that are likely to come from board members trigger a sense of anticipatory responsibility that cascade through the decision-making chains of the institution. Administrators and faculty leaders who interact with the board in committees and other contexts become very conscious of whether or not the announced goals of the strategy are being satisfied. Since its campus interlocutors know that the board will be provided information about progress in reaching the goals, anticipatory actions will ordinarily be taken to respond effectively to expected board queries. Thus, the actual and anticipated interrogatories of the governing board are a potent factor in the implementation of strategic goals. Because the board is the legal guarantor of the mission of the institution, it can play a decisive symbolic and actual role in the exercise of its fiduciary and leadership responsibilities to ensure the institution's future (Morrill 2002).

As the board receives assessments of the organization's results, it can take an active stance in monitoring performance. If the assessments raise issues, the board's monitoring becomes the basis for pressing for more information, and for seeking to know what is being done to resolve a problem or to reach a goal. Effective and active oversight depends on good systems of assessment, which in turn lead to questions about ways to improve performance to ensure results. The board does not intervene directly in a faculty or administrative responsibility, except in extremis. But its level of engagement increases if important goals continue to be delayed or missed. Its antennae go up if problems persist or are avoided. In keeping with its proper form of responsibility, it can take a variety of steps to ensure results, from asking for reports to adopting resolutions, creating task forces, and setting deadlines for action. The administrators and faculty members who interact directly with the governing board will feel the pressure of accountability to address strategic issues that the board has addressed. Ultimately, it is the president, the board's primary executive partner, who will be held to account to answer for problems that are subject to resolution, but not resolved, and to attain goals that are attainable, but not yet attained (Morrill 2002). In its own assessment of the president, the board uses the goals of the strategy as a central benchmark of performance.

Renewing the Work of the Board

When boards see their role strategically, a new kind of vitality and purposefulness are released. They feel their own unique and ultimate responsibility for translating the institution's narrative of identity into a narrative of aspiration. Their intentions find a new perspective through the methods of strategic leadership. Suddenly a course proposal is more than the arcane language of a professor, but a building block in the institution's effort to create a distinctive program that creates comparative educational advantage. Now plans for a new building are not just about cost and space but are as well part of a legacy of shared meaning and a new tool of education to reach strategic goals. The deliberations of the board and its committees display a new coherence, a clearer purpose, and a renewed level of commitment. That commitment in turn contributes to the board's enhanced ability to ensure the implementation of the institution's strategy as a way to guarantee its educational effectiveness and its viability in a world of change. Strategic momentum takes hold in the work of the board itself (Morrill 2002).

STRATEGIC INTEGRATION AND MOMENTUM

We have seen on numerous occasions that strategic leadership is an integrative discipline as well as a systemic process. Because it is rooted in the discovery and articulation of values, it always refers back to humans as agents and the choices that they make based on their underlying commitments. This pattern of seeking deeper connections defines the method at every turn. Strategic thinking finds the continuities between the past and the future by knowing and telling the institution's story as the basis of its vision. A concern for meaning and values embraces the effort to create a culture of evidence that will collect and use data that have strategic significance. The need for resources articulated in the strategy is integrated with plans to obtain them. The goals of the various strategies are assessed by an embedded process of evaluation and frequently connect to one another in broad patterns of relationship. Goals and priorities always come with price tags, so plans have to be translated into operating budgets. As we have seen, processes of communication and systems of implementation are efforts to motivate and coordinate the translation of decisions into actions. Strategic evaluation transforms its findings into new goals to improve results continuously. In all these ways, strategic leadership is an integrative and systemic process of sense making and sense giving.

In order to implement its goals, strategic leadership discerns multiple relationships and is ready to create permanent or temporary integrative mechanisms of decision making. Frequently, special committees or task forces are needed to address connected issues. These cross-departmental groups of faculty and staff draw together the members of departments and units, who must work cooperatively to implement strategies. They may become a continuing community of practice that develops self-consciousness and meets periodically. Because of their shared interest and expertise, they can contribute to one another's knowledge and growth (Wenger and Snyder 2000). When student learning or other critical values move to the center of the strategic agenda, then the isolated points of view of separate departments and faculty committees have to give way to the unified perspectives of cross-disciplinary task forces and strategy councils. Strategic leadership creates supple, resilient, and coherent networks of collaborative practice and leadership, decision making, and implementation.

Strategic Momentum

As we have seen, there is no doubt that an environment of constrained or declining resources creates severe challenges to successful strategy and leadership. Violent swings in resources from year to year at both public and private institutions make the work of strategy immensely difficult and complex. Under some extreme conditions, crisis management may have to replace strategic leadership for a time. But in most cases, the future of the institution itself will depend on strategies to address the resource problem at its source. If systematic restructuring of an institution's programs proves to be necessary, or if contingency planning becomes a continuing requirement, it is far better to approach the task as a strategic challenge than simply a political or managerial problem.

Happily, colleges and universities do not ordinarily find themselves in a crippling or chaotic environment. Possibilities present themselves continually in many different forms, sometimes under the guise of challenges, at other times as ready opportunities. Strategic leadership should be prepared to seize the promise of these circumstances. Skilled strategists know that every plan should include some worthy and significant goals that are within reach and can be rapidly achieved. "What helps strategic transformation succeed is a series of small wins" (Keller 1997, 168). When the designs of the strategy begin to take hold and possibilities are realized or threats are overcome, something quite remarkable begins to take hold in institutions. Energy and confidence that build a sense of momentum are released, creating a magnifying effect of achievements upon one another. In describing the experience of great companies, Collins uses the concept of "breakthrough" to denote that point when momentum takes hold and builds on itself: "Each piece of the system reinforces the other parts of the system to form an integrated whole that is much more powerful than the sum of the parts" (2001, 182). In describing turnaround situations at institutions with widely different missions, the contributors to *Academic Turnarounds* (MacTaggart 2007a) describe the ways that achieving financial stability, creating new self-images, and developing innovative academic initiatives intertwine and reinforce each other to achieve momentum.

Now the wisdom of establishing measurable goals that are demanding but attainable begins to be rewarded. Those responsible for the achievements feel a sense of control over their circumstances and are absorbed by their commitment to the tasks at hand. Intentions stated publicly and then fulfilled create credibility and trust in the strategy process and in those participating in it and leading it. Achievements in one sphere trigger accomplishments in others, as a synergy of success takes hold. The cycle of success translates from resources to programs, to new plans, to enlarged support, to more opportunities for students and faculty, and to enhanced reputation in a virtuous circle driven by strategic leadership (Keller 1997; cf. Lawrence and Cermak 2004).

In studying examples of successful strategy programs, one finds that the participants in the process often seek to express the ways that leadership and momentum are rooted in coherent and connected processes of strategic choice and action. As Dooris, Kelley, and Trainer reflect on these cases, they conclude: "Strategic planning—wisely used—can be a powerful tool to help an academic organization listen to its constituencies, encourage the emergence of good ideas from all levels, recognize opportunities, make decisions supported by evidence, strive toward shared mission...and actualize the vision" (2004, 10). In a word, even though they do not use the term, good strategy is leadership.

Strategic leadership depends on many individuals, so it is experienced as a collaborative and communal achievement. Problems and issues will still present themselves, sometimes as frustration that the pace of success is not even more accelerated. Yet it also becomes clear that the distrust and anxiety that often take hold when people do not know where the institution is headed largely disappear. People now see strategy as a valid enterprise because it delivers on its promises. It responds to several layers of human need by defining aspirations that are worth commitment, and by using an organized collaborative method to achieve them. Strategic leadership not only sets a direction for the future but also takes the organization toward its destination. In doing so, it embodies many of the capacities, satisfies the needs, and produces the benefits that describe the phenomenon of relational leadership.

PART IV

The Limits and Possibilities of Strategic Leadership

CHAPTER  12

Conflict and Change: The Limits and Possibilities of Strategic Leadership

We have learned that change and conflict are at the heart of leadership, and these issues have shaped the background and the foreground of this text. If strategic leadership in colleges and universities is about anything, it is about systematically negotiating the forces of change and the realities of structural conflict. It is time to bring the dynamics of these issues into self-conscious focus and to explore the capacities of strategic leadership to deal with them.

One of the central purposes of this section is to determine realistically the organizational times and circumstances when strategic leadership will be a more useful or less useful method of decision making. The reader will know that all methods have both possibilities and limits as well as conditions under which they are particularly effective or minimally so. Such is the case for strategic leadership. Our aim is to weigh the difference that strategic leadership makes under various conditions of change, crisis, and conflict. If we can understand with some precision the capacity of strategic leadership to deal with change and conflict, then a campus will be able to have realistic expectations about what the process can and cannot accomplish.

STRATEGIC LEADERSHIP AND STRUCTURAL CONFLICT

Like all organizations, colleges and universities are filled with conflict. The word itself calls to mind opposition between and among individuals and groups along a social and political spectrum that ranges from polite disagreements to intense personal hostilities, from political infighting to bitter public controversies, from negotiation to violence. Conflict is everywhere on campuses and elsewhere because people, with their contending values, interests, personalities, and points of view, are everywhere. As long as resources are limited and humans are finite, conflict will be at the center of human experience.

All these aspects of conflict shed light on the qualities, skills, and knowledge that individuals who carry leadership responsibilities should possess in order to deal with it. Dialogue, negotiation, and methods of conflict resolution are a leader's indispensable tools. Yet it has become clear in this study that no matter how successful a leader might be in resolving political, policy, and personality clashes, there are deeper structural conflicts in the governance of academic institutions that resist easy reconciliation. Structural conflict does not necessarily require antipathy between the parties but is a tension in the values to which the organization is committed. It appears both in contrasting orientations as to what should count in making choices and in the tensions enmeshed in the way those choices are made. Conflicts in basic values and paradigms cannot be reconciled by a leader's political skills and administrative talents alone but require the resources of strategic thinking and leadership.

Reconciling Conflicts in Values and Paradigms

We can examine some aspects of the dynamic of reconciling opposing values in a recent study of international business leadership. Although the authors we discuss use a different terminology than ours, their work gives a number of examples of the methods of strategic leadership in resolving conflicts between different cultural paradigms and contrasting organizational values.

Fons Trompenaars and Charles Hampden-Turner (2002) explore contrasting cultural value systems, including the classic conflict between cultures that define achievement in individualistic as opposed to communitarian terms. Western countries, especially the United States, emphasize achievement by the individual, while most Asian cultures put primary stress on group accomplishments. In dealing with a culturally diverse workforce, creative managers know that cultural value systems and paradigms run too deep to be drastically changed, since they involve a whole pattern of seeing and understanding the world from the ground up. Rather than confounding workers by imposing an incentive plan from another culture, effective managers try to reconcile differences between value systems. For example, they might try to develop a reward system that measures and recognizes individual achievement in terms of what it contributes to a team. The interactions of the team, in turn, can be designed to provide opportunities for individual growth and creativity. The energy and motivation of the group is then stimulated by new forms of recognition of their achievements as a team, perhaps in competition with other teams (Trompenaars and Hampden-Turner 2002).

Vicious Circles and Virtuous Circles

Trompenaars and Hampden-Turner analyze a series of conflicts in cultural and organizational values and their resolution in terms of what they call "vicious circles" and "virtuous circles." In a vicious circle, a single cultural system is imposed on another, and the results are a reinforcing downward spiral of problems. For example, if only individuals are recognized in tasks requiring teamwork, performance declines for both the individual and the group. In virtuous circles, on the other hand, there is a new "third thing" that emerges from the conflict. It has its own reinforcing patterns of success because it has drawn positive features from different value systems to create higher levels of performance—in this case, a team with distinctive and productive cultural norms of its own. The answer is not to create a series of disjointed compromises between the different cultural systems, but to find a new integration of values and ways of thinking.

Trompenaars and Hampden-Turner use a number of case studies to show how value reconciliation functions in a variety of other challenging organizational contexts, not just clashes in cultural values. Many of these have to do with issues of purpose and vision. We learn, for instance, that the genius of the business idea behind Dell Computer involves a reconciliation of opposites. Dell entered the personal computer market late, when many of the supply channels to the consumer were already filled with competitors' brands. In response, it came upon a new idea for the computer world: direct sales to the customer. The challenges were many. How could less personal service command competitive prices? How could the customer's desire for a machine built to order be combined with the techniques of mass production? In traditional strategic thinking, there would have been but two choices. Either you provide low-cost products or you offer expensive premium models designed to meet the customer's tastes. Yet Dell embraced both sides of the dilemma. Since its cost structure is less than half of that of its competitors, it can sustain an advantage in pricing. It also offers customized products through direct differentiated relationships with its customers, powerfully aided by the Internet. "One important reason Dell can do both is that it orders its components in mass quantities from its suppliers, achieving economies of scale, and also co-designs its computers with its intended customers... in unique, customized configurations" (Trompenaars and Hampden-Turner 2002, 245). This is a virtuous circle, contradictory on its face, of mass customization.

THE STRATEGIC RESOLUTION OF STRUCTURAL CONFLICT IN COLLEGES AND UNIVERSITIES

One should ask what companies that make products or offer commercial services, even sophisticated ones, have to do with higher education. The answer is, more than one might think. In all these cases there is evidence of a method of conceptual analysis and problem solving that is intimately tied to a set of strategic master images concerning the purpose and the vision of the organization in a changing environment. In drawing on these resources of self-definition and purpose, which typically circulate around narratives of identity, the resolution of the value conflicts shows conceptual depth and complexity, subtle differentiation, and creative insight. They reveal the ability of participants to gain intellectual distance from their challenges, to reposition their own reflections, and to think about their own thinking, all of which are characteristics of learning organizations. It is just this kind of intellectual virtuosity that is part of the discipline of strategic leadership in higher education. When a powerful sense of strategic direction takes hold within an organization, new resources of thought and imagination become available. The continuing tensions in policies and purposes have a stock of strategic insights on which to draw to create virtuous circles of understanding to resolve conflicts and to find shared commitments.

Strategic thinking in colleges and universities always encounters a series of implicit or explicit conflicts in governance, mission, and vision. Some of them track the fundamental value conflict in the decision-making system itself, reflecting the tension between autonomy and authority, intrinsic and instrumental values, or the paradigms that accompany them. Others lie within the academic sphere alone, while others, such as policies relating to social and academic student life, cross two or more decision-making zones. The organizational culture and the missions of many institutions of higher learning are balanced between purposes such as the following, which illustrate various forms of conflict, tension, and complementarities, especially in the context of a changing world (Morrill 1990):

- Teaching and research
- Liberal and professional education
- General education and disciplinary specialties
- Access and selectivity
- Diversity and community
- Need-based aid and merit scholarships
- Undergraduate and graduate studies
- Central and regional campuses
- Religious and secular values
- Local needs and national ambitions
- Legacy and change
- Student social life and academic life
- The academic core and the academic periphery
- Centralization and decentralization
- Equal resources and selective excellence
- Assessment as value added or as a level of achievement
- Academic selectivity and athletic competitiveness
- Openness and confidentiality
- Authority and participation

Teaching and Research

Let us look at a couple of examples to see how a process of strategic inquiry can become a form of conflict resolution. No one in higher education will argue that teaching and scholarship can be disconnected. Scholarship in some form, whether published or otherwise, is essential to the currency and vitality of teaching and student learning. Almost all academicians also will argue that a professor's scholarship or creative activity must eventually be made available in some public arena so that its significance can be assessed through peer review.

When the value of scholarship becomes defined by the originality, volume, and influence of publications (and their equivalents), its relationship to teaching and learning becomes more problematic. The conflict is not over the importance of scholarship to good teaching, which is a given, but over the type and quantity of scholarship that a particular institution will value. The conflict has several dimensions, but among them are the time of the faculty member and the resources of the institution that are available for research. It seems to follow, for instance, that original and influential scholarship is essential for professors in universities with missions in doctoral and advanced professional education. Reflecting this, graduate professors may only teach several courses a year, often with the help of teaching assistants, and they can rely on an extensive research infrastructure. Yet college professors who teach only undergraduates in three or four large classes each semester will be hard pressed to find the time and the resources to do a large amount of research and publication on a regular basis, whether or not they are inclined to do so.

If institutional missions regarding scholarship and teaching have not been differentiated and translated into appropriate resources, policies, and expectations, a vicious circle develops. The dominant model of the profession and the prestige of research turn the circle toward a commitment to publication, leaving less time and energy for teaching and the enhancement of student learning, which may suffer as a result. But so does scholarship, because ordinarily, little that has wide influence can be achieved when it is sandwiched in among other exhausting duties, and when it lacks time, resources, and rewards. Most importantly, the forms of scholarship that might enrich teaching and contribute most to the development of the professor are frustrated by the prevailing model.

The possibilities for reversing the vicious circle can be found in a clear conceptual analysis that is differentiated strategically in terms of institutional mission and context. The first step in doing so is to clear away the models about teaching and scholarship that have been imported unconsciously from other institutions. The next is to draw out the most fruitful connections between them suggested in the institution's distinctive strategic profile.

The benefit of removing faulty assumptions through clear and cogent conceptual analysis is illustrated in *Scholarship Reconsidered*, the well-known study by Ernest Boyer (1990b) that appeared some years ago. By sorting out the different forms of scholarship and affirming them in terms of various institutional missions, Boyer struck a vibrantly responsive chord among faculty members. As he differentiated the dominant model of the scholarship of discovery from applied scholarship, the scholarship of integration, and the scholarship of teaching, he also opened the imagination of many academics to see new patterns of relationship between teaching and scholarship. Beyond aligning policies with practices that reward a variety of forms of scholarship, he pointed the way toward creating virtuous circles of connection between scholarship and teaching. If expectations are textured in terms of institutional mission and vision, such as student involvement in faculty research, then scholarship, teaching, and student learning find novel and productive ways to reinforce and complement each other in virtuous circles.

Faculty Roles and Responsibilities

These reflections on teaching and scholarship lead in many related directions, revealing the systemic character of strategic thinking. One of the issues that they entail is the re-conceptualization and redelineation of individual faculty roles and responsibilities. The process is already underway in many institutions, though usually on a piecemeal basis. If faculty members are to have differential workloads in teaching, research, and service, there must be a careful definition of responsibilities in terms of what Linda McMillin (2002) describes as a "circle of value" between the faculty member and the institution. In terms of workload issues, a faculty member's teaching, scholarship, and service add value to a department, which in turn adds value to the institution. The final turn of the circle involves the institution adding value to the faculty member by providing resources and support for the individual's changing responsibilities and evolving professional interests. In sum, the idea of differential workloads will not be effective if it is based simply on an individual's preferences and desires, but only if it takes into account the needs and opportunities of all three parties, the person, the academic unit, and the institution (McMillin 2002).

Strategic conceptualization brings to this task a way of locating the issues precisely at the point of intersection between the institution and its environment. It brings the question back to the distinctive values, purposes, and competencies of academic organizations as they have been formed in the real world over time. Strategic leadership defines the needs, capacities, and possibilities of the organization and of its academic professionals simultaneously and in relation to one another. It sets in place a method of strategic differentiation that is able to define commitments that reconcile the perennial conflict between professional autonomy and the needs of the organization. Although the structural conflict in values will never disappear, it can become a virtuous circle of possibility rather than a vicious cycle of frustration.

Liberal and Professional Education

There is a large variety of conflicts in academic decision making where strategic leadership can provide new insights. The continuing tension between liberal education and professional studies is, for example, open to far more creative solutions than are typically brought to bear on it. As noted in *Greater Expectations*, "Liberal education is an educational philosophy rather than a body of knowledge, specific courses, or type of institution" (Association of American Colleges and Universities 2002, 25).

The more one sees rigorous learning as the acquisition of intellectual powers, cognitive skills, values, competencies, and dispositions mediated by a variety of subjects, the less significant the dichotomy between liberal arts and professional fields seems. The connections between the two can be constructed through the articulation of a shared set of demanding educational objectives. From this perspective, liberal education shows itself to be powerfully practical, and professional studies to involve a series of crucial theoretical issues. Studies of both the theoretical and practical issues in leadership, professional ethics, quantitative reasoning, organizational culture and behavior, policy development, problem solving, and decision making provide examples of contexts for interdisciplinary work involving the social sciences, humanities, and professional fields (cf. Bok 2006). If an institution develops a major strategic initiative to excel in creating a productive and distinctive relationship between the theory and practice of liberal and professional education, it could achieve a goal of enduring importance that creates a virtuous circle out of a traditional sphere of conflict. With little doubt, it will find that its passion for the task will come from threads of connection to its own existing or emerging practices and the distinguishing characteristics that are rooted in its identity.

These examples of the tensions between teaching and research and liberal and professional education suggest a method that can be applied to a large variety of similar polarities. In creating an authentic and compelling sense of institutional purpose and vision, the process of strategic leadership is able to meet a series of demanding requirements. It requires intellectual self-consciousness and conceptual depth, speaks to the human need for coherence, provides a sense of common enterprise, analyzes changing trends in education, and articulates worthwhile possibilities for the future that grow out of a legacy. In doing so, it motivates and obligates members of the organization to come together around common goals. As leadership must, it also shoulders the task of reconciling conflict. Being strategic, it brings to each form of conflict a sense of the larger world and the institution's place in it. It gathers these insights into a disciplined process of sense making that create new integrations that end tiresome debates and in new articulations of values that transcend the conflict. Academic commitments to quality and autonomy become embodied in organizational forms and practices that are necessary to them, and those forms in turn bear the imprint of intrinsic values. As a source of both responsibility and shared meaning, the institution's narrative of identity and aspiration empowers the continuous effort to create new forms of authentic balance, synthesis, and commitment. We often use its methods of building consensus even when we do not do so consciously and systematically.

ADVERSARIAL LIMITS TO STRATEGIC LEADERSHIP

As any practitioner of strategy will quickly acknowledge, the success of the process depends on conditions that it cannot provide for itself. Strategic leadership cannot function optimally or sometimes at all in the context of deep mistrust and hostility. If the governing board is in turmoil, if faculty and administration have taken up battle positions, or if large factions of the faculty are at war with each other, then strategic leadership will not be effective. A foundation of basic goodwill and a modicum of trust are the prerequisites and can be the results of the multiple inquiries, deliberations, and collaborations that drive the process. It is often better not to start the work of strategy until the right circumstances are created, rather than to have it succumb to dysfunction.

Strategic leadership ultimately depends on a fundamental consensus about the values that the organization exists to serve. Wide variations in the interpretations of the exact content of those values are possible, but shared commitment to them is necessary. The many leaders and participants in the strategy process can do little to enjoy the benefits of strategic leadership unless they share the common ground of commitment to the institution, a high regard for academic process and values, and respect for one another. A good strategy process can do many things, but it cannot be expected to change the passions, ideologies, or values in which individuals have grounded their identities.

STRATEGIC LEADERSHIP AND CHANGE

As we have seen throughout this inquiry, a growing consciousness of the pervasiveness of change and the need for higher education to respond effectively to it have become central themes in a large variety of recent studies and projects (Bok 2006; Friedman 2005; Newman, Couturier, and Scurry 2004; Zemsky, Wegner, and Massy 2005), among them a major undertaking of the American Council on Education called "On Leadership and Institutional Transformation," which issued a series of five reports, *On Change*, from 1998 to 2002. Then there are the various projects and publications of the Pew Roundtables and the Knight Collaborative, which offer reports and analyses on key issues of educational policy and practice, especially related to new market realities, beginning in the early 1990s and continuing for more than a decade, and form the basis for the work by Zemsky, Wegner, and Massy (2005). In several articles and studies related to the "Project on the Future of Higher Education," Alan Guskin and Mary Marcy (2002, 2003) argue that colleges and universities must take on the challenge of change by reducing soaring instructional costs themselves, or others will do it for them.

The emphasis on change differs significantly in each of these studies. Some concentrate on broad external forces such as information technology, global competition, and proprietary educational providers, while others focus more on institutional change as an intentional process. Policy makers seem to be the intended audience for some of the studies, while in other cases it is faculty members or academic administrators. Above all, no one reading these reports, and the many others like them, could ever conclude that contemporary higher education in America is a special intellectual preserve free of the full-bodied realities of economic, social, cultural, educational, and technological change. Echoing a perspective offered repeatedly throughout this work, they show that colleges and universities have a contextual identity like every other institution and are enmeshed in nets of social forces and webs of accountability.

Resistance to Change

Enough has been written here and elsewhere about the difficulty of planned change in higher education that it requires little new argumentation. One of the ironies of change in colleges and universities is that it occurs continually, but by no means uniformly, in the work of individual faculty members and many academic units. Yet the institutions that house these changes at the micro level often face agonies of change at the macro level, especially in academic programs and policies.

We have traced how the well-known characteristics of professional autonomy, loose coupling, shared governance, and fragmented decision making produce organizations that resist change, especially if the change has not been initiated by academic professionals themselves. The general human tendency to resist the threat of the unfamiliar is especially evident in academic communities. Since academicians define themselves through their professional identities, change frequently challenges important sources of self-respect.

The reports and projects we have referenced offer trenchant diagnoses of the need for change, offer worthy proposals to improve institutional performance, and describe successful change processes. Yet one has to wonder whether they have seized the critical importance of effective methods of interactive and integral strategic leadership as the enabler of intentional and sustained change. In most studies, there is frequent reference to the responsibilities of official leaders, but much less to the ways change occurs as part of a reciprocal direction-setting leadership process. Bok (2006) writes sagely about the ways presidents and deans can use their positions to define a vision for the improvement of undergraduate education, including the assessment of student learning. If enthusiasm for these tasks does not take root among the faculty, however, it is doubtful that top-down strategies will be sustainable or widely influential. *On Change V* insightfully describes some aspects of a reciprocal leadership process, yet undoubtedly because the report is focused on the change process, it tends to describe change as if it were an end in itself (Eckel, Hill, and Green 2001).

Many of the things that official leaders do to encourage and effect change are precisely the components of an integral approach to strategy, which provides the content of change. They facilitate change by anchoring it in legacies and cherished academic values, and by building trust and taking the long view. They also help people to develop new ways of thinking by encouraging reflection on hidden assumptions, values, and familiar ways of doing things. Effective leaders of change listen to those involved in the process and learn from dissenting views. They also are sensitive to issues of collaborative process, create a sense of urgency for change, and communicate widely about the issues (Eckel, Green, and Hill 2001). They root their exercise of authority in a process of relational leadership.

In an illuminating subsequent study, *Taking the Reins*, Eckel and Kezar (2003) describe how six of the twenty-six American Council on Education institutions reached the level of what they call transforming change, change that was pervasive, deep, and intentional and altered the culture of the institution over time. The book presents five basic characteristics that seem essential to transformation: "(1) senior administrative support, (2) collaborative leadership, (3) flexible vision, (4) staff development, (5) visible action" (Eckel and Kezar 2003, 78).

Note the prominence on this list of factors that we have identified as critical to strategic leadership, especially the motifs of action, collaboration, vision, and senior administrative support. In addition to these, the authors analyzed other interlocking characteristics in the decision-making culture of the institutions that contributed to transforming change. Perhaps the key element is the way participants found new ways of constructing meaning about change, or what we have often called sense making.

Although the *Change* reports and *Taking the Reins* use different language than ours, their findings parallel precisely many of the components of integral and integrated strategic leadership. This conclusion hinges on understanding strategy comprehensively, not as a method to change a program's market position. Although interactive leadership is recognized, what seems less central in their accounts is a systematic description of the possibilities of leadership as an engaging reciprocal process that can mobilize commitment to enact strategic change. The effectiveness of those who hold positions of authority is essential, but more is required to create a leadership method that can be embedded in the institution and is not only activated when change is required. The ultimate goal is to implement leadership as a *system* of interaction that is framed by an integrative discipline and collaborative process of strategic decision making.

Strategic leadership can serve as a vehicle for effecting change in institutions of higher education, both through its content and its methods. It can be the missing link between proposals that involve change and their enactment. It makes intentional change a function of strategic change and thereby builds the change agenda into the leadership process through which an institution designs its future in a challenging world. If, for example, assessment is to improve the quality of student learning, leadership has to be embedded in organizational processes and relationships to achieve and sustain the change. A faculty will dismiss out of hand all the alluring models of assessment at other institutions unless they are part of a decision-making process that relates to the values, beliefs, and circumstances of their own institution.

Based on the perspectives provided in this analysis, it is clear that strategic leadership brings a large array of resources to the demands and tasks of collegiate change. As we have seen, these include:

- An emphasis on patterns of awareness and reflection that discern the contextual identity of institutions of higher learning, including their interaction with the driving forces of change

- An interpretation of leadership that is focused on issues of human agency and sense making, and that sets an agenda for change with an awareness of its threats to personal and professional values

- A sensitivity to institutional identity, story, and legacy, thus affirming heritage while preparing for change

- A collaborative process of strategic thinking and decision making, which builds legitimacy for change and embeds it in a structured process of choice

- A process of transparency in sharing information of all kinds about the institution, which raises the awareness of the institution's strengths and weaknesses

- The articulation of a vision for the future that reduces uncertainty and provides motivation

- The development of a set of measurable goals that give a specific contour to change and provide an integrated sense of direction

- A plan for communication about change and for the implementation of goals that establishes confidence and credibility and builds a sense of momentum for the future

THE NATURE OF STRATEGIC CHANGE

In order to avoid confusion and uncertainty about the intent of a strategy process and to define expectations for strategic change accurately, it is important to be clear about the various forms and dimensions of change. To do so, it helps to consider two fundamental aspects of change, the scope of change and the time it takes for change. Each aspect in turn has its own dynamics that produce varying degrees of change. As to time, the speed of change can be considered in terms of the poles of rapid versus gradual change, while its duration ranges from enduring to temporary change. With regard to its scope, we can distinguish between the breadth of change as pervasive or limited, while the element of depth considers change that ranges from deep to superficial. Needless to say, many similar terms and phrases can substitute for those suggested here (Eckel, Green, and Hill 2001).[1]

The Scope of Strategic Change

These categories help us to understand the differences between strategic change and other forms of change on a campus, including those that are operational or experimental, or that involve a response to crisis. Many operational changes are limited or minor adjustments in day-to-day management policies and practices, such as a change in the prerequisites for a course or a modification to the software in one office. Were the changes in the software system to affect the whole campus, the project would become a broad change, though it may be a superficial one. It affects a lot of people, but most of them in minor ways. Deep changes affect basic organizational capabilities and characteristics, though they can be limited in the scope of their influence and might apply to only one or two academic or administrative units. If the change is so significant in both scope and depth that it reaches the level of a basic competency across the institution, then it becomes a strategic issue. Issues of strategic change can never be defined with precision and finality because the meaning of change in the collegiate world is fluid and symbolic. The different categories of change help us to understand that strategic change takes us toward the deep and pervasive issues of change that confront an institution.

Time and Strategic Change

When we consider the reference points of the time of change, we discover characteristics of strategic change that are counterintuitive. Although strategic change in the corporate world is often rapid, pervasive, and enduring (consider successful mergers and acquisitions), the same ordinarily does not hold true for the academic programs and identities of colleges and universities. In itself, there is no reason to think that gradual (sometimes called incremental) change cannot be enduring, profound, and pervasive. These characteristics are precisely the ones that Burns (2003) uses to define transforming change, and he notes that it may occur over long periods of time. Eckel and Kezar (2003) suggest that institutions engaged in transformational change see it as a continuing process, even after five-and-a-half years. In his study of entrepreneurial universities, Burton Clark (1998) concludes that several decades were required for their transformations to occur, and in examining several turnaround situations, Adrian Tinsley (2007) suggests that transformational change is incremental.

Some writers on change tend to contrast transforming leadership with incremental change, while the true contrast may be with rapid, temporary, and operational change that lacks a strategic focus (Lick 2002). As a case in point, consider our earlier example of the internationalization of a university. If an achievement is truly strategic and transforming, it represents a pervasive, deep, and enduring change. Being pervasive or comprehensive, it touches most departments and programs in the institution, and in being deep or profound, it will alter the way that many courses are designed and taught, as well as the experiences of many faculty and students. Its scope will show itself in a change in the population of the university, and over time in deep shifts in the norms and culture of the organization. Yet the change process will not be rapid, but gradual and incremental. It will take at least a decade or two for the institution to accomplish many of the central tasks of strategic change of this magnitude, and the work will never be entirely accomplished because changes in the outside world will continue to necessitate changes inside the organization.

The Characteristics of Strategic Change

The explanation for some of the characteristics of strategic change can be found in several of the defining features of strategic leadership that we have considered, including the notions of strategic vision and strategic intent. The concept of intent is an apt one, for it captures the motifs of purposefulness and self-awareness, which are defining components of human agency. Implicated as well are the themes of will and commitment, the motivation to attain worthwhile goals in order to fulfill the organization's best possibilities. Understood in this way, a vision clearly fosters enduring change that will be as deep and broad as is required to respond to the strategic situation at hand. If the challenges and opportunities produce a compelling vision that requires deep, enduring, and pervasive change, strategic leadership will seek to mobilize resources and commitment to accomplish that goal. Over time, with clearly marked milestones of continuing progress, the result will be transforming change.

Given the enormously variable circumstances and identities of each institution, strategic change has several forms and possibilities. Some colleges and universities dominate their environments with the resources they command and the positions they hold. Respond to change they must, but they often do so with a flexibility, deliberateness, and circumspection that others cannot afford. The need to respond to change is inescapable, but it is often masked by adaptive and conservative impulses, especially in the academic sphere proper.

At the other end of the spectrum are institutions whose capacity for change is driven by an innovative vision or by vulnerability in enrollment or finances—witness organizations rapidly adding new programs for adults in multiple locations, new job-related offerings, or distance-learning programs that make novel uses of technology. Thus, the speed, depth, and scope of change that are required of a given college or university to reach its objectives are widely variable. For some institutions, rapid, bold, and profound changes are not on the horizon, nor do they necessarily need to be. For all these reasons, institutions frequently move in cycles of change. A period of intense innovation is followed by a time for consolidation, preparatory to the next cycle of more intensive change. Thus, in being genuinely strategic, intentional change will be legitimately variable by place, time, and circumstance. Woe to the institution, however, that mistakes its place in the cycle of change or uses its apparent strength to dismiss the forms of change to which it must respond. Self-delusion and complacency are denials of leadership, both among leaders and those who are led. Serious threats to institutions can lead to crises if they are covered up by neglect or timidity. Strategic leadership as a form of consciousness is designed precisely to discern the most compelling and dangerous signs of the times and to convert them into opportunities for change. The common belief that the deepest changes usually only occur through crisis may be correct. Yet effective strategy programs provide the tools to avoid the worst of a crisis before it takes hold. Strategy can and must be decisive when the times require it, using its methods and insights to reveal both threats and opportunities as they develop.

Some of these thoughts on strategic change can be illustrated by a quick glance at institutional histories. Perhaps the most common pattern of fundamental change is for institutions of higher learning to make a series of circumscribed but deep changes that create an evolutionary transformation of organizational mission. As major universities gradually emerged from small "colonial" colleges in the last several decades of the nineteenth century, for example, change followed a common pattern. New disciplines and new professional schools were added to the core of existing classical fields, eventually creating the multi-universities that we know today (Veysey 1965). In one regard the changes were circumscribed, because a new school or program did not alter existing activities themselves. Yet the cumulative changes over time created institutions that were drastic transformations of their former selves. In more recent decades, many universities have transformed themselves in a parallel way by adding research institutes, interdisciplinary centers, professional education programs, satellite campuses, and international affiliates. The examples show that even though the time required achieving it may span several decades, a transforming level of strategic change may be reached.

Change, Crisis, and the Limits to Strategic Leadership

As we have discovered, strategy is intended to discern and prevent impending crises, and it should insist that risk management plans be developed systematically to prepare for emergencies. The attention to possible calamities is increasingly a requirement of risk management and is a useful method for testing the strengths and limits of organizational capacities. Deep knowledge of the strategic identity of an organization includes sharpened sensitivity to threats to its reputation, finances, campus infrastructure, human resources, and leadership. Yet when a state budget allocation is suddenly cut by 20 percent or a fire ravages "Old Main," a crime wave hits the campus, a controversy shatters confidence in the president, or hurricanes and floods destroy the campus, long-term strategy gives way to crisis leadership. The vision will have to be put on hold so that the crisis and the pain that may be involved can be confronted.

As these examples make clear, the analytical and disciplined protocols of strategic leadership move in a different orbit than the rapid, symbolic, and unilateral interventions often required during a crisis or an emergency. No doubt, some groups and persons can be effective in both strategic leadership and crisis leadership, others not. No doubt, too, the story of a place and its vision for the future will need to be invoked to reassure a community in a crisis and to help it find its bearings as the emergency subsides. Nonetheless, as much as strategy defines the need to prepare for them, strategic leadership is not driven by unforeseen and disruptive solitary events.

As has also become evident, strategic leadership is limited in other ways. Because strategies take their root in legacies and flower in visions that draw on the special capacities of the members of an academic community, they are not usually the vehicle for revolutionary change. There are logical limits to the content and the work of strategy. If the proposed content of the strategy nullifies the organization's identity and the capacities of the existing faculty and staff, then the proposal for change is not a strategy of *that* community but of some other real or hypothetical organization. Similarly, narratives can be altered and transformed, but they cannot be replaced. Radical change of this nature represents the transition to a new identity, which may occur, for example, as an external authority such as a state governing board decides to turn a technical college into a major university in a short period of time. Whatever the form and nature of change, there finally is a point at which the discussion is logically no longer about options within a given strategy, but about change to an entirely new identity. Strategic leadership is not able to make rapid or radical revolutions in higher education, for to do so is to contradict the values and organizational identity that are in place. It can find ways to rapidly transplant some vital organs, but not the self of the institution.

EMBEDDED LEADERSHIP

Taken together, these comments on strategic change suggest that a set of basic conditions must be fulfilled for it to be successful and continuous. Significant and persistent attention has to be given to creating leadership and decision-making systems for colleges and universities that are far more resilient and responsive to change than is currently the case.

Leadership for change requires institutions of higher learning to embed and distribute responsive and responsible processes of strategic decision making among committees, teams, and communities throughout the organization. This task is indispensable for mending the worn patchwork of decision-making patterns that characterize today's institutions. For this to occur, a new sense of shared responsibility for effective leadership and governance must take hold and shape the enterprise's culture of collaborative governance. In such a context, obligations are felt by all parties in the process (Tierney 2000). Leaders empower and respond to the needs of their followers, but followers have the responsibility to do the same for leaders, so that at times their roles become interchangeable. It will require the commitment of the faculty, administration, students, and the governing board to answer to one another for the quality of their shared leadership and followership in collaborative systems of decision making. Participants in the process grant designated leaders, whether the head of a committee or the president, a chance to be heard and recognize a legitimate role for authority, creating a sense of mutual responsibility sometimes lacking in academic communities (cf. Burns 2003). In discussing leadership and the distress that usually comes with the adaptation to change, Heifetz notes: "The long-term challenge of leadership is to develop people's adaptive capacity for tackling an ongoing stream of hard problems" (1994, 247).

Out of better and more responsive ways to make decisions will spring more effective and responsible decisions. Ultimately, according to Burns, it happens that in such a pattern of embedded leadership, "Instead of identifying individual actors simply as leaders or simply as followers, we see the whole process as a *system* in which the function of leadership is palpable and central but the actors move in and out of leader and follower roles" (2003, 185).

Leadership and change are difficult and complex issues in all organizations, but they are especially so in institutions of higher learning. The deep commitment of academic professionals to the power of learning as their center of value must be made organizationally resilient for it to flourish in the future. Without new approaches to governance, to leadership, and to management, that future will be more frustrating and traumatic than it needs to be, with the encroachment of managerial and commercial models of decision making ever more in evidence. Much is at stake in safeguarding the vitality of academic work and in retaining its sense of calling, as Clark reminds us. As a calling, it "constitutes a practical ideal of activity and character that makes a person's work morally inseparable from his or her life. It subsumes the self into a community of disciplined practice and sound judgment whose activity has meaning and value in itself, not just in the output or profit that results from it" (Bellah, Madsen, Sullivan, Swidler and Tipton quoted in B. R. Clark 1987, 274). The academy requires effective and widely distributed leadership to sustain the power and vitality of this vision.

NOTE

1. My discussion of these points has been influenced and oriented by the *Change V* report, however, I use different terminology and come to different conclusions.

CHAPTER 13

Conclusion: The Strategic Integration of Leadership

The time has come to take stock of the enterprise of strategic leadership. As suggested earlier, at one level, this work is an effort to reinterpret strategic decision-making processes that occur in some form in every institution. Strategic thinking may be tacit or self-conscious, fragmented or systematic, episodic or continuous. Nonetheless, it would be hard to claim that an institution could function without defining itself and its place in the world through decisions about its future. Some forms of strategy and reciprocal leadership have to be in place for academic organizations to function at all.

RECAPITULATION

Starting with these givens, I have attempted to reconceptualize the strategy process based on an understanding of leadership as a method of direction setting and sense making rooted in narratives, values, and paradigms. Based on those meanings, I have tried to show how a systematic approach to strategic leadership offers a coherent and promising method for decision making in colleges and universities.

The reconceptualization of the strategy process leads to its reformulation. More than inventing a set of new practices, I have aimed to discover new meanings, relationships, and possibilities in existing ones. I have suggested that the process and the discipline of strategic leadership must be woven into the protocols and structures of collaborative governance. The reformulation changes the form of strategy by providing it with a comprehensive, systematic, systemic, and integrated agenda for implementation. As the process unfolds, it can become both embodied and embedded in the life and work of the organization. In doing so, it exemplifies and enacts many of the characteristics of relational leadership by building trust and commitment among members of the organization (cf. Kezar 2004).

THE DISCIPLINE OF STRATEGIC LEADERSHIP

Although always somewhat artificial when they are separated from their natural connections in practice, we can distinguish the components of strategic leadership to understand it more fully. In doing so, we can also recapitulate and systematize the findings and claims of the preceding sections of this work. I have argued that strategic leadership is a collaborative and integrative process and discipline of decision making that enables an organization to understand, define, and adopt shared purposes, priorities, and goals that are based on the group's identity and vision. It involves the following elements and assumptions:

- **Human agency and values.** When strategy is prosecuted as a discipline of leadership, it becomes an integral process of human agency. As a consequence, strategic leadership requires the critical awareness, articulation, and enactment of values as organizational patterns of identity and commitment.

- **Organizational culture and paradigms.** In the process of discovering an institution's identity, the discipline of strategic leadership brings to awareness the culture of an institution as a system of beliefs, values, and practices. It seeks to become explicitly conscious of organizational paradigms: the presuppositions that guide decisions, the norms that orient action, and the assumptions that shape beliefs.

- **Narrative and vision.** To elicit the possibilities of leadership, strategy draws on the power of the organizational story as a sense-making and sense-giving narrative of identity and aspiration. The story and the vision articulate shared beliefs, commitments, and goals that create a sense of mutual responsibility and common purpose, reconciling structural tensions in the academic system and culture of decision making.

- **Data and information.** Strategic leadership is data driven and information rich. It uses a variety of strategic indicators and methods of quantitative reasoning to define an institution's characteristics and display its contextual possibilities and challenges.

- **Responsiveness and responsibility.** Contextual responsibility is the defining mind-set of strategic thinking and leadership. It continuously seeks information about the trends in the wider social, political, economic, educational, and technological contexts. Strategic leadership defines its purposes and priorities through a paradigm of responsive interpretation of and responsible interaction with the world as it is and will be.

- **Conceptual thinking.** Strategic leadership requires a deep conceptual understanding of the meaning of the changing environment, organizational purposes and values, and the distinguishing elements, educational programs, and commitments of the institution, many of which are in tension with one another.

- **Integrative thinking.** Given all the forms and dimensions of knowledge and understanding that it involves, strategic leadership is a quintessentially integrative discipline. The claims that it advances and the goals that it sets require the synthesis of information, concepts, and meanings that come in a variety of forms from many sources.

- **Decision making.** As a discipline of decision making, strategic leadership displays the peculiar integrative and sovereign power of decisions. They take place as enactments that synthesize a wide range of factors. Rarely the consequence of rational calculation or deductive logic alone, decisions carry the deep imprint of culture, commitments, and political influences.

- **Systemic thinking.** Not only is strategic decision making integrative at the two levels of knowledge and of decision, it is also systemic. It understands that insights and decisions in one domain of an organization are connected to others as part of a system.

THE PROCESS OF STRATEGIC LEADERSHIP

This recapitulation of strategic leadership as a discipline is enlarged, enriched, and exemplified as we consider the organizational systems and processes that enable and enact it. We have seen that strategic leadership as a process involves a variety of mechanisms, methods, steps, and procedures.

- **Collaboration.** Reciprocal leadership and decision making require dialogue and interaction between groups and individuals in order to interpret the meaning of the organization's context and mission. Many strategic insights and possibilities are a collaborative achievement, often not available to individuals working in isolation.

- **Governance.** The process of strategic leadership requires effective mechanisms of governance that overcome the complexity and fragmentation of decision making in higher education. A strategy council or its equivalent has to be empowered to recommend a coherent strategic agenda for the institution's future.

- **Legitimacy.** The mechanisms of strategic governance must not only be effective but must also satisfy campus norms of collegial decision making. Ultimately it falls to the governing board and the president to ensure that the mechanisms and methods of strategic governance, strategic leadership, and strategic management meet the canons of both legitimacy and effectiveness.

- **Design.** The strategy process and its mechanisms must be carefully designed and organized to ensure effectiveness. Persons who are assigned key roles should have appropriate levels of interest, skill, and knowledge, and the president and other top officers must be committed to the tasks of strategy.

- **Systemic methods.** Both as a discipline and as a process, strategic leadership is systemic and discerns the connectedness of the activities and programs of the organization. As a result, it drives strategic management to be integrative and seeks to build a momentum of accomplishment through continuing assessment and improvements in quality as a learning organization.

- **Embedded process.** The processes of strategic leadership develop relationships that create trust and respect among participants and encourage confidence and empowerment among both leaders and followers. Over time, the practices of strategic leadership become embedded in patterns of initiative and systems of responsibility throughout the organization.

This summary of the elements of strategic leadership also reveals a way to integrate several of the major approaches to the study of leadership and decision making in higher education. At various points, we have explored the insights that can be drawn from studies of collegiate culture concerning the significance of symbolism, narratives, and sense making. At other places we have reviewed the findings and the counsel of those who see strategy as a set of management practices. The literature on collegial governance and the empirical and conceptual studies of presidential and other forms of leadership have also been a focus of our attention. Our aim has been to integrate these diverse and valuable threads of research, theory, and practice into a model of leadership as a reciprocal process of sense making, sense giving, and enactment.

We can perhaps do no better to illustrate the potential integration of these conceptual and practical motifs than by returning to Burton Clark's (1998) study of entrepreneurial universities. In these contexts, he notes how a powerful institutional *idea* links up participants and spreads to practices and processes of decision making that create enduring and distinctive *beliefs*, eventually creating a new *culture*. Strong cultures reinforce practices and create a unified *identity*, which can in time become a *saga*, encapsulating the sense of distinctive organizational achievements. I see these administrative, conceptual, and cultural elements described by Clark as components that can be integrated through a systematic method of strategic leadership.

THE DIALECTICS OF LEADERSHIP

There are many perspectives from which this proposal for strategic leadership can be questioned. Some will disagree with our approach because they do not resonate with its conceptual framework and methods of argumentation. Others will be skeptical because they resist all forms of strategy, and yet others will await a large-scale empirical study to support the usefulness of the approach—a complex and difficult one, given the many variables involved (cf. Dooris, Kelley, and Trainer 2004). On a more practical level, some will find that the recommendations for changes in governance, the strategy process, and management systems are not possible or realistic, at least in their circumstances. Others will continue to be most comfortable with the way they have consistently used strategic planning to good effect as a tool of management. For all these reasons and others, many decision makers might suggest that various combinations of the political, symbolic, collegial, or administrative models of leadership are most useful and effective. A number of leaders, including many presidents, prefer to be more independent and spontaneous than is suggested by the collaborative system required in a discipline of leadership.

One of the most persistent questions about strategic leadership will come in response to the claim that an important dimension of leadership can be practiced as a process and an applied discipline. Returning to some of our earlier themes, we note again that we are still conditioned to think of leaders as exceptional individuals who hold substantial positions of power, generally because of the unusual qualities or qualifications they possess. Though the weight of modern scholarship centers on quite different notions of leadership, on an everyday basis we tend to reflect within inherited habits of thought. As a consequence, we doubt claims that some aspects of leadership could be a process and a discipline, when it seems so manifestly to be a matter of special abilities and characteristics. If a discipline, it could be taught and learned.

Even those scholars who vigorously endorse the study of leadership do not necessarily intend to establish the case that it is a discipline of practice, as opposed to one of reflection. They advance the claim that leadership can be taught as a method of inquiry, as a "multidiscipline," as "leadership studies," which in itself is controversial (Burns 1978, 2003). Although it may be implied in the work of a number of scholars, it is quite another thing to argue that we can teach explicitly for the exercise of leadership as a discipline of decision making.

Yet, as I have tried to show, strategic leadership is a way to integrate practices, methods, insights, and knowledge *about* leadership into an applied discipline *for* the exercise of leadership. To be sure, authority and the attributes, expertise, and practices of leaders should be understood as the conditions on which strategic leadership depends and the resources it needs to be effective. To use a common but helpful distinction on which we shall rely, strategic leadership can function only if these necessary conditions are satisfied. Yet necessary are not sufficient conditions and it is many of the latter that strategic leadership provides as a discipline and process of decision making.

Resources: Authority, Talent, and the Tasks of Leadership

We can illustrate the dimensions of the relationship between necessary and sufficient conditions with reference to authority, a topic we have considered on several occasions. To be sure, strategic leadership in colleges and universities depends on authority to be successful. Yet since leadership is a reciprocal process that finally depends on the consent, involvement, and commitment of a broad cross-section of a campus community that enjoys substantial decision-making autonomy, authority alone cannot constitute leadership. We can see it as a critical resource for leadership (Burns 1978).

A similar relationship between necessary and sufficient is evident in the way a wide variety of talents and characteristics that are associated with leaders actually function within a leadership process. The capacity to communicate and to inspire, qualities of courage and tenacity, ability to resolve conflict and solve problems, and the possession of expert knowledge and experience are the kinds of attributes one finds in leaders. These characteristics, again, are clearly necessary but not sufficient for leadership. For without a value centered structure within which to orient them to a common task, and to fulfill a high purpose, they can become distorted and disoriented. If the defining goal of leadership becomes the power and self-aggrandizement of the leader, then these valuable personal resources can become the snares and delusions of a demagogue or dictator. A defining commitment to fulfilling human needs and possibilities shows itself to be essential to leadership, serving as a moral criterion for the process. The criterion helps us to differentiate the special characteristics and dynamics of leadership as a discipline of purpose, not just of power (Burns 1978, 2003.)

In a similar way, the recent emphasis on the practices and relational processes of leadership represent an important resource, but one that needs to be supplemented by the system of a discipline. Many contemporary theorists suggest practices that involve sensitivity to the needs and values of followers, the requirement to develop a vision, and willingness to challenge standard practices (Kouzes and Posner 1990). All these tasks are indeed facets of the leadership relationship and conditions of its effectiveness. Yet, without a more structured intellectual framework and systematic process in which to set them, they can become a loosely related list of individual acts and practices that lack connection. They can easily be overtaken by the press of events, forgotten in the crush of institutional business or lost in the urgencies of implementation.

THE STRATEGIC INTEGRATION OF LEADERSHIP

We can see some of these same patterns of relationship in returning to a topic we reviewed earlier concerning the various frames or styles of presidential leadership in colleges and universities: the political, administrative, collegial, and symbolic. We learned that each of them offers a vital perspective for understanding and exercising leadership, yet none of them is adequate to the task of integration if it functions in isolation or sequentially.

Strategic Leadership and Political Leadership

To illustrate, consider the capacity to persuade, to create coalitions, to reward and punish, to splinter the opposition, to use power creatively and at times coercively, all of which are the stuff of classical political leadership. These are tools that are required in any organizational context, and many colleges and university leaders depend on them as tactics and skills required for much of their effectiveness. If campus relationships turn hostile or adversarial, the political, and/or the administrative frames of leadership often become dominant because they offer the safety net of authority. There may be no other choice.

The process of strategy itself requires political deftness in its development and operation, for it has to be inserted into a real world of political relationships and patterns of influence. Moreover, strategy, if carefully done, becomes in itself a powerful vehicle of political legitimacy. It is highly collaborative, uses information transparently, and focuses on issues and tasks through collegial methods. By its very existence, collaborative strategy makes its own political statement that the academy's most important values of process and substance matter. It empowers people to address issues of consequence and to seek new opportunities, and in so doing it builds trust. A good strategy process penetrates and gives a new form to the political frame.

But strategy transcends political considerations because it defines the contours of the future in terms of the enduring commitments of the organization. Without fidelity to core values, politics becomes blind. As both our national and campus political lives teach us, it can degenerate into systematic distortions, an ugly contest of egos, and character assassination. These weapons are in evidence on some campuses, as much as in the capital. For its practices to remain responsible, politics has to be redeemed by purpose, and purpose has to reflect fundamental values. When politics are integrated into strategic leadership it functions within a process bounded by a legacy, oriented to a vision, and infused with substantive values.

Strategic Leadership and Administrative, Collegial, and Symbolic Leadership

As we touch on the other leadership frames or styles—the administrative, the collegial, and the symbolic—we find similar patterns of relationship with strategic leadership. The other forms provide necessary conditions and resources that are refashioned and reoriented when they are drawn into the larger dialectic of integration that strategic leadership provides.

To pursue another example, without a good administrative infrastructure, strategy will go nowhere. Good data are needed, effective staff support is required, administrative control systems must be adequate, and the organizational capacities have to be in place to implement goals. At one level, strategy itself is simply a set of administrative practices and methods. Yet administrative effectiveness is clearly not sufficient for the motivation and engagement that are required in strategic leadership. It does not always welcome or understand change, cannot overcome the structural conflict to which it is a party, and easily falls prey to routine. More than administrative expertise and good management are required to serve the evolving needs and possibilities of academic organizations. Under the impress of strategic leadership the management frame refashions its sense of the world, gains a purchase on change, and finds more motivating and integrated tools with which to do its work.

The other two frames of leadership, the collegial and the symbolic, are also essential. As we have seen repeatedly, strategy has to satisfy the norms and secure the benefits of shared governance to be effective and legitimate, so collegiality is an important condition of the process. Academic expertise in teaching, learning, and scholarship has to drive the organization. Our argument has stressed emphatically that strategic leadership is rooted in the power of symbolic leadership, especially in its use of institutional narratives and in its congruence with organizational cultures.

Each of these dimensions is present within strategic leadership, but as part of a larger process of decision making and meaning that changes them in the process. Whereas strategic leadership gives purpose to political and administrative styles of leadership, it offers structure and systems of responsibility to its symbolic and collegial forms. Without an integrated system of decision making within which to function, these other approaches can remain ineffectual. Collegiality offers the form but not the content of decisions required to respond to change, so strategic leadership alters its forms while respecting its norms. At times the intricate protocols of governance become intractable or an elegant excuse for inaction. Symbolic thinking draws heavily on the indispensable power and meaning of institutional stories and culture, but it cannot by itself systematize or enact what it believes. It often tends to resist change by holding up images of a golden past that will never return.

Strategic leadership draws the other forms of leadership into a system that creates a true interpenetration of the approaches, a powerful integration of purpose and action. It moves beyond a serial or sequential application of different leadership methods that would deal with some issues in one way and others in another, moving from case to case with skills and insights that lack coherence. Mixing styles without an inner logic can lead to one method becoming dominant, distorting the other approaches to fit its perception of reality. Leaders often live comfortably for long periods with distorted interpretations of their organizations, squelching information that challenges their primary frame of reference. Their sense of personal effectiveness as leaders often becomes tied to their dominant models of perception. Changing models, and allowing new insights and new learning to take hold, becomes a threat to personal and professional self-worth.

The Integration of Leadership

Strategic leadership, on the other hand, seeks a genuine synthesis of the different frames of leadership. It draws together all the hard realities of an institution's choices and circumstances around a sense-making narrative and sense-giving vision of the purposes that it serves, with the organization as the agent of that vision. The various frames then function as subsystems within a systematic method that uses, modifies, and transforms them to implement an integrative strategy. As we have seen throughout the course of our inquiry, strategic leadership creates the mechanisms of governance, forms of authority and administrative systems it requires to do its work. It systematically unites power with purpose, vision with action, shared values with shared governance, and narratives of identity with administrative systems. As an integrative frame of meaning, strategic leadership allows us to see what is there in varying degrees but is often hidden—a complex but real integration and interpenetration of an institution's systems of decision making.

Learning Strategic Leadership

One of the reasons that strategic leadership is a process with broad application is that it functions as an applied discipline. This means that its various components can be taught and learned both practically and theoretically, from the insights needed to understand institutional cultures, to the development and interpretation of strategic indicators, to knowing and telling the institution's story. To be sure, some practitioners of the discipline will be far more skilled than others in using it. But that is always the case in every field or discipline, especially those that involve various forms of practice. Talent and skill are indispensable. They weigh very heavily in the leadership equation. Yet few of us will ever qualify as transforming leaders or brilliant strategists, and fewer still will do so by the possession of exceptional natural gifts. Nonetheless, most of us can learn a process and discipline that substantially expands our given abilities to provide direction for an organization or some part of it. As a discipline and systematic process it is able to institutionalize effective practices of leadership that otherwise are subject to the vagaries of circumstance.

In making these claims, we assume that organizations use some wisdom in selecting various individuals to serve in formal positions of leadership and responsibility, whether as the chair of a committee or as president. Many of the skills, attributes, and values that we reviewed briefly early in our study are precisely the characteristics that drive the choice of certain individuals for these various responsibilities of leadership. It is fair to assume that many of the qualities that we associate with leadership are spread quite widely though not evenly through the population. Finding a person with the qualities and skills that match the needs of a position at various times and under different circumstances is a crucial and demanding task. At the same time, we are often surprised and pleased to see how most people rise to the challenges of the responsibilities that they are given.

As individuals come into leadership roles, from president on down the hierarchy, the question they often ask themselves silently in the dark of night is, "What am I doing here? How am I supposed to run this committee, or this department, or this organization? Do I have the tools to do this work? Are my authority, experience, and skill adequate to the task?"

When the inevitable challenges to the individual's leadership first arrive, the haunting questions intensify, sometimes in a form that is less helpful and relevant than it might appear to be. Under pressure leaders may become fixated on whether they have the repertoire of insights, qualities, and abilities needed for the job, even though most of those are not quickly or easily subject to modification. Or they may turn to detailed analyses of the formal powers and prerogatives of their office, as they wonder whether and how to assert their authority. Although these queries may be authentic and conscientious and are sometimes relevant, they are often misplaced. The more authentic questions usually are "How do I use the talents, methods and authority that I already have to do the job?" and "How do I best go about the task of exercising leadership in systematic ways that both respond to and motivate others?" It is in response to precisely these questions that the process and methods of strategic leadership present themselves as a coherent and promising alternative. It offers a structured and integrative discipline of decision making that can be learned through experience and reflection, by practice and study.

This ordering of the problem also puts into perspective the dialectical relationship between strategic leadership as a discipline and the personal attributes of leaders. We can see, once again, that they provide a threshold that must be crossed for strategic leadership to be practiced effectively, defining the difference between unacceptable and acceptable ranges of talent for leadership. If the basic conditions are not satisfied, the method will be frustrated. The fact that a leader must satisfy basic standards and have certain qualities is no clearer than in the realm of values. Leaders must stand for something to do anything. In the applied discipline of leadership, decisions must include the stamp of authenticity of the decision maker.

Typically, of course, persons who fail to meet these thresholds are not selected to exercise authority, and if they are, they are likely to be weeded out quickly. In most circumstances, persons are chosen for leadership precisely because they display attributes and skills of leadership well beyond the qualifying level. Under these conditions, the individual's talents as a leader are mobilized and amplified by the rigor and system of a collaborative process. The practitioner of the art and science of strategic leadership discovers new ways to make sense of personal and collective experience and to influence the course of events. In turn, the process reaches higher levels of effectiveness due to a leader's superior abilities, genuine virtuosity, or passionate degree of commitment.

Leadership as Sense Making

To be successful, however, strategic leadership does not require heroic, flawless, or extraordinary leaders. When it takes hold in the decision-making culture of an organization, it reveals the meaning of leadership itself. Leadership comes to be understood as a necessary dimension in the development of the social identities and organizational capacities of human beings. The roots of leadership are not in hierarchies of power but in methods of sense making that are part of the human condition. They are tied to human needs and values as they necessarily come to expression in cultural systems and social relationships. The dramatically diverse political and cultural artifacts that surround leadership in different societies and organizations around the globe are predictable aspects of the extraordinary range of human social experience. They arise, however, from something more fundamental than the diversity itself. Humans live through social and cultural systems of sense making that preserve and enhance what they care deeply and decisively about, those institutions, beliefs, and relationships in which they invest themselves to give purpose to their striving. Ultimately, the leadership of organizations, including colleges and universities, is about sustaining the values through which humans define themselves and find meaning in social forms. As a transforming narrative process, strategic leadership never ceases to explore the meanings that are hidden in familiar places and events, values and purposes. At its fullest, it enables a homecoming of the spirit. Through narrative, echoing T. S. Eliot, we "arrive where we started, and know the place for the first time" (Eliot 1943).

From this perspective it becomes especially clear why both leadership and responsibility have to be effectively and widely shared in organizations of higher learning. As integral strategic leadership takes hold in a college or university, the values that it serves and the vision that it offers move to center stage. Conflicts and distractions over protocols and position are relegated to the wings. So engaging is the educational task of transforming human possibilities, so absorbing is the quest for learning, so compelling is the errand of meeting human needs, that people experience the powerful norms of a community that serves a magnificent common cause. In such a community it becomes nearly impossible to draw sharp lines between those who lead and those who follow. There is more than enough work to go around, and more than enough responsibility to be shared by different individuals and groups in different ways at different times.

BIBLIOGRAPHY

Ackerman, L. D. *Identity is Destiny: Leadership and the Roots of Value Creation*. San Francisco: Berrett-Koehler, 2000.

Alfred, R., et al. *Managing the Big Picture in Colleges and Universities: From Tactics to Strategy*. Westport, CT: ACE/Praeger, 2006.

American Association of University Professors. American Council on Education and Association of Governing Boards of Universities and Colleges. "Statement on Government of Colleges and Universities." In *Organization and Governance in Higher Education*, ed. M. Peterson, E. E. Chaffee, and T. H. White, 157–163,. 4th ed. Needham Heights, MA: Ginn Press, 1991.

Argnese, L. J., Jr. "Repositioning for Success." In *Presidential Essays: Success Stories. Strategies That Make a Difference at Thirteen Independent Colleges and Universities*, ed. A. Splete, 8–15. Indianapolis, IN: Lumina Foundation, 2000.

Associated New American Colleges. "A Primer on the Associated New American Colleges," http://www.anac.org (accessed July 2004).

Association of American Colleges and Universities. *Greater Expectations: A New Vision for Learning as a Nation Goes to College*. Washington, DC: Author, 2002.

Association of American Colleges and Universities. *Our Students' Best Work: A Framework of Accountability Worthy of Our Mission*. Washington, DC: Author, 2004.

Association of Governing Boards of Universities and Colleges. *Institutional Governance Statement*. Washington, DC: Author, 1998.

Association of Governing Boards of Universities and Colleges. *The Leadership Imperative: The Report of the AGB Task Force on the State of the Presidency in American Higher Education*. Washington, DC: Author, 2006.

Association of Governing Boards of Universities and Colleges. *Renewing the Academic Presidency: Stronger Leadership for Tougher Times*. Washington, DC: Author, 1996.

Astin, A. W. *Four Critical Years: Effects of College on Beliefs, Attitudes, and Knowledge*. San Francisco: Jossey-Bass, 1977.

Astin, A. W. *What Matters in College: Four Critical Years Revisited.* San Francisco: Jossey-Bass, 1993.

Banta, T. W., ed. *Building a Scholarship of Assessment.* San Francisco: Jossey-Bass, 2002.

Barazzone, E. L. "Back from the Brink." In *Presidential Essays: Success Stories. Strategies That Make a Difference at Thirteen Independent Colleges and Universities,* ed. A. Splete, 21–30. Indianapolis, IN: Lumina Foundation, 2000.

Bass, B. M. *Bass and Stodgill's Handbook of Leadership.* 3rd ed. New York: Free Press, 1990.

Bass, B. M., and B. J. Aviolio. "Transformational Leadership: A Response to Critiques." In *Leadership Theory and Research,* ed. M. M. Chemers and R. Ayman, 49–80. San Diego: Academic Press, 1993.

Bass, B. M., and R. E. Riggio. *Transformational Leadership.* 2nd ed. Mahwah, NJ: Erlbaum, 2006.

Baylor University. "Baylor 2012: Ten Year Vision, 2002–2012." Waco, TX: Author, 2002.

Benjamin, R., and S. Carroll "The Implications of the Changed Environment for Governance in Higher Education." In *The Responsive University: Restructuring for High Performance.* (ed.) W.G. Tierney, 92–119. Baltimore, MD: 1998.

Bennis, W. *On Becoming a Leader.* New York: Basic Books: 1989, 2003.

Bennis, W., and B. Nanus. *Leaders: Strategies for Taking Charge.* 2nd ed. New York: Harper Business, 1997.

Bensimon, E. M. "The Meaning of 'Good Presidential Leadership': A Frame Analysis." In *Organization and Governance in Higher Education,* ed. M. Peterson, E. E. Chafee, and T. H. White, 421–431. 4th ed. Needham Heights, MA: Ginn Press, 1991.

Bensimon, E. M., and A. Neumann. "What Teams Can Do." In *Organization and Governance in Higher Education,* ed. M. C. Brown, 244–257. 5th ed. Boston: Pearson Custom Publishing, 2000.

Bensimon, E. M., A. Neumann, and R. Birnbaum. "Higher Education and Leadership Theory." In *Organization and Governance in Higher Education,* ed. M. Peterson, E. E. Chafee, and T. H. White, 389–398. 4th ed. Needham Heights, MA: Ginn Press, 1991.

Berberet, J. "Transforming Ugly Ducklings: Marketing and Branding New American Colleges." In *Academic Turnarounds: Restoring Vitality to Challenged American Colleges and Universities,* ed. T. MacTaggart. Westport, CT: ACE/Praeger, 2007.

Berquist, W. *The Four Cultures of the Academy.* San Francisco: Jossey-Bass, 1992.

Birnbaum, R. "The End of Shared Governance: Looking Ahead or Looking Back." In *Restructuring Shared Governance in Higher Education,* ed. W. G. Tierney and V. M. Lechuga, 5–22. No. 127. San Francisco: Jossey-Bass, 2004.

Birnbaum, R. *How Academic Leadership Works.* San Francisco: Jossey-Bass, 1992.

Birnbaum, R. *How Colleges Work.* San Francisco: Jossey-Bass, 1988.

Birnbaum, R. *Management Fads in Higher Education.* San Francisco: Jossey-Bass, 2001.

Birnbaum R. "Responsibility without Authority: The Impossible Job of the College President." In *Higher Education: Handbook of Theory and Research,* ed. John C. Smart, 5: 31–56. New York: Agathon, 1989.

Bligh, M. C., and J. R. Mendl. "The Cultural Ecology of Leadership: An Analysis of Popular Books." In *The Psychology of Leadership: New Perspectives on Leadership,* ed. D. M. Messick and R. M. Kramer, 11–52. Mahwah, NJ: Erlbaum, 2005.

Bok, D. *Our Underachieving Colleges.* Princeton, NJ: Princeton University Press, 2006.

Bok, D. *Universities in the Marketplace: The Commercialization of Higher Education.* Princeton, NJ: Princeton University Press, 2003.

Bollag, B. "True to Their Roots." *Chronicle of Higher Education*, March 25, 2005.

Bolman, L. G., and T. E. Deal. *Reframing Organizations*. San Francisco: Jossey-Bass, 2003.

Borg, M. J. *Meeting Jesus Again for the First Time: The Historical Jesus and the Heart of Contemporary Faith*. New York: HarperCollins, 1994.

Bornstein, R. *Legitimacy in the Academic Presidency*. Westport, CT: ACE/Praeger, 2003.

Boyer, E. "The New American College." *Perspectives*, 24, no. 1–2 (1994): 6–11.

Boyer, E. "Press Release for Publication of *Campus Life*." Princeton, NJ: Carnegie Foundation for the Advancement of Teaching, 1990a.

Boyer, E. *Scholarship Reconsidered: Priorities of the Professoriate*. Princeton, NJ: Carnegie Foundation for the Advancement of Teaching, 1990b.

Bridgewater College. "Strategic Plan." Bridgewater, VA: Author, 2002.

Brown, D. G., ed. *University Presidents as Moral Leaders*. Westport, CT: ACE/Praeger, 2006.

Brown, M. C., ed. *Organization and Governance in Higher Education*. 5th ed. Boston: Pearson Custom Publishing, 2000.

Brown University. "The Plan for Academic Enrichment." 2004. http://www.brown.edu/web/pae/plan.html (accessed June 2004).

Bruner, J. *Making Stories: Law, Literature and Life*. Cambridge, MA: Harvard University Press, 2002.

Bryson, J. *Strategic Planning for Public and Nonprofit Organizations: A Guide to Strengthening and Sustaining Organizational Achievement*. Rev. ed. San Francisco: Jossey-Bass, 1995.

Burgan, M., R. Weisbuch, and S. Lowry. "A Profession in Difficult Times." *Liberal Education*, 85, no. 4 (1999): 7–15.

Burke, J. C., ed. *Achieving Accountability in Higher Education: Balancing Public, Academic, and Market Demands*. San Francisco: Jossey-Bass, 2005.

Burns, J. M. *Leadership*. New York: Harper and Row, 1978.

Burns, J. M. *Transforming Leadership*. New York: Atlantic Monthly Press, 2003.

Carnegie Mellon University. "Carnegie Mellon's Strategic Plan." 1998. http://www.cmu.edu/splan/initiatives.html (accessed July 2004).

Chaffee, E. E. "Three Models of Strategy." In *Organization and Governance in Higher Education*, ed. M. Peterson, E. E. Chaffee, and T. H. White, 225–238. 4th ed. Needham Heights, MA: Ginn Press, 1991.

Chaffee, E. E., and S. W. Jacobson. "Creating and Changing Institutional Cultures." In *Planning and Management for a Changing Environment: A Handbook on Redesigning Postsecondary Institutions*, ed. M. Peterson, D. D. Dill, L. Mets, et al., 230–245. San Francisco: Jossey-Bass, 1997.

Chaffee, E. E., and W. G. Tierney. *Collegiate Culture and Leadership Strategies*. Washington, DC: ACE/Macmillan, 1988.

Chait, R. P., T. P. Holland, and B. E. Taylor. *The Effective Board of Trustees*. Phoenix, AZ: ACE/Oryx, 1993.

Chait, R. P., W. P. Ryan, and B. E. Taylor. *Governance as Leadership: Reframing the Work of Nonprofit Boards*. Hoboken, NJ: John Wiley and Sons, 2005.

Chickering, A. *Education and Identity*. San Francisco: Jossey-Bass, 1969.

Ciulla, J. *The Ethics of Leadership*. Belmont, CA: Wadsworth, 2002.

Ciulla, J. "Leadership Ethics: Mapping the Territory." In *Ethics: the Heart of Leadership*, ed. J. Ciulla, 3–24. Westport, CT: Quorum Books, 1998.

Ciulla, J., T. Price, and E. Murphy, eds. *The Quest for Ethical Leaders*. Northampton, MA: Elgar, 2005.

Clandinin, D. J., and F. M. Connelly. *Narrative Inquiry: Experience and Story in Qualitative Research*. San Francisco: Jossey-Bass, 2000.

Clark, B. R. *The Academic Life: Small Worlds, Different Worlds*. Princeton, NJ: Carnegie Foundation for the Advancement of Teaching, 1987.

Clark, B. R. *Creating Entrepreneurial Universities: Organizational Pathways of Transformation*. Oxford: IAU/Pergamon, 1998.

Clark, B. R. *The Distinctive College: Antioch, Reed, and Swarthmore*. Chicago: Aldine, 1970.

Clark, B. R. Foreword. In *Planning and Management for a Changing Environment: A Handbook on Redesigning Postsecondary Institutions*, ed. M. Peterson, D. D. Dill, L. Mets, et al. San Francisco: Jossey-Bass, 1997.

Clark, B. R. "The Organizational Saga in Higher Education." In *Organization and Governance in Higher Education*, M. Peterson, E. E. Chaffee, and T. H. White, 46–52. 4th ed. Needham Heights, MA: Ginn Press, 1991.

Clark, K. E., and M. B. Clark. *Choosing to Lead*. Charlotte, NC: Leadership Press, 1994.

Clark, K. E., and M. B. Clark, eds. *Measures of Leadership*. West Orange, NJ: Leadership Library, 1990.

Cohen, M. D., and J. G. March. *Leadership and Ambiguity*. 2nd ed. Boston: Harvard Business School Press, 1986.

Coleman, M. S. "Implementing a Strategic Plan Using Indicators and Targets." In *Pursuing Excellence in Higher Education: Eight Fundamental Challenges*, ed. B. D. Ruben, 117–127. San Francisco: Jossey-Bass, 2004.

Coles, R. *The Call of Stories: Teaching and the Moral Imagination*. Boston: Houghton Mifflin, 1989.

Collins, J. *Good to Great and the Social Sectors*. Boulder, CO: Jim Collins, 2005.

Collins, J. *Good to Great: Why Some Companies Make the Leap . . . and Others Don't*. New York: HarperCollins, 2001.

Commission on Colleges. *Accreditation Guidelines*. Atlanta, GA: Southern Association of Colleges and Schools, 2002.

Connor, R. *Teagle Foundation Annual Report*. New York: Teagle Foundation, 2004.

Cope, R. G. "College Strategic Capabilities: Five Sources of Comparative Advantage." Paper presented at the Snowmass Institute, Snowmass, CO, 1994.

Cope, R. G. *High Involvement Strategic Planning: When People and Their Ideas Matter*. Oxford: Basil Blackwell and the Planning Forum, 1989.

Davies, G. "The Importance of Being General: Philosophy, Politics and Institutional Mission Statements." In *Higher Education: Handbook of Theory and Research*, ed. John C. Smart, 2, 85–103:. New York: Agathon Press, 1986.

Davis, J. R. *Learning to Lead: A Handbook for Postsecondary Administrators*. Westport, CT: ACE/Praeger, 2003.

Denning, S. *The Leader's Guide to Storytelling: Mastering the Art and Discipline of Business Narrative*. San Francisco: Jossey-Bass, 2005.

DePree, M. *Leadership Is an Art*. New York: Doubleday, 1989.

Diamond, R. M., ed. *Field Guide to Academic Leadership*. San Francisco: Jossey-Bass, 2002.

Dickeson, R. C. *Prioritizing Academic Programs and Services: Reallocating Resources to Achieve Strategic Balance*. San Francisco: Jossey-Bass, 1999.

Dill, D. "Focusing Institutional Mission." In *Planning and Management for a Changing Environment: A Handbook on Redesigning Postsecondary Institutions*, ed. M. Peterson, D. D. Dill, L. Mets, et al., 171–190. San Francisco: Jossey-Bass, 1997.

Dodd, A. H. "Accreditation as a Catalyst for Institutional Effectiveness." In *Successful Strategic Planning: New Directions for Institutional Research*, ed. M. J. Dooris, J. M. Kelley, and J. F. Trainer, 13–25. No. 123. San Francisco: Jossey-Bass, 2004.

Dooris, M. J., J. M. Kelley, and J. F. Trainer. "Strategic Planning in Higher Education." In *Successful Strategic Planning: New Directions for Institutional Planning*, ed. M. J. Dooris, J. M. Kelley, and J. F. Trainer, 5–11. No. 123. San Francisco: Jossey-Bass, 2004.

Duderstadt, J. "Governing the Twenty-first Century University: A View from the Bridge." In *Competing Conceptions of Academic Governance; Negotiating the Perfect Storm* (ed.) W. G. Tierney, 137–157. Baltimore, MD: Johns Hopkins Press, 2004.

Duke University. "Executive Summary." *Building on Excellence*. Durham, NC: Office of the Provost, 2001.

Duryea, E. D. "The Evolution of University Organization" In *Organization and Governance in Higher Education*, ed. M. Peterson, E. E. Chaffee, and T. H. White, 3–16. 4th ed. Needham Heights, MA: Ginn Press, 1991.

East Lancashire Training and Enterprise Council. http://www.nvq5.com (accessed July, 2004).

Eckel, P., M. Green, B. Hill, and W. Mallon. *On Change III—Taking Charge of Change: A Primer for Colleges and Universities*. Washington, DC: American Council on Education, 2000.

Eckel, P., M. Green, and B. Hill. *On Change V—Riding the Waves of Change: Insights from Transforming Institutions*. Washington, DC: American Council on Education, 2001.

Eckel, P., B. Hill, and M. Green. *On Change I—En Route to Transformation*. Washington, DC: American Council on Education, 1998.

Eckel, P., B. Hill, M. Green, and W. Mallon. *On Change II—Reports from the Road: Insights on Institutional Change*. Washington, DC: American Council on Education, 1999.

Eckel, P., and A. Kezar. *Taking the Reins: Institutional Transformation in Higher Education*. Westport, CT: ACE/Praeger, 2003.

Eliot, T. S. "Little Gidding." In *Four Quartets*, New York: Harcourt, 1943.

Erwin, T. D. "Standardized Testing and Accountability: Finding the Way and the Will." In *Achieving Accountability in Higher Education: Balancing Public, Academic, and Market Demands*, ed. J. C. Burke, 125–147. San Francisco: Jossey-Bass, 2005.

Ewell, P. T. *Making the Grade: How Boards Can Ensure Academic Quality*. Washington, DC: Association for Governing Boards of Universities and Colleges, 2006.

Ferren, A. S., and W. W. Stanton. *Leadership Through Collaboration*. Westport, CT: ACE/Praeger, 2004.

Fiedler, F. E., "The Leadership Situation and the Black Box in Contingency Theories," In *Leadership Theory and Research: Perspectives and Directions*, ed., M. M. Chemers and R. Ayman, 2–28. San Diego: Academic Press, 1993.

Fish, S. "What Did You Do All Day?" *Chronicle of Higher Education*, November 24, 2004.

Fisher, J. L. *Power of the Presidency*. San Francisco: Jossey-Bass, 1984.

Fisher, J. L., and J. V. Koch. *The Entrepreneurial College President*. Westport, CT: ACE/Praeger, 2004.

Fisher, J. L., and J. V. Koch. *Presidential Leadership: Making a Difference*. Phoenix, AZ: Oryx, 1996.

Fisher, J. L., and M. W. Tack. *Leaders on Leadership: The College Presidency*. San Francisco: Jossey-Bass, 1988.

Fisher, J. L., M. W. Tack, and T. J. Wheeler. *The Effective College President*. New York: ACE/Macmillan, 1988.

Frances, C., G. Huxel, J. Meyerson, and D. Park. *Strategic Decision Making*. Washington, DC: Association of Governing Boards of Universities and Colleges, 1987.

Freedman, M., and B. B. Tregoe. *The Art and Discipline of Strategic Leadership*. New York: McGraw-Hill, 2003.

Friedman, T. *The World Is Flat*. New York: Doubleday, 2005.

Gaff, J. G., J. L. Ratcliff, et al., eds. *Handbook of the Undergraduate Curriculum: A Comprehensive Guide to Purposes, Structures, Practices, and Change*. San Francisco: Jossey-Bass, 1997.

Ganz, M. "Why David Sometimes Wins: Strategic Capacity in Social Movements." In *The Psychology of Leadership: New Perspectives and Research*, ed. D. M. Messick and R. M. Kramer, 209–238. Mahwah, NJ: Erlbaum, 2005.

Gardner, H. *Changing Minds: The Art and Science of Changing Our Own and Other People's Minds*. Boston: Harvard Business School Press, 2004.

Gardner, H. *Leading Minds: An Anatomy of Leadership*. New York: Basic Books, 1995.

Gardner, J. *On Leadership*. New York: Free Press, 1990.

Gardner, W. L., et al. "'Can You See the Real Me?' A Self-Based Model of Authentic Leader and Follower Development." *Leadership Quarterly*, 16 (2005): 343–72.

Geiger, R. L. *Knowledge and Money: Research and the Paradox of the Marketplace*. Stanford, CA: Stanford University Press, 2004.

George, R. *Authentic Leadership: Rediscovering the Secrets to Creating Lasting Value*. San Francisco: Jossey-Bass, 2003.

Gilligan, C. *In a Different Voice: Psychological Theory and Women's Development*. Cambridge, MA: Harvard University Press, 1982.

Gioia, D. A., and Thomas, J. B. "Sense-Making during Strategic Change in Academia" In *Organization and Governance in Higher Education*, ed. M. C. Brown, 352–378. 5th ed. Boston: Pearson Custom Publishing, 2000.

Gmelch, W., and V. Miskin. *Chairing an Academic Department*. Madison, WI: Atwood Press, 2004.

Goethals, G. R. "The Psychodynamics of Leadership: Freud's Insights and Their Vicissitudes." In *The Psychology of Leadership: New Perspectives and Research*, ed. D. M. Messick and R. M. Kramer, 97–112. Mahwah, NJ: Erlbaum, 2005.

Goethals, G. R., and G. L. J. Sorenson, eds. *The Quest for a General Theory of Leadership*. Northampton, MA: Elgar, 2006.

Goethals, G. R., G. J. Swenson, and J. M. Burns, eds. *Encyclopedia of Leadership*. 4 vols. Thousand Oaks, CA: Sage, 2004.

Green, T. F. "Evaluating Liberal Learning: Doubts and Explorations." *Liberal Education*, 68, no. 2 (1982): 127–38.

Green, M. F., and S. A. McDade, *Investing in Higher Education: A Handbook of Leadership Development*. Phoenix, AZ: Oryx Press, 1994.

Greenleaf, R. *Servant Leadership*. New York: Paulist Press, 1977.

Gumport, P. J. "Academic Structure, Culture and the Case of Feminist Scholarship In *Organization and Governance in Higher Education*, ed. M. C. Brown, 508–520. 5th ed. Boston: Pearson Custom Publishing, 2000.

Gunsalis, C. K. *The College Administrator's Survival Guide*. Cambridge, MA: Harvard University Press, 2006.

Guskin, A. E., and M. B. Marcy. "Dealing with the Future Now: Principles for Creating a Vital Campus in a Climate of Restricted Resources." *Change*, July/August 2003, 10–21.

Guskin, A. E., and M. B. Marcy. "Pressures for Fundamental Reform: Creating a Viable Academic Future." In *Field Guide to Academic Leadership*, ed. R. M. Diamond, 3–13. San Francisco: Jossey-Bass, 2002.

Hackman, J. R. "Rethinking Team Leadership or Team Leaders Are Not Music Directors." In *The Psychology of Leadership: New Perspectives and Research*, ed. D. M. Messick and R. M. Kramer, 115–142. Mahwah, NJ: Erlbaum, 2005.

Hamel, G. "The Concept of Core Competence." In *Competence-Based Competition*, ed. G. Hamel and A. Hune,11–34. Hoboken, NJ: John Wiley and Sons, 1994.

Hamilton, N. "Are We Speaking the Same Language? Comparing AAUP and AGB." *Liberal Education*, 85, no. 4 (1999): 24–31.

Hartley, M., and L. Schall. "The Endless Good Argument: The Adaptation of Mission at Two Liberal Arts Colleges." *Planning for Higher Education*, 33, no. 4 (2005): 5–11.

Healy, P., and S. Rimer. "Amid Uproar, Harvard Head Ponders Style." *New York Times*, February 26, 2005.

Healy, P., and S. Rimer. "Harvard President Vows to Temper His Style with Respect." *New York Times*, February 23, 2005.

Heath, D. *Growing up in College: Liberal Education in College*. San Francisco: Jossey-Bass, 1968.

Heifetz, R. *Leadership without Easy Answers*. Cambridge, MA: Belknap Press, 1994.

Heilman, B. "The Era of Transformation." Presentation to the Osher Institute at the University of Richmond, VA, March 2005.

Hickman, G., ed. *Leading Organizations*. Thousand Oaks, CA: Sage, 1998.

Hicks, D. A., and T. L. Price. "A Framework for a General Theory of Leadership Ethics." In *The Quest for a General Theory of Leadership*, ed. G. R. Goethals and G.L.J. Sorenson, 123–151. Northampton, MA: Elgar, 2006.

Hill, B., M. Green, and P. Eckel. *On Change IV—What Governing Boards Need to Know and Do About Institutional Change*. Washington, DC: American Council on Education, 2001.

Hogg, M. A. "Social Identity and Leadership." In *The Psychology of Leadership: New Perspectives and Research*, ed. D. M. Messick and R. M. Kramer, 53–80. Mahwah, NJ: Erlbaum, 2005.

Hollander, E. P. "Legitimacy, Power, and Influence: A Perspective on Relational Features of Leadership." In *Leadership Theory and Research: Perspectives and Directions*, ed. M. M. Chemers and R. Ayman. San Diego: Academic Press, 1993.

Hoppe, S. L., and, B. W., Speck (eds.) *Identifying and Preparing Academic Leaders: New Directions for Higher Education*. No. 124. San Francisco: Jossey-Bass, 2003.

Hortado, S. "The Campus Racial Climate (1992)." In *Organization and Governance in Higher Education*, ed. M. C. Brown, 182–202. 5th ed. Boston: Pearson Custom Publishing, 2000.

House, R. J., and Shamir, B. "Toward the Integration of Transformational, Charismatic, and Visionary Theories." In *Leadership Theory and Research: Perspectives and Directions*, ed. M. M. Chemers and R. Ayman, 81–107. San Diego: Academic Press, 1993.

Hoyt, C. L., G. R. Goethals, and R. E. Riggio. "Leader-Follower Relations: Group Dynamics and the Role of Leadership." In *The Quest for a General Theory of Leadership*, ed. G. R. Goethals and G.L.J. Sorenson, 96–122. Northampton, MA: Elgar, 2006.

Hughes, R. L., R. C. Ginnett, and G. J. Curphy. "Power, Influence, and Influence Tactics." In *The Leader's Companion*, ed. T. Wren, 39–47. New York: Free Press, 1995.

Hunt, C. M., Oosting, K. W., Stevens, R., Loudon, D., and Migliore, R. H. *Strategic Planning for Higher Education*. New York: Haworth Press, 1997.

Jasinski, J. "Strategic Planning via Baldridge: Lessons Learned." In *Successful Strategic Planning: New Directions in Institutional Research*, ed. M. J. Dooris, J. M. Kelley, and J. F. Trainer, 27–31. No. 123. San Francisco: Jossey-Bass, 2004.

Jenkins, K. *International Education in an Altered World*. Washington, DC: Association for Governing Boards of Universities and Colleges, 2002.

Juniata College. "The Strategic Plan for Juniata." Huntingdon, PA: Author, 2001.

Keller, G. *Academic Strategy: The Management Revolution in American Higher Education*. Baltimore: Johns Hopkins University Press, 1983.

Keller, G. "The Vision Thing." *Planning for Higher Education*, 23 (1995): 8–14.

Keller, G. "Examining What Works in Strategic Planning." In *Planning and Management for a Changing Environment: A Handbook on Redesigning Postsecondary Institutions*, ed. M. Peterson, D. D. Dill, L. Mets, et al.,158–170. San Francisco: Jossey-Bass, 1997.

Keller, G. "A Growing Quaintness: Traditional Governance in the Markedly New Realm of U.S. Higher Education." In *Competing Conceptions of Academic Governance: Negotiating the Perfect Academic Storm*, (ed.) W.G. Tierney, 158–176. Baltimore, MD: Johns Hopkins Press, 2004.

Kelley, J. M., and J. F. Trainer. "A Team Approach to Goal Attainment: Villanova University." In *Successful Strategic Planning: New Directions for Institutional Research*, ed. M. J. Dooris, J. M. Kelley, and J. F. Trainer, 97–104. No. 123. San Francisco: Jossey-Bass, 2004.

Keohane, N. *Higher Ground: Ethics and Leadership in the Modern University*. Durham, NC: Duke University Press, 2006.

Kerr, C., and M. L. Gade. *The Many Lives of Academic Presidents: Time, Place and Character*. Washington, DC: Association of Governing Boards of Universities and Colleges, 1986.

Kezar, A. "Pluralistic Leadership: Incorporating Diverse Voices." *Journal of Higher Education*, 71, no. 6 (2000): 722–43.

Kezar, A. "What Is More Important to Effective Governance: Relationships, Trust, and Leadership or Structures and Formal Process?" In *Restructuring Governance in Higher Education: New Directions for Higher Education*, ed. W. G. Tierney and V. M. Lechuga, 35–46. No. 127. San Francisco: Jossey-Bass, 2004.

Kirp, D. L. *Shakespeare, Einstein, and the Bottom Line*. Cambridge, MA: Harvard University Press, 2003.

Kotter, J. *Leading Change*. Boston: Harvard Business School Press, 1996.

Kouzes, J., and B. Posner. *Jossey-Bass Academic Administrator's Guide to Exemplary Leadership*. San Francisco: Jossey-Bass, 2003.

Kouzes, J., and B. Posner. *The Leadership Challenge*. San Francisco: Jossey-Bass, 1990.

Krahenbuhl, G. *Building the Academic Deanship: Strategies for Success*. Westport, CT: ACE/ Praeger, 2004.

Kuh, G. "Imagine Asking the Client: Using Student and Alumni Surveys for Accountability in Higher Education." In *Achieving Accountability in Higher Education: Balancing*

Public, Academic, and Market Demands, ed. J. C. Burke, 148–172. San Francisco: Jossey-Bass, 2005.

Kuh, G., J. Kinzie, J. H. Schuh, E. J. Whitt, et al. *Student Success in College: Creating Conditions That Matter*. San Francisco: Jossey-Bass, 2005.

Kuh, G., J. H. Schuh, E. J. Whitt, et al. *Involving Colleges: Successful Approaches to Fostering Student Learning Outside the Classroom*. San Francisco: Jossey-Bass, 1991.

Kuh, G., and E. Whitt. "Culture in American Colleges and Universities." In *Organization and Governance in Higher Education*, ed. M. C. Brown, 160–169. 5th ed. Boston: Pearson Custom Publishing, 2000.

Lawrence, F. L., and C. H. Cermak. "Advancing Academic Excellence and Collaboration through Strategic Planning." In *Pursuing Excellence in Higher Education: Eight Fundamental Challenges*, ed. B. D. Ruben, 233–240. San Francisco: Jossey-Bass, 2004.

Leslie, D., and E. K. Fretwell. *Wise Moves in Hard Times: Creating and Managing Resilient Colleges*. San Francisco: Jossey-Bass, 1996.

LeVan, S. "Vision 2008." Presentation to the Albemarle Corporation, Richmond, VA, November 2005.

Levin, R. C. "Preparing for Yale's Fourth Century." *Yale Alumni Magazine*, December 1996, 10.

Levine, D. N. *Powers of the Mind: The Reinvention of Liberal Learning in America*. Chicago: University of Chicago Press, 2006.

Lick, D. "Leadership and Change." In *Field Guide to Academic Leadership*, ed. R. M. Diamond, 27–47. San Francisco: Jossey-Bass, 2002.

Light, R. *Making the Most of College: Students Speak Their Minds*. Cambridge, MA: Harvard University Press, 2001.

Longin, T. "Institutional Governance: A Call for Collaborative Decision-Making in American Higher Education." In *A New Academic Compact: Revisioning the Relationship between Faculty and Their Institutions*, ed. L. A. McMillin and J. Berberet, 211–221. Boston, MA: Anker Publishing, 2002.

MacTaggart, T., ed. *Academic Turnarounds: Restoring Vitality to Challenged American Colleges and Universities*. Westport, CT: ACE/Praeger, 2007a.

MacTaggart, T. "Turnarounds in Public Higher Education." In *Academic Turnarounds: Restoring Vitality to Challenged American Colleges and Universities*, ed. T. MacTaggart. Westport, CT: ACE/Praeger, 2007b.

Mallon, W. "Disjointed Governance in University Centers and Institutes." In *Restructuring Shared Governance in Higher Education: New Directions for Higher Education*, ed. W. G. Tierney and V. M. Lechuga, 61–74. No. 127. San Francisco: Jossey-Bass, 2004.

March, J. A. *A Primer on Decision-Making: How Decisions Happen*. New York: Free Press, 1994.

McAdams, D. P. *The Stories We Live By*. New York: Guilford Press, 1993.

McMillin, L. A. "Faculty Workload: Differentiation through Unit Collaboration." In *A New Academic Compact: Revisioning the Relationship between Faculty and Their Institutions*, ed. L. McMillin and J. Berberet, 87–110. Boston: Anker, 2002.

Meacham, J., and J. G. Gaff. "Learning Goals in Mission Statements: Implications for Educational Leadership." *Liberal Education*, 92, no. 1 (2006): 6–13.

Mehl, R. *De l'Autorité des Valeurs* [On the authority of values]. Paris: Presses Universitaires de France, 1957.

Messick, D. M. "On the Psychological Exchange between Leaders and Followers." In *The Psychology of Leadership: New Perspectives and Research*, ed. D. M. Messick and R. M. Kramer, 81–96. Mahwah, NJ: Erlbaum, 2005.

Mets, L. "Planned Change through Program Review." In *Planning and Management for a Changing Environment: A Handbook on Redesigning Postsecondary Institutions*, ed. M. Peterson, D. D. Dill, L. Mets, et al., 340–359. San Francisco: Jossey-Bass, 1997.

Mintzberg, H. *The Rise and Fall of Strategic Planning*. New York: Free Press, 1994.

Mintzberg, H. *The Structuring of Organizations*. Englewood Cliffs, NJ: Prentice Hall, 1979.

Mintzberg, H., B. Ahlstrand, and J. Lampel. *Strategy Safari: A Guided Tour through the Wilds of Strategic Management*. New York: Free Press, 1998.

Mintzberg, H., J. Lampel, J. B. Quinn, and S. Goshal. *The Strategy Process*. Upper Saddle River, NJ: Prentice Hall, 2003.

Moore, R. M. "The Rising Tide: 'Branding' and the Academic Marketplace." *Change*, May/June 2004, 57.

Morrill, R. L. "Academic Planning: Values and Decision Making." In *Ethics and Higher Education*, ed. W. May, 69–83. New York: ACE/Macmillan, 1990.

Morrill, R. L. "Centre College of Kentucky." In *Successful Strategic Planning: Case Studies*, ed. D. W. Steeples, 33–43. San Francisco: Jossey-Bass, 1988.

Morrill, R. L. *Strategic Leadership in Academic Affairs: Clarifying the Board's Responsibilities*. Washington DC: Association of Governing Boards of Universities and Colleges, 2002.

Morrill, R. L. *Teaching Values in College: Facilitating Ethical, Moral and Value Awareness in Students*. San Francisco: Jossey-Bass, 1980.

Morrill, R. L. "The Use of Indicators in the Strategic Management of Universities." *Higher Education Management*, 12, no. 1 (2000): 105–12.

Morrison, J. L., and I. Wilson. "Analyzing Environments and Developing Scenarios for Uncertain Times." In *Planning and Management for a Changing Environment: A Handbook on Redesigning Postsecondary Institutions*, 204–229, ed. M. Peterson, D. D. Dill, L. Mets, et al. San Francisco: Jossey-Bass, 1997.

Morse, S. *Smart Communities: How Citizens and Local Leaders Can Use Strategic Thinking to Build a Brighter Future*. San Francisco: Jossey-Bass, 2004.

Nanus, B. *Visionary Leadership: Creating a Compelling Sense of Direction for Your Organization*. San Francisco: Jossey-Bass, 1992.

National Association of State Universities and Land-Grant Colleges. Task Force on International Education. "A Call to Leadership: the Presidential Role in Internationalizing the University." Washington, DC: Author, 2004.

Neumann, A. "Strategic Leadership: The Changing Orientation of College Presidents." *Review of Higher Education*, 12 (1989): 137–51.

Neumann, A., and R. S. Larson. "Enhancing the Leadership Factor in Planning." In *Planning and Management for a Changing Environment: A Handbook on Redesigning Postsecondary Institutions*, ed. M. Peterson, D. D. Dill, L. Mets, et al., 191–203. San Francisco: Jossey-Bass, 1997.

Newman, F., L. Couturier, and J. Scurry. *The Future of Higher Education: Rhetoric, Reality and the Risks of the Market*. San Francisco: Jossey-Bass, 2004.

Newsom, W., and C. P. Hayes. "Are Mission Statements Worthwhile?" *Planning for Higher Education*, 19, no. 2 (1990): 28–30.

Nickel, M. "Historic Plan to Transform Brown Builds upon Earlier Initiatives." *Brown University George Street Journal*, March 2004, 1, 4–7.

Niebuhr, H. R. *The Meaning of Revelation*. New York: Macmillan, 1941.

Niebuhr, H. R. *The Responsible Self*. New York: Harper and Row, 1963.

O'Toole, J. *Leading Change: Overcoming the Ideology of Comfort and the Tyranny of Custom*. San Francisco: Jossey-Bass, 1995.

O'Toole, J. *Making America Work: Productivity and Responsibility*. New York: Continuum, 1981.

Padilla, A. *Portraits in Leadership: Six Extraordinary University Presidents*. Westport, CT: ACE/Praeger, 2005.

Paris, K. A. "Moving the Strategic Plan off the Shelf and into Action at the University of Wisconsin." In *Successful Strategic Planning: New Directions for Institutional Research*, ed. M. J. Dooris, J. M. Kelley, and J. F. Trainer, 121–128. No. 123. San Francisco: Jossey-Bass, 2004.

Pascarella, E. T., and P. T. Terenzini. *How College Affects Students: A Third Decade of Research*. San Francisco: Jossey-Bass, 2005.

Pascarella, E. T., and P. T. Terenzini. *How College Affects Students: Findings and Insights from Twenty Years of Research*. San Francisco: Jossey-Bass, 1991.

Penley, L. E. "A Response to President Hearn's Essay: Models for Moral Leadership: From Wile E. Coyote to Homer." In *University Presidents as Moral Leaders*, ed. D. G. Brown, 177–181. Westport, CT: ACE/Praeger, 2006.

Perry, W. G. *Forms of Intellectual and Ethical Development in the College Years*. New York: Holt, Rinehart and Winston, 1970.

Peters, T. J., and R. H. Waterman, Jr. *In Search of Excellence: Lessons from America's Best-Run Companies*. New York: Harper and Row, 1982.

Peterson, M. "Using Contextual Planning to Transform Institutions." In *Planning and Management for a Changing Environment: A Handbook on Redesigning Postsecondary Institutions*, ed. M. Peterson, D. D. Dill, L. Mets, et al., 127–170. San Francisco: Jossey-Bass, 1997.

Peterson, M., E. E. Chaffee, and T. E. White, eds. *Organization and Governance in Higher Education*, 4th ed. Needham Heights, MA: Ginn Press, 1991.

Peterson, M., D. D. Dill, L. Mets, et al., eds. *Planning and Management for a Changing Environment: A Handbook on Redesigning Postsecondary Institutions*. San Francisco: Jossey-Bass, 1997.

Peterson, M., and M. Spencer. "Understanding Academic Culture and Climate." In *Organization and Governance in Higher Education*, ed. M. Peterson, E. E. Chaffee, and T. E. White, 140–152. 4th ed. Needham Heights, MA: Ginn Press, 1991.

Pfeiffer University. "Strategic Plan for the Future of Pfeiffer University." 2001. http://www.pfeiffer.edu. (accessed July 2004).

Polkinghorne, D. E. *Narrative Knowing and the Human Sciences*. Albany: State University of New York Press, 1988.

Price, T. *Understanding Ethical Failures in Leadership*. Cambridge: Cambridge University Press, 2005a.

Price, T. Princeton University. "Central Purposes of Princeton University." *Wythes Committee Report*, April 2000. http://www.princeton.edu/pr/reports/withes (accessed July 2004).

Puka, B. "Teaching Ethical Excellence: Artful Response-Ability, Creative Integrity, Character Opus," *Liberal Education*, 91, no.3, (2005) 22–25.

Ramsden, P. *Learning to Lead in Higher Education*. New York: Routledge Farmer, 1998.

Rand Corporation/Council for Aid to Education, Collegiate Learning Assessment. http://www.cae.org/content/pro_collegiate.htm (accessed July 2004).

Rhodes, F. *The Creation of the Future: The Role of the American University*. Ithaca, NY: Cornell University Press, 2001.

Rhodes College. "Becoming the Best." *The Campaign for Rhodes College*, Memphis, TN: Author, 2003.

Ricoeur, P. *Oneself as Another*. Trans. K. Blamey, Chicago: University of Chicago Press, 1992.

Ricoeur, P. *Philosophie de la Volonté* [Philosophy of the will]. Vol. 1, *Le Volontaire et l'Involontaire* [The voluntary and the involuntary]. Paris: Aubier, 1950.

Ricoeur, P. *Time and Narrative*. 2 vols. Trans. K. McLaughlin and D. Pellauer. Chicago: University of Chicago Press, 1984–1986.

Roanoke College. "The 2002 Plan." Roanoke, VA: Author, 1993.

Rost, J. "Leaders and Followers Are the People in This Relationship." In *The Leader's Companion*, ed. J. T. Wren 189–192. New York: Free Press, 1995.

Rost, J. *Leadership for the Twenty-first Century*. New York: Praeger, 1991.

Rowley, D. J., H. D. Lujan, and M. G. Dolence. *Strategic Change in Colleges and Universities: Planning to Survive and Prosper*. San Francisco: Jossey-Bass, 1997.

Rowley, D. J., and H. Sherman. *From Strategy to Change: Implementing the Plan in Higher Education*. San Francisco: Jossey-Bass, 2001.

Ruben, B. "Devoting More Attention and Resources to Leadership: Attracting, Developing, and Retaining Outstanding Leaders." In *Pursuing Excellence in Higher Education: Eight Fundamental Challenges*, ed. B. Ruben, 288–308. San Francisco: Jossey-Bass, 2004a.

Ruben, B., ed. *Pursuing Excellence in Higher Education: Eight Fundamental Challenges*. San Francisco: Jossey-Bass, 2004b.

Savage, J. E. "Revisions in Faculty Governance." Providence, RI: Brown University Task Force on Faculty Governance, 2003.

Schein, E. H. *Organizational Culture and Leadership*. 2nd ed. San Francisco: Jossey-Bass, 1992.

Schmidtlein, F. A., and T. H. Milton. "College and University Planning: Perspectives from a Nation-Wide Study." *Planning for Higher Education*, 17, no. 3 (1988–1989): 1–19.

Schuster, J. H., D. G. Smith, K. A. Corak, and M. M. Yamada. *Strategic Governance: How to Make Big Decisions Better*. Phoenix, AZ: ACE/Oryx, 1994.

Schwartz, P. *"The Art of the Long View: Planning for the Future in an Uncertain World*. New York: Doubleday, 1991.

Secor, R. "The Committee on Institutional Cooperation's Academic Leadership Program." In *Pursuing Excellence in Higher Education: Eight Fundamental Challenges*, ed. B. D. Ruben, 241–48. San Francisco: Jossey-Bass, 2004.

Senge, P. M. *The Fifth Discipline: The Art and Practice of the Learning Organization*. New York: Doubleday, 1990.

Sevier, R. A. *Strategic Planning in Higher Education: Theory and Practice*. Washington, DC: Case Books, 2000.

Shaw, G., R. Brown, and P. Bromiley. "Strategic Stories: How 3M Is Rewriting Business Planning." In *Harvard Business Review on Advances in Strategy*, 51–69. Boston: Harvard Business School Publishing, 2002.

Shaw, K. A. *The Intentional Leader.* Syracuse, NY: Syracuse University Press, 2006.

Shinn, L. "A Conflict of Cultures: Governance at Liberal Arts Colleges." *Change,* January/ February 2004, 19–26.

Shulman, L. "Counting and Recounting: Assessment and the Quest for Accountability." *Change,* January/February 2007, 20–25.

Simsek, H. "The Power of Symbolic Constructs in Reading Change in Higher Education." In *Organization and Governance in Higher Education,* ed. M. C. Brown, 589–604. 5th ed. Boston: Pearson Custom Publishing, 2000.

Simsek, H., and K. S. Louis. "Organizational Change as Paradigm Shift." In *Organization and Governance in Higher Education,* ed. M. C. Brown, 550–565. 5th ed. Boston: Pearson Custom Publishing, 2000.

Splete, A., ed. *Presidential Essays: Success Stories. Strategies That Make a Difference at Thirteen Independent Colleges and Universities.* New Agenda Series. Indianapolis, IN: Lumina Foundation for Education, 2000.

Steeples, D. W., ed. *Successful Strategic Planning: Case Studies.* San Francisco: Jossey-Bass, 1988.

Stettinius, W. Strategy presentation to the board of directors of the Library of Virginia Foundation. Richmond, VA, 2005.

Sweet Briar College, "The President's Perspective." Sweet Briar College, VA: Office of the President, 2004.

Tabatoni, P. "Issues on Management of Institutional Policies for Quality in Universities." *Journal of the Association of European Universities,* 107 (1996): 41–54.

Taylor, B., and W. Massy. *Strategic Indicators for Higher Education.* Princeton, NJ: Petersons's, 1996.

Taylor, B., J. Meyerson, L. Morrell, and D. Park, Jr. *Strategic Analysis: Using Comparative Data to Understand Your Institution.* Washington, DC: Association of Governing Boards of Universities and Colleges, 1991.

Taylor, C. *Sources of the Self: The Making of the Modern Identity.* Cambridge, MA: Harvard University Press, 1989.

Tierney, W. G., ed. *Competing Conceptions of Academic Governance: Negotiating the Perfect Academic Storm.* Baltimore: Johns Hopkins University Press, 2004.

Tierney, W. G. "Critical Leadership and Decision-Making in a Postmodern World." In *Organization and Governance in Higher Education,* ed. M. C. Brown, 537–549. 5th ed. Boston: Pearson Custom Publishing, 2000.

Tierney, W. G. "Mission and Vision Statements: An Essential First Step." In *Field Guide to Academic Leadership,* ed. R. M. Diamond, 49–58. San Francisco: Jossey-Bass, 2002.

Tierney, W. G. "Symbolism and Presidential Perceptions of Leadership." In *Organization and Governance in Higher Education,* ed. M. Peterson, E. E. Chaffee, and T. E. White, 432–440. 4th ed. Needham Heights, MA: Ginn Press, 1991.

Tierney, W. G., and V. M. Lechuga, eds. *Restructuring Shared Governance in Higher Education: New Directions for Higher Education.* No. 127. San Francisco: Jossey-Bass, 2004.

Tinsley, A. "Academic Revitalization: Fulfilling the Turnaround Promise," In *Academic Turnarounds: Restoring Vitality to Challenged American Colleges and Universities,*" ed. T. MacTaggart. Westport, CT: ACE/ Praeger, 2007.

Toma, J. D., G. Dubrow, and M. Hartley. *The Uses of Institutional Culture: Strengthening Identification and Building Brand Equity.* ASHE Report, 31, no. 2. San Francisco: Jossey-Bass, 2005.

Townsley, M. "A Practical Guide to Financial Metrics." In *Academic Turnarounds: Restoring Vitality to Challenged American Colleges and Universities*, ed. T. MacTaggart. Westport, CT: ACE/Praeger, 2007.

Trainer, J. F. "Models and Tools for Strategic Planning." In *Successful Strategic Planning: New Directions for Institutional Research*, ed. M. J. Dooris, J. M. Kelley, and J. F. Trainer, 129–138. No. 123. San Francisco: Jossey-Bass, 2004.

Trollinger, R. "A Distinctive College: Saga, Values, and the Message About Centre," In *On Becoming A More Perfect Centre*, ed. C. Wyatt and R. Trollinger, 12–23. Danville, KY: Centre College, 2003.

Trompenaars, F., and C. Hampden-Turner. *Twenty-one Leaders for the Twenty-first Century*. New York: McGraw-Hill, 2002.

Troutt, W. E. "President's Message: The Rhodes Vision." *Magazine of Rhodes College*, Spring, 1, 2003.

Tyler, T. R. "Process-Based Leadership: How Do Leaders Lead?" In *The Psychology of Leadership: New Perspectives and Research*, ed. D. M. Messick and R. M. Kramer, 163–189. Mahwah, NJ: Erlbaum, 2005.

University of Connecticut. "University's Vision, Mission, Values, and Goals." *University Strategic Plan*. 2000. http://www.uc2000.uconn.edu/strategicplan/vision (accessed July 2004).

University of North Carolina at Greensboro. "The UNCG Plan." Greensboro, NC: Author, 1998.

University of Richmond. "Development Comparisons 1998–2001." *University of Richmond Factbook*. Richmond, VA: Office of the President, 2003a.

University of Richmond. "Transforming Bright Minds." *The Campaign for Richmond*, Richmond, VA: Author, 2003b.

Van der Heijden, K. *Scenarios: The Art of Strategic Conversation*. Chichester, UK: John Wiley and Sons, 1996.

Veysey, L. *The Emergence of the American University*. Chicago: University of Chicago Press, 1965.

Virginia Commonwealth University. "Strategic Plan for the Future of Virginia Commonwealth University." 1997. http://www.vcu.edu/provost/plan (accessed July 2004).

Watson, D. *Managing Strategy*. Buckingham, UK: Open University Press, 2000.

Weick, K. "Educational Organizations as Loosely Coupled Systems." In *Organization and Governance in Higher Education*, ed. M. Peterson, E. E. Chaffee, and T. H. White, 103–117. 4th ed. Needham Heights, MA: Ginn Press, 1991.

Weick, K. *Making Sense of the Organization*. Oxford: Blackwell, 2001.

Weick, K. *Sense-Making in Organizations*. Thousand Oaks, CA: Sage, 1995.

Wenger, E. C., and W. M. Snyder. "Communities of Practice: the Organizational Frontier." *Harvard Business Review*, January/February 2000, 139–45.

Wergin, J. "Academic Program Review." In *Field Guide to Academic Leadership*, ed. R. M. Diamond, 241–255. San Francisco: Jossey-Bass, 2002.

Wergin, J. "Taking Responsibility for Student Learning: The Role of Accreditation." *Change*, January/February 2003, 30–33.

Williams College. *1997 Reaccreditation Self-Study*. Williamstown, MA: Author, 1997.

Wilson, R. "The Dynamics of Organizational and Academic Planning." *Planning for Higher Education*, 34, no. 2 (2006): 5–17.

Wren, J. T., ed. *The Leader's Companion*. New York: Free Press, 1995.

Wren, J. T. "A Quest for a Grand Theory of Leadership." In *The Quest for a General Theory of Leadership*, ed. G. R. Goethals and G.L.J. Sorenson, 1–38. Northampton, MA: Elgar, 2006.

Wyatt, C. "Defining the Centre Experience." *On Becoming a More Perfect Centre.* ed. C. Wyatt and R. Trollinger, 7–8. Danville, KY: Centre College, 2003.

Yankelovich, D. "Ferment and Change: Higher Education in 2015." *Chronicle of Higher Education*, November 25, 2005.

Yukl, G., and R. Lepsinger. *Flexible Leadership.* San Francisco: Jossey-Bass, 2004.

Zemsky, R., G. Wegner, and W. Massy. *Remaking the American University: Market-Smart and Mission-Centered.* New Brunswick, NJ: Rutgers University Press, 2005.

INDEX

About the Author

RICHARD L. MORRILL, after ten years as president of the University of Richmond, became chancellor and distinguished university professor of ethics and democratic values in 1998. He previously served as president of Centre College from 1982 to 1988 and of Salem College from 1979 to 1982. He is the author of *Teaching Values in College* (1980) and *Strategic Leadership in Academic Affairs: Clarifying the Board's Responsibilities* (2002). Morrill received degrees from Brown University in history, magna cum laude, and from Yale University in religious thought before completing his doctoral work at Duke University in religion and ethics. He studied for a year in Paris as an undergraduate and has been honored by the French government with membership in the Order of Academic Palms and the Order of National Merit. He currently serves on several corporate and not-for-profit boards and as a consultant on governance, strategy, and leadership to colleges and universities.